MODERN SCEPTICISM.

MODERN SCEPTICISM.

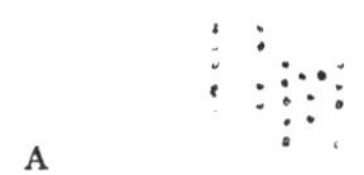

A

COURSE OF LECTURES

DELIVERED AT THE REQUEST OF THE

CHRISTIAN EVIDENCE SOCIETY,

WITH AN EXPLANATORY PAPER

BY THE RIGHT REVEREND

C. J. ELLICOTT, D.D.,

LORD BISHOP OF GLOUCESTER AND BRISTOL.

NEW YORK:

ANSON D. F. RANDOLPH AND CO.,

770, BROADWAY.

MDCCCLXXI.

Issued in this Country
by special arrangement with the English Publishers,
MESSRS. HODDER AND STOUGHTON.

PREFACE.

THE following Lectures, delivered at the request of the Christian Evidence Society, are now, for the convenience of the reader, gathered together into one volume, and earnestly commended to his serious consideration.

A short account of the general designs of the Society, of the plan of the Lectures, and the reasons for their appearing in a different order from that in which they were delivered, will be found in an explanatory paper which the Bishop of Gloucester and Bristol has been kind enough to draw up at the request of the Committee. Though placed, as last written, at the end of the volume, the attention of the reader should be early directed to this paper.

The Committee take this opportunity of offering their best thanks to the eminent men who have found time, in the midst of their varied and laborious avocations, to lend such able and efficient service to the great cause in hand,—the maintenance of the truth of the Christian Revelation.

HARROWBY,

Chairman of Committee.

CONTENTS.

DESIGN IN NATURE.

BY THE MOST REVEREND

THE LORD ARCHBISHOP OF YORK.

DESIGN IN NATURE.

"ALL things are full of God," said the father of Greek philosophy. "We have no need of the hypothesis of God," said a modern French astronomer. It is with the latter saying, which is descriptive of the attitude of modern science at this time, that the present address will have to do. Atheism no doubt exists; but far more common is the mode of thinking which would dispense with all questions about the Divine nature in dealing with the world and its phenomena; which considers that the introduction of the name of God into scientific research, complicates what is simple, obscures the rules of observation, introduces controversies that are useless to science, restrains the free course of inductive reasoning by an apprehension of consequences, and entangles physical inquiry which leads to sure and clear results, with mental and with spiritual inquiry which have produced nothing but disputation. Those who hold such views would think it unphilosophical to deny, just as they would regard it to affirm, the existence of God. But the popular mind is not equal to nice distinctions; and it seems almost the same thing to most people to deny the existence of God as to exclude the thought of Him when exploring His creation.

I am not without hope that a few words delivered here upon "the argument from design," as it is called, may tend to diminish the growing estrangement between science and religion, and at the same time to revindicate for religion her legitimate share in matters of scientific interest.

I may undertake that the subject, however unworthily treated in other respects, shall be discussed without bitterness, and with a fitting respect for those who have done so much for physical science during the present generation.

It is necessary to sketch in a few sentences that field of creation with which the argument from design has to do. The world presents to us four kingdoms or classes of facts. One of these, and the first in point of order, is the mineral kingdom. A few so-called elements, as metals, earthy bases, and the like, acted upon by certain forces, known to us as gravitation, motion, heat, electricity, magnetism, chemical affinity, have formed the mountain and the valley, the wind and the clouds, the sea margin and the cave; in a word, all the grand substructure on which the higher kingdoms are to take their places. Modern science has discovered however, that these physico-chemical forces are interchangeable or convertible; that retarded motion turns to heat, as in the railway break, that heat generates electricity, and the electric current magnetises the iron round which it passes. Not only this, but each force generates a certain equivalent of another—so much and no more; and no force is lost, though a force may pass from an active to a potential state. For example, two tuns of water are raised by evaporation from the sea, and one of them falls in rain in a valley drained by a river, and in its downward motion back to the sea it will turn the water-wheel, lift the tilt-hammer, bear the barge swiftly in its current, leap over the rocky ledge a foaming cataract, and in all these it is only sending back a portion of the force which was spent upon its evaporation; and the real source of all this work is, and must be, the sun's heat. And ere the water rests again in the sea it will have accounted for the whole of the force, neither less nor more, that had operated upon it; part of it in friction on its bed and in consequent heat; part of it in tasks imposed by human skill. The other tun of water shall fall into some land-locked tarn, high in the hills, where it cannot at once render back its force in work or duty, but the force is there, held in suspense or in reserve. Water lifted from the sea level to the valley of the Engadine, a mile higher, has used much of the sun's heat; it will restore that heat or some equivalent force, as soon as you make a way for it to the sea level again; and it will have parted with all the force, neither more nor less, which raised it to that height. That forces are convertible, and that whether converted or not they are conserved, so that nothing is lost, are propositions demonstrated. It is not, I believe, demonstrated, but it is a probable supposition, that all forces are but one force manifested in different modes.

Then as to the material elements on which these forces work; the hydrogen, carbon, iron, lime, and the like, the name of elements must be held to mean no more than that they have not as yet been resolved into simpler substances. Of their ultimate composition we know nothing. They may be so many modifications of an ultimate matter; but whether this ultimate matter exists, whether it be, as modern materialists tell us with such confidence, eternal and indestructible, whether impenetrability be one of its properties, whether it be not a kind of polar opposite to the physico-chemical forces, and engendered with them, so that in a different universe, with other forces at work, there must have been different elements, these are all questions of mere speculation, incapable of proof. The physical enquirer has bound himself to consider only the facts which he can observe; and when he tells us that matter is eternal, and that therefore creation is impossible, he is deserting the ground where alone he is strong. Bishop Berkeley's and Collier's denial that matter truly exists is quite as probable as this affirmation. But both alike are speculative guesses and not science.

There is a second kingdom to add to the first. The world is not a mere agglomeration of rocks and mountains, seas and lakes. Before the physical forces had completed their work, a new force had been added to them; that of life. The bare rocks became clothed with living moss. In marshy places, warm and moist, a rich vegetation grew and decayed. Along the slopes the interlacing roots of grasses detained the particles of soil which would otherwise have been washed down to some lower bed. The vegetable world, with thousands of varieties, clothed and adorned the stony earth. England's greatness in the present was taken order for in those ages when her coal measures were formed out of the forests which grew rank and died in a climate different in all respects from that which forms the subject of our daily animadversion.

Third in order comes the Animal Kingdom. I do not attempt to define life, whether animal or vegetable, with exactness. Every one has failed in that attempt. As a rough description of animal life, it may, perhaps, suffice to say that the living being is one endowed with sensation and spontaneous motion, of which each of the parts contributes something to the continuance of the whole, and is in turn preserved or defended by the whole. If those who find fault with this, look for another definition in Dr. Whewell's comprehensive work,* they will find my excuse in the variety and the inadequacy of the definitions there collected. The animal life spread out over the globe from the first is profuse, is beautiful and various. The oolitic limestone and the white chalk are almost wholly made up of shells of Foraminifera. On the river Columbia is a bed of clay 500 feet thick, which consists largely of the shells of Diatoms, if, indeed, these are to be ranked in the animal kingdom. The shells of the Foraminifera, which can only be examined by the microscope, exhibit wonderful variety and beauty. Still more remarkable in this respect are the Polycystina, whose shells, as figured in Mr. Ponton's book, recall censers and vases, jewelled crosses and stars, pendants and tripods, such as a London goldsmith would do well to reproduce. Until the microscope was invented no eye can have explored this wonderful dust. The shells of both these humble tribes, the Foraminifera and Polycystina resemble the shells of other animals much higher in the scale of organization; but nearly as they are related in organization to each other, the forms are very different, and each in itself presents a wonderful diversity

* "Philosophy of the Inductive Sciences."

of forms. In higher families of animals there are the same characters. The globe teems with life in earth, and air, and water. If you will permit me, so early in my argument, to speak of the Maker of them all, I will say that the creative power is inexhaustible in invention, both of useful and beautiful parts. And in the ceaseless activity of these creatures, great and small, we recognise the physical happiness which accompanies so much life. It is a chorus of thanksgiving and praise, from pool and jungle, from tree-top and soft grass, from the creatures that revel in the life that God has given them.

In demanding the right to regard man as the fourth kingdom of nature, I am aware that some may demur to the claim. No doubt he must take rank in the kingdom of the animals, by reason of his identity with animals in all the vital functions. Disparaging things have been said of his brain; and Moleschott has remarked, I think, that all its finest things are but modified phosphorus after all. "No phosphorus, no thinking!" The slight projection on the outer margin of the ear has lately assumed portentous proportions. The possession of that precious relic, which has turned up suddenly like the locket of the long lost child in a stimulating novel, proves our kinship to the Simian race, from some balder specimens of which we are supposed to have descended, and gives us a place on an unsuspected family tree.

But, after all that has been said by the naturalists to teach us humility, there do remain some facts, which entitle man to a separate place, to one at least of which the modern school have given greater prominence than before. They are these. Man can control nature. He can read nature and understand it. He has a power of self-regulation, which we call conscience. And he can and does think much about God.

As to the power of man to control nature, I prefer to employ the words of Mr. Wallace, one of the first to put forward what is called "the law of natural selection," who will not be suspected of claiming any transcendental place or privilege for man. "With a naked and unprotected body," he says, man's intelligence "gave him clothing against the varying inclemencies of the seasons. Though unable to compete with the deer in swiftness, or with the wild bull in strength, it has given him weapons wherewith to capture and overcome both. Though less capable than most other animals, of living on the herbs and the fruits which unaided nature supplies, this wonderful faculty taught him to govern and direct nature to his own benefit, and to make her produce food for him when and where he pleased. From the moment when the first skin was used as a covering, when the first rude spear was formed to assist in the chase, the first seed sown or root planted, a grand revolution was effected in nature, a revolution which in all the previous ages of the world had had no parallel, for a being had arisen who was no longer necessarily subject to change with the changing universe, a being who was, in some degree, superior to nature, inasmuch as he knew how to control and regulate her action, and could keep himself in harmony with her, not by a change in body, but by an advance in mind. Here, then, we see the true grandeur and dignity of man. On this view of his special attributes we may admit that even those who claim for him a position and an order a class or a sub-kingdom by himself, have some reason on their side. He is indeed a being apart, since he is not influenced by the great laws which irresistibly modify all other organic beings. Nay, more, this victory which he has gained for himself gives him a directing influence over other existences. Man has not only escaped natural selection himself, but he is actually able to take away some of that power from nature which before his appearance she universally exercised. We can anticipate the time when the earth will produce only cultivated plants and domestic animals; when man's selection shall have supplanted natural selection; and when the ocean will be the only domain in which that power can be exerted, which for countless cycles of ages ruled supreme over the earth."*

* Mr. Wallace, in the "Anthropological Journal," 1864; see also Lubbock's "Prehistoric Times," last chapter.

Thus eloquently and forcibly speaks Mr. Wallace; and I do not stop now to criticise the exaggeration of language which treats the law of natural selection as supreme ruler of the earth. Let me say a few words next upon man's power to reflect on, and to understand nature. For this was the second mark by which man was distinguished from the animal creation, with which he has so much in common.

Man alone is capable of an unselfish interest in the world around him; that is, an interest that does not bear immediately on his bodily wants. How far he has carried this interest, let modern science bear witness. The common feat of foretelling all the eclipses of sun and moon for a given year, is performed for our almanack yearly, without exciting surprise or gratitude. Yet it means that man can so follow the heavenly bodies in their path, for years and years to come, for all the years that are gone, that he can tell, without fear of error, on what day the cone of shadow thrown by the sun-lighted earth into space, shall sweep over the face of the moon and blot out her light, completely or a little. But this is an old triumph, hardly worth quoting, but for its aptness to impress all kinds of minds. A clerk in one of our public offices, using only such leisure as official work allowed, has told us lately wonders about the composition of the sun; and here in London, armed with a little instrument (the spectroscope), this distinguished man has been able to ascertain that in yonder photosphere the same elements are found which the chemist seeks and finds in the crust of our little earth. What proofs can be more convincing of the fitness of man to play his part in the scene in which he is placed? His senses are adapted to the facts he is to observe; his eye to light, his ear to sonorous vibrations, his touch to resistance and to weight. But the naked organ soon falls short of his wishes. And soon the microscope unfolds the beautiful forms of the Polycystina shells, the minute fibril of the muscle, and the components of the blood of life. The telescope brings near the world of stars, and resolves the bright mist into clusters of distinct orbs. The balance weighs quantities of matter too small for the touch to appreciate. And lastly, the spectroscope takes the picture, so to speak, of chemical phenomena too distant to be realised by these means; and so the composition of the heavenly bodies, about which the most sanguine observer twenty years ago would have admitted that we should never know anything firmer than conjecture, is already the subject of exact observation.

The names of Homer, Plato, and Shakspeare remind us how marvellously the world is imaged and reproduced in the minds of some great men, and of the share which we smaller men can take in their work by an admiring sympathy. A production of art, whether literary, pictorial, or plastic, is a creation. The things of Troy were not so touching nor so grand in their reality as they became in the form which the poet gave them. Legend enters largely into the stories of Macbeth and Hamlet. The histories are shadowy, but the plays are substantial; they contain some touch of truth. Old and young read them, and lend to the author all their feelings to work on as he will. Weigh this fact well. It seems to me to show so plainly that man's constitution has been fitted by foresight and preparation for the place in earth that he was to fill.

Supposing that Moleschott was right in his startling aphorism, "Without phosphorus there is no thought," what a wonder are we forced to recognise here. The rage of Achilles, the death of Socrates, the resolute wickedness of Lady Macbeth, the character of her husband, so weak in his crime, so grand in his remorse and ruin; the refined and gentle Hamlet, forced by a preternatural command to assume the character of an avenger; to all these the presence of phosphorus in the brain is indispensable. How comes so small a cause to work such grand effects. It is sufficiently wonderful to hear Joachim discourse eloquent music upon the simplest of instruments, a violin; take away the violin and substitute a bit of wood; if the music still continues, what was before a wonderful exercise of skill is now miraculous.

If great thoughts are but phosphorus burnt in the closed stove of a poet's brain, I am more ready than ever to admire that creative wisdom which could bring this out of that, which could so dispense with ordinary means in His highest productions. But the aphorism is not true as it stands. I believe there is no free phosphorus in the brain. "Without lime, no thought; without oxygen, no thought; without water, no thought." All these are true, and they import a well-known fact, that man who thinks is a creature in a material world, and that certain forms of matter are needful to his existence as an organised being.*

"Two things are awful to me," said Kant, "the starry firmament and the sense of responsibility in man." In his "Metaphysics of Ethics" he has treated this sense of responsibility with singular logical power. It is one of the marks that separate man from all other creatures. No doubt this principle has allowed men to come to very wrong and absurd conclusions. Because the savage practises cannibalism, and knows no rules of chastity but those which flow from the husband's right of property in the wife, it is inferred that the savage has no moral sense. It would be as fair to infer that because England once traded in slaves, fought cocks, baited bulls, and oppressed the native races in India and

* Moleschott, "Circulation of Life:" Letter XVIII., with Liebig's opinion there quoted.

her colonies, therefore there was no sense of right and wrong in England. It is for the existence of the principle that I contend, and not for its perfect education and enlightenment. The principle is that something is right to will and to do, and something is not right. The existence of the principle is proved if the poor savage of whom I spoke would consider his manhood disgraced by fleeing, even for his life's sake, before the foe, or by suffering one cry to escape him under the tortures, wherewith his captors are doing him to death. The education of this principle is a different matter; no one could say that even now his conscience was completely educated. "So act that your principle of action would bear to be made a law for the whole world,"* is a noble maxim; but it requires knowledge and light, as well as right intention. If you twit us with the fact that men have been cruel, impure, capricious, and absurd in their conduct, we answer that they had still a right and a wrong. One who has the sense of sight may find himself compelled to live in some narrow cleft or ravine, where there is little to see, but the sense is there still. The bathing-men at Pfeffers, with the earth closed almost over their heads, see little of the scenery of Switzerland: but they have eyes not the less. We are claiming for men now, not the fine

*Kant, "Metaphysics of Ethics."

sweep of moral prospect, but the moral sense of sight; and this is never wanting. Upon this sense every artifice has been used to make it lock like something else;* for until it can be so transformed, it is a powerful witness for another world than this. The commonest explanation is that it is only a principle of enlightened self-interest. Study it for yourself in the savage, in the little child; you will find that these two principles run on different lines.

The last mark of man, that distinguishes him from all animals is, that he believes in God. One half the human race at this moment profess some creed in which God is the great first cause, the Creator and Governor of the world. Of the other half, hardly any are quite without religion. "Obliged as I am," says M. Quatrefages, in words which I have had occasion to quote elsewhere,† "even by my education, to pass in review the races of men, I have sought for atheism in the lowest and in the highest, but nowhere have I met with it, except in an individual, or at most in some school of men, more or less known, as we have seen in Europe in the last century, and as we see at the present day. Everywhere and always the masses of the people have escaped it." But for my present argument it is not neces-

* See, for example, Renouvier, "Science de la Morale," 1869.

† "Limits of Philosophical Enquiry." 1868.

sary to insist that a right belief in God prevails. There is a belief in God, and it cannot have come from experience or observation of visible facts. You may lower the position of man, by comparing him to the apes, and by chemical analysis of his brain; all the more wonderful is it that a creature in such sorry case should pretend to hold communion with the divine. His feet are in the earthy clay, but his head is lifted up towards heaven. Heir to a hundred maladies, the sport of a hundred passions, holding on this life, so chequered in its complexion, but for a few days, this creature cries out of his trouble: "God exists; and he can see and hear me."

Man, if I have proved my position, stands quite alone at the head of the kingdoms of nature, alone in his power of controlling it, alone in his appreciation of its beauty, alone in the self-government of conscience, the first of all the creatures of God, to pronounce the name of Him who had made all things, in a world which for ages had been blind to its Maker, and thankless because blind.

Now it has become, and will probably continue to be, a question of the deepest interest to mankind, how these four kingdoms came into being. And at present there is a tendency towards a theory purely material and mechanical. It is so in Germany, the country of Büchner, Vogt, and Moleschott; it is so in France, where Comte and Littre have written; it is so here in England, where it is needless to quote distinguished names. I purpose, in the remainder of this lecture, to attempt an interpretation of the facts before us, quite different from this prevalent notion; and also to show how vicious and how inadequate in a scientific point of view the system known as materialism appears to be. The time is all too short for such a purpose: but any address like this can only aim to scatter germs of thought, not to present a system.

That the creation was gradual, appears alike from the account of the Bible and from scientific observation. Matter and motion must have existed before the ball of earth was formed; and the physico-chemical forces must have been in full play when the first lichen clothed the rocks, or the first plants were formed in the sea. The first appearance of life on the globe was a mighty step in creation, and from this point the question of design becomes a very urgent one. Observe: the plant world is a new world, with a series of wonders all its own. There was nothing in the heat of the sun, nor in the earth's motion or magnetic currents, to give any promise or presage of the marvels of the forest. Supposing that we admit that these were evolved by law, that is to say, that as a matter of fact plants only appeared where certain conditions of light and heat and moisture combined to favour them, and that wherever these conditions were combined they never failed to appear. The question next arises whether matter and force evolved them from their own inherent nature, or force and matter were created with the intention to produce them, so that the plant was intended and prepared then when the other forces began to stir the formless void. Is the plant world the accidental or necessary outcome of the forces that made the mineral world? or must we say that it bears marks of design? Here we must observe that it is a wider and richer world than that which preceded it: more full by far of forms of beauty and grace, each of them sustained by a vascular system of which the mineral world affords no parallel. You stand before the gnarled and twisted oak that rises out of the feathering ferns; you never think that this giant of two centuries, endued with a certain power of self-protection against the storms of two hundred years, is an accidental product. It is so grandly strong, so richly clothed with a myriad leaves, alike but yet in something different each from each. The cattle count upon its friendly shade; the fowls of the air make it their resting-place. This a result of certain motions in the universe and certain properties of matter, not designed at all, foreseen by no eye? To no one would such a thought naturally occur. The world, full in its first stage of marks of order and purpose, shows more of the same marks in its second and more complicated state. The change that has taken place is not towards confusion and exhaustion from unforeseen defects in mechanism, but a higher development. The mineral kingdom was wonderful; that it should be able to clothe itself with a mantle of verdure, and pass into another kingdom much more complex, heightens the wonder. But then comes the further change, the pouring out of animal life upon the globe. Was this too an inevitable consequence of physical forces? All the animal creation teems with marks of purpose. Consider only some of the contrivances by which the fowls of the air are fitted for their peculiar life. Describing a night of extreme coldness, the poet says:

> "The owl, for all her feathers, is a-cold."

That warm covering of the bird must be portable as well as warm; it weighs about an ounce and a half. But the covering of birds would be useless to them if the showers to which they must be exposed were absorbed by the plumage, so that it became a heavy clinging mass. An oily secretion makes it waterproof; we have all seen the duck free itself by one shake from every trace of its recent bath. The heavy skeleton that befits pedestrian creatures, would disable the bird from flight; so it is provided with tubes of thin bone, surrounding a cavity filled with air. Its pinions must be light as well as strong; observe how the light barbs of the feather have roughened edges so that they form one strong continuous surface, almost impervious to the air which they strike. The air in the bones of birds and in other cavities of the body, heated too by an inner warmth much greater than that of man, contributes something to their buoyancy. Their speed and endurance are enormous. It is said that the swallow's flight is ninety miles an hour. One long stretch across the North Sea brings the sea-fowl from Norway to Flamborough Head; they rest for a short time after this flight, and pass inland, not the worse for their exploit. You may infer from the beak of a bird its habits and its food. The bill of a woodpecker is a pointed tool, tipped with hardest horn, to break open the bark of the tree for insects. The flat bill of the duck has plates of horn at the side; an excellent instrument for straining off the water and retaining the food. The bill of the snipe is long, and narrow, and sensitive, to pierce the marshy ground, and feel after its food. We might go on for hours multiplying such instances, and from every part of the field of creation.

Now, any mind in its natural state knows that in human works such adaptations could only proceed from contrivance, and is willing to regard these in the same way as proofs of design in creation. The physicist has to tutor himself to a different view. All these things are evolutions, under pressure of circumstances, of the original forces of creation. For example, out of certain birds tenanting marshy places, one has a somewhat larger beak, and this gives him an advantage in piercing the ground for food; and so his share of food is larger, and his strength and courage greater, and he has a freer choice of a mate; and so the long beak grows longer in the next generation, and the grandson's beak is longer than the son's, from the same causes; and thus the law works, until in course of time there stands confessed a new species—a perfect snipe. Is the scientific theory better in this case than the popular? It is not. It does not account for the facts so well. But is not our belief that God made the fowl of the air with fitting instruments for a peculiar life because He saw that it was good, and wished all portions of His varied earth to be the scene of the joy and energy of appropriate tenants, a mere hypothesis? The worship of God is universal, and exists without any explicit opinion that He is the Creator, the first Cause. Because you are able to conceive of Him, and are willing to accept Him as the Ruler of your will and conscience, He must exist. Does this seem too rapid an assumption? Consider the alternative. If He exists not, the sound of worship has gone up from all lands in vain, and in vain have all good men consecrated their lives to an obedience to the law of duty. Were such deceit felt to be possible, a darkness that might be felt would settle upon our spirits, and the hands would indeed hang down, and the feeble knees be paralyzed, and a strict silence on all moral subjects become us best. But we must see with such eyes as God has given us; and scepticism about faith and conscience is perhaps as unprofitable as scepticism about touch and sight. God exists then, it is assured to us by the common faith of mankind, by the highest law within ourselves. And as He exists, to Him, and to no other, must we assign the place of Creator. There cannot be two Gods. I cannot give my conscience to one as its guide, and adore another for the wisdom of the universe God exists then, and His existence is not merely assumed in order to account for marks of design in nature. And we maintain that the easier supposition is also the truer. These marks of purpose are what they appear to be, tokens of the wisdom of God. "Thou hast made heaven, the heaven of heavens with all their host, the earth and all things that are therein, the sea and all that is therein, and thou preservest them all."*

If I were to venture to express in a few sentences the belief of a man of ordinary education upon this subject I should say that God alone is and can be the first cause of this universe, the mover of its motion, the giver of its life. The wise purposes which shine forth for us in

* Nehem. ix. 6.

nature, were in the mind of God from the first act of creation. In saying that He has wrought by laws, we do not detract from His power; we seem rather to enhance it to our minds in attributing to Him constancy as well as wisdom. A law is not a restraint; it is a fixed manner of working. To say of a painter that he never produces any but fine works, does not affirm that he is less free than an inferior artist; just because producing bad work is no power or privilege but a defect. And so, when we admit that God works by law, and expect to find the same spectrum from the sun's rays, which we have once made with our own prism, at every time and in every place where the sun's light shines, and so on, we do not narrow the power of the Great Artificer, unless it can be shown that caprice is a privilege and a good. The subject of miracles is not here to be discussed; I will only observe that they are presented to us as parts of a great purpose for the good of man; and that our Lord refused, when He was tempted, to work wonders out of wilfulness, or only to astonish. The extreme jealousy of scientific men of admitting any allusion to theology, in connection with the course of nature, proceeds from erroneous conceptions of God. Mr. Wallace, whom I have already quoted with respect, is ready to admit that the Creator works in the beginning as the founder of the laws on which the world is to proceed; but he is afraid of admitting that there has been continual interference and re-arrangement of details.* But this eminent naturalist attributes to us a conception of the Most High which we do not hold, nay, which we energetically reject. If the laws were wise and good, whence would come the need of interference or re-arrangement? Who are we that we should bid God speak once, and forbid Him twice to speak? The laws of nature are God's laws, and God's laws are His utterance of Himself through the speech of nature. God is the same yesterday, to-day, and for ever; and so His laws remain the same. They are, if I may say so without irreverence, the veil and vesture over the form of God, too bright in itself for us to look on; they take their outline from Him who is beneath them. You may continue your researches in full confidence that the laws will stand sure, not because you have the slightest guarantee as a man of science that these laws will never be interfered with; such a guarantee you have on your own principles no right to ask. You are to observe that the facts are so; that they shall eternally be so is not for you, for that is all beyond experience. But the wisdom that made the laws needs not to revise its work, and erase and insert and amend its code. In the days of creation God saw that it was good; the eye that so approved it

* See Duke of Argyll's "Reign of Law."

changes not. Until the purpose that runs through the ages is completed the laws will stand sure. But each new kingdom of nature has introduced a change amounting to a revolution, which neither the theologian nor the naturalist regards as an interference or a caprice. When the principle of plant-life was introduced, the mineral world became the material on which the plant-life worked; it gathered into itself the lower elements, carbon, silica, nitrogen, and used them as means of its own organic life. The plant partook of the nature of the class below it, whilst it dominated and used that class. This same took place when animal life was introduced. The beautiful plants become the material whereon the animal life worked, the food whereby it sustained itself. It was the same when man was added, in whom instinct is replaced by reason, and ethical action supervenes over action by impulse and appetite. Each of these kingdoms has much in common with that which is below it. The animal is in many respects a plant; for the diatomaceous creatures one knows hardly in which kingdom to find their place. The man is an animal in much, and perhaps his animal instincts play a larger part in the world's history and in his own development than we are wont to allow. But each higher step brings in something wholly new. "An animal," says Hegel, "is a miracle for the vegetable world." Each step is a revolution in one point of view; but then the lower state prepared itself for the higher, prophesied, so to speak, of its coming, and the higher seated itself so easily on the throne prepared for it, that we do not wonder to find it there. You call it evolution; we call it a creative act. We think that God exists, and if He acts anywhere it must be in this, the universe of things. Ἐξ ἑνὸς τὰ πάντα γίγνεσθαι is an old saying long before Christianity. But you and we may work by the same calculus and rules of observation. The facts are the same, the interpretation of what is behind them is different. Nor need we deny that the principle of which Mr. Wallace spoke as "supreme in the world," has its truth and its use in explaining the facts of creation. It never raised an inert mineral mass into a vegetable organism; it never raised a plant into an animal. It never raised an ape into a man. No facts have yet been produced that go to prove any such leaps, and if our logic is to be improved in anything by the light of experience, it is in this, that facts should be recorded and generalised, but not assumed. But that climatic conditions, and the struggles for life, have modified species, and worked out new varieties, or new species, we may fearlessly admit; it is one more proof, perhaps, that the world is a meet school and training ground for the creatures placed in it for discipline. But a law is not a god; it never ruled supreme; never was other than one precept out of many in the Divine code of the world.

It has become the fashion with some naturalists to speak of God as "the Unknowable." Mr. Martineau has finely observed, somewhere, that this name is self-contradictory; for we affirm by the use of it that we know so much, that He cannot be known. I go much further. It assumes the existence of God, and in the same breath separates us from Him for ever. Theologians have ever been ready to confess that God cannot be known in His own essence to creatures such as we. "Lo! these are parts of His ways: but how little a portion is known of Him? but the thunder of His power who can understand?"* An uninspired writer speaks the same language as the inspired. "For us that are men to talk about divine things is as when the unmusical discourse of music or civilians of strategy."† But shall we then sit down in despair, and no more look up to God? We shall be untrue to our own best instincts; we shall not have used all our means of enlightenment. I grant that the mere contemplation of God in nature is not enough. Like the pillar of cloud of old, it is at once light and darkness; a light to us in contemplating the book of nature, a darkness to our hearts, shut in with their own sins and sorrows. Naturalists have never done justice, as it seems to me, to

* Job xxvi. 14.

† Plutarch, "De Justitia."

the most important facts of man's nature. Not only can he study nature, but he can act in it and upon it. And this power of action assures him of his freedom. Possessed of this gift, that places him a little lower than the angels, he knows that he can use it either way. He may follow his own foolish vanity, his own evil wishes, and set up for his own law, and be his own God; or he may return to Him, whence he came out, and offer to God the homage of his own will, of his love, and his obedience. To one who has performed this great act God is no more "the Unknowable." In the mutual commerce of two wills, two spirits, the finite and the infinite, the finite rises more and more, and sees more and more of Him who has manifested Himself to us in His creation of the world out of free love, in His creation of a free being to rule in the same world, crowned with glory and honor, in His giving that free being a law of duty wherewith to rule himself, in His having planted in him hopes and longings that will be satisfied only in eternity.

Yes; man is humble and low. By every organ, and by every fibre he is mated with some analogous creature in the brute world. He surpasses them in the variety of his ailments, and the profundity of his pains. He is part of a system, which naturalists tell us is hastening towards night and death;* the motion of the power of nature tending plainly

* Buchner.

towards universal rest. But

> "Placed on this isthmus of a middle state,
> A being darkly wise and rudely great,"

he has that in him which unites him to another sphere. To be able to conceive of God at all; to have within him a will and a power of worship, these make him one with God, and assure him against death and darkness. To deny oneself this privilege of viewing the earth in its relation to God, to shut out God artificially from that sphere where the natural understanding has always found Him without assistance, is a pedantry for which we shall surely suffer. God will find us out. There is often a certain irritation in those who would exclude Him from their sphere of view. They lose their philosophic calmness when they speak of religious things. These are the tokens of past conflicts and past quarrels, of a soul that might know more of God if it had not refused. God is reflected in the world, in the man's intelligence, in his conscience, in his will. "Whither shall I go from His presence?" we seem to be saying. It is better to be able to say, "Whom have I in heaven and earth but Thee?"

PANTHEISM.

BY THE

REV. J. H. RIGG, D.D.,

PRINCIPAL OF WESTMINSTER TRAINING COLLEGE.

PANTHEISM.

A HUNDRED years ago the controversy of Christianity in England was with Deism, and in France with Atheism; while at that time the transcendental infidelity of Germany was as yet undeveloped, and the name of Spinoza was nowhere held in honour. Now, however, deistic infidelity appears to be obsolete, and it is universally felt by those who have entered truly into the thought and controversies of the age, that the question for the present is between Christian Theism and that style of philosophy which recognises an impersonal divinity in all things.

Deism grants too much to the Christian. If a man really believes in a living and personal God, a Divine Maker and Ruler of the universe, with a moral character and will, he finds it hard to deny the possibility and probability of a revelation, and impossible to maintain the impossibility of miracles. Having been obliged to yield thus far to the Christian argument, the deist is unable thereafter to withstand the positive evidence in favour of Christianity. Moreover Deism is beset by the same difficulties in effect which surround the Christian revelation, without its lights, its consolations, its blessings. The man, therefore, who rejects Christianity seldom finds his resting-place in Deism. He becomes a pantheist or an atheist.

Naked atheism, however, is a repulsive creed. It is a heart-withering negation. It touches no sympathy; it stimulates no play of intellect; under the deadly chill of its unlighted vacancy, imagination cannot breathe. There is nothing about it refined, or subtle, or profound. It is the barest and hardest form of infidelity, and has been professed by the coarsest minds. It demands no effort to comprehend its one universal negation and it taxes no skill to expound it. It is an arid and barren, a cold and dreary, hypothesis, which no genius, not even that of Lucretius, could make attractive. The old illustration is conclusive as to its absurdity. It would be immensely less monstrous to maintain that the Iliad, in its full perfection, might have been the product of the "fortuitous concourse" of the letters of the Greek alphabet, than that this infinitely wonderful and glorious universe is the result of the "fortuitous concourse of atoms." Stark atheism, therefore, however it may have flourished in the heartless and hopeless France of a hundred years ago, was never likely to take root in the soil of European scepticism as the alternative of Christianity. In England it has had very few votaries. Nor has atheism, as such, ever found favour in the land of Luther and Melancthon, the favourite soil of mysticism and pietism. English deism and Scottish scepticism did, indeed, produce potent effects in Germany a hundred years ago; but the result was neither deism, nor such scepticism as that of Hume, nor atheism, but a dreamy idealistic pantheism. And now Germany, with a disastrous fidelity, by an infusion into our literature of its pantheistic unbelief, has repaid to Britain the debt which it contracted by its importation of English deism and Scottish scepticism. At the present moment a pantheistic philosophy is the philosophy in which unbelief for the most part invests itself in England.

Hence the task which falls to me to-day cannot but be felt by myself to be one of very grave importance. I could unfeignedly have wished that it had fallen into other and more competent hands. Perhaps, however, I may venture to claim two qualifications which may, in some measure, help to fit me for dealing with the subject on which I have to speak. One is, that the subject of Pantheism is one which has much and frequently exercised my thoughts for many years past, ever since I learnt from the writings of

Coleridge, Hare, and others the meaning of what Hare spoke of as the "fascination of Pantheism;" ever since I was led to the study of philosophy and its development, and especially of the thoughts of the early Greek wrestlers with the mysteries of being, of the Alexandrian Neo-Platonists, and of the modern thinkers of Germany, who have filled with transcendental exhalations of verbal dialectics the vacuum in speculation which had been created by the destructive logic of Kant. The other qualification which I venture to claim for my task to-day is that I have some knowledge of the difficulties of thought and belief which may lead honest men to become pantheists; that I understand the manner of thought of one who has become entangled in the mazy coil of pantheistic reasonings; at all events, that I know that honest searchers after truth *may* reluctantly become intellectually pantheists, while yet their heart longs to retain faith and worship towards a personal God. If, therefore, one necessary condition of true success in argument is an intellectual and, as far as possible, a moral sympathy with one's opponents, that condition, I believe, is fulfilled in my case. And I cannot but think that all Christian controversialists ought to feel a tender sympathy towards honest thinkers who are involved in the bewildering confusions of a philosophy which they do not love, even although they may, after many a struggle and in sadness of heart, have succumbed at length to Pantheism as the only conclusion of controversy in which they are able to abide.

My subject to-day is not the history of Pantheism, but its principles. The history could not be dealt with in one lecture; the principles, I hope, may. And whatever may be the intellectual genesis, the descent and derivation, or the special character, of any particular form of Pantheism, all its forms will be found to coincide in certain respects. The semi-Hegelian of Oxford, and the pantheist who falls back on the lines of Mr. Herbert Spencer's speculations as his place of defence, may both be regarded as standing on common ground for the purpose of my present argument.

In attempting a criticism of the principles of Pantheism, the first thing to be done is to obtain as clear an idea as possible of what is to be understood by Pantheism, as distinguished from Theism on the one hand, and from Atheism on the other. There can be no doubt that the difficulties, both metaphysical and moral, which attach to the conception of a personal God, the Creator and Governor of the universe, have, more than any other cause, constrained thoughtful men who have pondered the problem of the universe, to endeavour to escape from their perplexities and bewilderments by taking refuge in the notion of a diffused impersonal divinity. And it must be confessed that these difficulties are so oppressive and so staggering to our incompetent human reason, that they might well tempt the mere reasoner, the mere logician, the mere metaphysician, to give up faith in a personal God, if so to do were not really to involve one's self in more than equivalent difficulties of the very same class, besides many other difficulties, and in truth contradictions, both intellectual and also moral, which are involved in the pantheistic hypothesis. That the alternative is such as I have now stated, that the pantheistic hypothesis is necessarily beset with such difficulties and contradictions, will in part be shown by the inquiry which, as I have intimated, must needs come first of all in the criticism I am to attempt. An investigation of the meaning of Pantheism, of the characteristic idea proper to the intermediate hypothesis which rejects equally A-Theism and Theism, will open to view the metaphysical difficulties and contradictions involved in the hypothesis. I shall afterwards try to show the incompatibility of the principles of Pantheism with the true principles of natural science. The moral considerations belonging to the Christian controversy with Pantheism I shall reserve till the final stage in my argument.

Pantheism agrees with atheism in its denial of a personal Deity. Its divinity of the universe is a divinity without a will and without conscious intelligence. In what respect, then, does Pantheism really differ from atheism? If we eliminate from our idea of the divinity of the universe all consciousness, all sympathy, all will, what sort of a divinity remains, what sense of a present and real divine power is left to the man that shrinks from atheism? Atheism denies that in, or over, or with nature there is anything whatever besides nature. Does not Pantheism do the very same? If not, what is there, let the pantheist tell us, in nature besides nature? What sort of a divinity is that which is separate from conscious intelligence and from voluntary will or power? Is it said that though there be no Deity in the universe, yet there is a harmony, a unity, an unfolding plan and purpose, which must be recognised as transcending all limitation, as unerring, inexhaustible, infinite, and therefore as divine? Let us ask ourselves what unity that can be which is above mere nature, as such, and yet stands in no relation to a personal Lord and Ruler of the universe; what plan and purpose that can be which is the product of no intelligence, which no mind ever planned; what infinite and unerring harmony can mean, when there is no harmonist to inspire and regulate the life and movement of the whole. Do not the points of distinction which the pantheist makes between his philosophy and the bald tenets of the atheist amount in effect to so many admissions that the facts of the universe cannot be stated, that the phenomena of nature cannot be described, with anything like fidelity or accuracy, without the use of language such as has no real meaning unless it implies the existence and operation throughout universal nature of a supreme actuative and providential Mind and Will?

The least and lowest implication which is involved in Pantheism, the most elementary idea which the word pantheism can be held to connote, the barest *minimum* of meaning which the creed of the pantheist can be presumed to contain, is that there is in the whole of nature—in this universe of being—a *divine unity*. Let us then look at this word *unity*, and consider closely what it must mean.

Those who believe in a divine unity pervading all nature must imply that in the midst of the infinite complexity and variety of the universe there is everywhere to be recognised a grand law and order of nature—a method, plan, and harmony in the great whole, which must consequently be traceable through all the parts. But whose and whence is this grand law? Is it indeed a reality? Are all things fitted to each other, part to part, law to law, force to force, throughout the infinite depths of microscopic disclosures, throughout the infinite exuberance of nature's grandest provinces, throughout all space and all duration? Do all things work to meet each other? Is every several life-cell, each organic fibre, moving, tending, developing, making escapes or overtures, as if a separate angel of unerring sympathy and insight, of illimitable plastic skill and power, of creative energy and perfect providence, inhabited, inspired, and actuated it? Is it so that the man of science, who enters into communion with nature's actual life, and movement, and purpose, seems to see and feel divinities, unrestingly, unweariedly, in silent omnipotence, in infinite diffusion, everywhere at work, so that the reverent inquirer and gazer to whom this wondrous spectacle is unveiled, could almost, in his own pantheistic sense, adopt the invocation of Coleridge, and address the powers he sees at work in such words as these:

> "Spirits that hover o'er
> The immeasurable fount,
> Ebullient with creative Deity!
> *And ye of plastic power that interfused*
> *Roll through the grosser and material mass,*
> *In organizing surge! Holies of God!*
> (*And what if Monads of the Infinite Mind?*)"

Is it so? I ask. Then, what does such a real harmony and such universal correspondence and providence as this imply? Surely we must perforce adopt one of two alternatives. If we refuse to believe in One Ruling, Organizing, Creative Mind, One Living, Universal Mind and Will and Providence, which works through all, we must endow each separate being, or at least each form of life, with creative energy, illimitable and all-answering sensibility and sympathy, unerring wisdom, and veritable will. Nay, ultimately, as it seems to me, the alternative must be between accepting the faith in an infinite God, and attributing to even the particles of inorganic matter, amenable as these are to the laws of gravitation and chemical combination, a wisdom, will, and power of their own, the power of intelligence and of self-direction. As to what are called the laws of gravitation and of chemical combination, we know that a law, like "an idol," is "nothing in the world" but a name. "There is no power but of God; the powers that be, are ordained of God." A law is not a power; the laws of science do but define observed methods of movement or forms of customary relation between thing and thing.

Of one thing, at any rate, I think we may be sure, that a mere order of nature, ascertained though it may have been by the truest and surest induction, cannot have made and cannot sustain itself, cannot be self-originated and self-impelled. So also it is certain that a mere plastic universal power, apart from any creative or providential mind, however its products might seem to imply intelligence, could be animated by no conscious purpose, and could not be conceived as working with blind automatic certainty conformably to a grand cosmical plan or towards a providential end. And if the divinity of the pantheist is nothing more than a personified law or order of nature, his personification of this order or law can add nothing to its virtue or potency, can by no means transform it from a phrase into a living power, from a figure of speech into a real and intelligent force, can never constitute it into a divinity. The more I reflect upon the subject, the more assured the conclusion appears to be, that any conception of a real unity in and of nature is self-contradictory and unmeaning, except upon the assumption of a conscious and intelligent Creator. The unity of nature, to a man who denies the existence of a real God, cannot be a unity inherent in nature, cannot be a unity according to which nature itself has been planned, and is really working; it is an imputed unity, the conception of the pantheistic philosopher's own mind. Unity, indeed, as apprehended by us—and it can only be known through our apprehension of it—is essentially a conception, a relative idea. If one could conceive nature as existing destitute of a mind either to work on a plan, or to recognise a plan in working, in such nature there could be no unity. Unity in action implies a plan of voluntary working, and therefore a regulating mind. Unity of conception and exposition implies an intelligent observer. The unity of nature, if it be not the plan and work of the very God, can be nothing more than a scheme and conception which has been invented and imputed by man.

But perhaps it may be thought that the word unity,

as used by pantheists, should be understood rather as referring to the ultimate oneness and identity of all force throughout the universe, than to harmony of universal plan and purpose. Various as are the appearances of nature, and the modes in which the laws of nature operate, it may yet be set forth by the pantheist as his belief,—a belief, he will say, which the modern advance of science tends continually to establish as the true theory of the universe,—that all force is ultimately one, that the different forces of nature are mutually convertible and equivalent, that one energy of nature, Protean, universal, of infinite plasticity and power of variation or adaptation, pervades and actuates all things. It may be called gravitation, or electricity, or light, or heat, or nervous energy, or vital force; but ultimately and essentially it is one and the same; it is, to quote well-worn lines which will be held here strictly to apply—

> "Changed thro' all, and yet in all the same."

It

> "Warms in the sun, refreshes in the breeze,
> Glows in the stars, and blossoms in the trees;
> Lives thro' all life, extends thro' all extent,
> Spreads undivided, operates unspent:
> Breathes in our soul, informs our mortal part,
> * * * * * * * *
> To it no high, no low, no great, no small,
> It fills, it bounds, connects, and equals all."

Now if this be the pantheistic unity which is admitted by

men who deny a personal Deity, I will not stay to object that such a view is hardly consistent with the essential distinction in nature which even Professor Huxley and men of his school unwaveringly and powerfully maintain, between inorganic matter and living forms. It is more to my purpose to remark that it is much simpler and easier to believe in a personal God, than in such an impersonal divinity as this Protean Force. Every difficulty which belongs to the thought of God's existence belongs to this also. This force must be self-originated, must have been from everlasting, must be creative, omnipresent, providential, equal to all plans, purposes, contrivances, inspirations, which have been, or ever will be, in this dædalean and infinite universe; must be the source of all intelligence, though itself unintelligent; of all sympathy, although itself incapable of sympathy; must have formed the eye, though it cannot see, and the ear, though it cannot hear; must have blossomed and developed into personal intelligences, although personal intelligence is a property which cannot be attributed to it; must unquestionably be omniscient as well as omnipresent, or it could not, in its infinite convertibility, anticipate all needs, meet all demands, answer in absolute and universal harmony to every faculty, capability, and tendency of all things that are and all things that become. Now is it reasonable to object to the doctrine of a personal Deity because of its inconceivability and its stupendous difficulties, and yet to believe in such a primal, essential, immaterial, creative, infinite, blind and unintelligent force as this? Surely no contradiction could be greater. The conception of God as from everlasting *is* stupendous. But an infinite Protean Force from everlasting, destitute of intelligence and will, yet continually operative as the life, soul, wisdom, and providence, of all things, is nothing less than contradictory and absurd.

I can come to no conclusion, accordingly, but that Pantheism really only differs from atheism, in so far as it confesses that it is impossible to speak with ordinary propriety, or in any such way as to meet the necessities either of science itself or of the common sense and feelings of mankind, without employing theistic language. It has been said that hypocrisy is the homage which vice pays to virtue. So a profession of Pantheism is the tribute of compliance at least in speech, is the outward language of homage, which theism has power to extort from atheism. "Pantheism," as is said by the author of *Lothair*, "is but atheism *in domino*. Nothing," as the same writer adds, "can surely be more monstrous than to represent a creator as unconscious of creating."

Yes, Pantheism is but veiled atheism. Strip Pantheism of all involutions of thought and all investitures of language, and in its naked truth it stands forth as mere atheism.

Every form which Pantheism takes, every disguise which it assumes, to hide from itself and from the world its real character, is a testimony borne by atheism to the necessity which all men feel for assuming the existence of Deity; What Robespierre is reported to have said with reference to political government and national well-being, that if there were not a God, it would be necessary to invent one, is felt by pantheistic philosophers to be true in regard to nature. So monstrous a conception is that of this universe without a governing mind; so clearly and directly to the common sense of mankind do the infinite harmonies of the universe seem to imply a designing and governing Intelligence; so indubitably does the might and life of the universe, ever coming forth anew, ever springing up afresh, ever unfolding and advancing, imply a central living Power, One with the infinite governing Intelligence; that pantheists, in order to speak and write intelligibly, are compelled to invest nature with the qualities which they deny to the Deity, to attribute a spirit and intelligence to the whole machine, because they deny the existence of the great Mechanist; to personify a harmony and unity which is but an abstraction, which, on their own hypothesis, is but a grand accident, a result without a cause, because they refuse to believe in a personal God.

I am very far indeed from wishing to come under the

definition of what Mr. Hutton has spoken of as the "Hard Church," or to carry my positions merely by the use of the dilemma, yet I cannot refrain from saying, parenthetically, that the argument of the dilemma, carefully and truly applied, is not only always legitimate but often necessary, and I must affirm that it applies very closely in the present instance. The pantheist cannot maintain his position midway between atheism and theism. If he absolutely refuses to be a theist, it is necessary to show him that he will have to yield to the cruel necessity of acknowledging himself to be an atheist. Standing midway, his position is altogether untenable, from whichever side it is assailed. On the one side, the pantheist is condemned by the same arguments which condemn atheism; on the other side, the atheist may justly allege against the position of the pantheist the selfsame difficulties which both pantheist and atheist urge against theism.

But if pantheism be in reality only atheism, I may henceforth disregard the verbal distinction between the two, and bring forward considerations and arguments which apply indifferently to either. In pursuing the discussion I shall take up in detail some points of argument already, as to their general scope, more or less distinctly intimated in the preliminary considerations which I have advanced.

To explode any view of the world which excludes from it

the presence and government of a personal God, nothing more is needed than to realize and truly understand the atheistic view in its various aspects. Let us try the atheist's theory on the history of the universe, and see whether it can be made to fit, or must be broken in the attempt to fit it.

The will and interference of God, as the Lord and Ruler of the universe, is excluded. The universe is held to have been from the beginning without a shaping and ruling intelligence and will. No mind has presided over its destinies, has aminated its energies; no providence of Divine power and wisdom has guided its changes and progress, has renewed and replenished and sustained it. It follows that no power or will from beyond itself has ever touched the universe. Its own unaided and unguided powers have done all. If the universe did not make itself, it has developed itself: all that has been, or is to be, was included potentially in that which was at the beginning, and has unfolded in necessary order. The vision presented is to certain minds very fascinating: it is a vision of vast unbroken progress, of continual and infinite self-development. But let it be worked out, and let us consider what it really means. Such an hypothesis must lead us back, in the infinite dim distance of the original and indistinguishable past, into a universe-mist of germinal powers from which all has since developed.—But stay. Was this mist and expanse of universal nature in its *origines* all homogeneous and at one stage of existence? Then I have to ask, whence came it? What, going ever further and further back, where were the infinitely earlier, fainter, evanishing entities or powers, into which infinite creative force and potentiality was diffused? and what the one life and grand harmony of influences and impulses, tending towards an infinite goal of progress and perfection, which pervaded the whole? What does all this mean? Is this easier, simpler, more rational, than to believe in God from everlasting? Is anything gained in simplicity, comprehensibility, probability, or in scientific character, by denying that in the "increasing purpose" which "runs through the ages" there is any guidance of a divine intelligence or working of a divine will; and calling the whole process from first to last, from everlasting to everlasting, "development"? What is this word development but a name? Does the use of the word explain anything? Does the use of the word reduce the mystery of the universe to the simplicity of an axiom? Does the use of the word provide a simple equivalent for all that divine wisdom, power, and providence, have ever been imagined to do for the universe? Men call the mystery of being and becoming by the name of development, and then say that all things are effected by development, and that development explains all! Whereas this development of which they talk so familiarly, as though they understood all its secrets, and were privy to its infinitely various and mighty workings, and could unfold its source and meaning, is itself all the time the very mystery to be resolved and explained. Development is in truth as amazing and incomprehensible a mystery as creation. It seems to be but another word for creation. Only they who affect its use instead of the word *creation*, insist upon creation without a creator. The unintelligent and unconscious universe, on their view, is continually creating itself.

The hypothesis of development, however, is not only unintelligible and utterly devoid of reality, when criticized in its general principle; as might be expected, it altogether breaks down when it is tested in detail. Professor Huxley's protoplasm breaks it down. All the scientific evidence, as that eminent teacher of science showed at Liverpool last autumn, is opposed to the idea that protoplasm was developed out of inorganic matter. The hypothesis of spontaneous life-generation appears to be exploded. Science, at any rate, on its own positive principles, has no right whatever to pretend that life has ever been developed out of what was not living. Here, then, a great and, so far as science can help us to form a judgment, an altogether impassable barrier rises to view against any development hypothesis. At a certain stage in the history of the universe protoplasm, organized life, made its appearance on the scene, starting up as a perfectly new, an original, an undeveloped phenomenon. Before, all had been inorganic and dead; now Life was abroad in the world, destined to increase and multiply, and replenish the universe. Let those who deny divine and creative will and government, inform us whence came this life. It was not developed. Must it not have been created. If not, then whence, I ask, whence did it spring?

The argument which I have just urged should, as I venture to think, be conclusive even with those who know, and seek to know, nothing more of science than the order and method of its phenomenal processes. I will now bring forward a consideration which will, I hope, be admitted to have weight by those men of science—it is to be greatly lamented that there should be so few of these—who have studied the nature and working of the mind as well as the phenomena of sense. We have seen that protoplasm—that Life—was not developed out of inorganic matter, but appears to have been an entirely new and primary fact on the face of the universe. Life came in and appropriated, put to its own uses, bound up under its own seal, impregnated with its own specific virtue, the raw inorganic materials which it found in nature; but the power of Life itself was altogether new. A fact in some sort analogous to this confronts us in a higher sphere, in the sphere of living intelligence itself. I refer to the emergence of personal consciousness among the world of living creatures. To me it appears that the sense of personality is an altogether new and original fact, one which cannot be conceived as developed or developable out of any pre-existing phenomena or conditions. Whence it comes, or how it arises, I know not. But it appears to be, in and of itself, the assertion of an essential separateness between One's Self and all phenomena, all constituents, all conditions whatever. The sense of an I Myself, of Personality, asserts an antithesis between the Man, and all that the Man uses, takes up into his personality, makes his own. As Life binds up inorganic matter under its seal, but is not developed out of inorganic matter, so the voluntary and responsible Self binds up under the seal of its own personality all that belongs to the manifold life of its complex being. As life brings into the universe a new world of phenomena, higher and more manifold than those of mere inorganic matter, yet embodying and adopting these, so personality brings into the universe a new world of vastly higher and rarer phenomena than those of mere vitality, yet embodies and adopts these:—it introduces all that belongs to reflection and morality, giving birth to an intelligence and a world of thought, in which all the lower and anterior phenomena of the world become matters of cognisance, and are mirrored as objects of thought.

As I venture to think that this sense of personality, with

the new world of reflective consciousness and morality which it brings in, is a fact, starting up in the midst of a universe of anterior developments, such as all Mr. Darwin's solvents utterly fail to touch, a phenomenon which remains as far from explanation as before he wrote his last book, so it appears to me that the power of human speech is another fact starting up in the midst of the line of supposed developments which no hypothesis of evolution can afford any help towards explaining. Miraculously developed reason, something higher, as it seems to me, than any development of human reason our race has, in its highest culture, as yet put forth, must have been necessary in order to the invention of language by any race even of the most sagacious mammals. And yet, again, speech itself is a necessity, a necessary instrument, in order to the high development of reason. We have some idea what deaf mutes of our human family are like, when no painstaking and kindly culture has been bestowed on their intelligence, and temper, and affections, and conscience. Let us conceive the whole race of man to be, and to have been from the beginning, not indeed deaf, but congenitally and irreversibly dumb, with no more power of articulate expression than a horse, or let us say, a dog. What would the development of human reason have been under such conditions? How, then, is it possible to conceive that the wondrous faculty and instrument of speech was ever invented and perfected by mammals of infra-human faculty and development, and that they were afterwards through this invention developed yet more highly, until they attained to the dignity and advancement of humanity? Such infra-human mammals must have been more miraculously endowed in order to such an invention than ever man himself has been.

After all that Mr. Darwin has written, does or can any reasonable man or woman actually believe in the possibility,—*apart from the Divine Power and Will and Guidance*,—for that is the point,—of the self-development, the spontaneous upgrowth of articulate language? Let us study our quadrupedal familiars, for the sake of illustration and analogy. We see daily how our noble dogs strain and groan after speech, do all but speak: we mark their eloquent looks, their speaking gestures, their wonderfully expressive movements, how they watch us speak, and seem as if they understood what speech is to us, and as if they craved most longingly the power for themselves. We cannot but sympathetically admire the intelligent, the benevolent, the noble, the sagacious physiognomies which they show. If any creature ever could, would, or did develop speech in any rudimentary form, are not they just in the circumstances to do it? And when once rudimentally begun, however uncouthly and imperfectly, should not their organs continually improve by the continual effort and the increasing intelligence? Is it not immensely less hard of belief, and less difficult to imagine, that dogs should develop speech, than that man should have been developed from the larvæ of the *ascidiæ?* Yet is there even a beginning made towards the canine development of articulate language, or does any living man believe that such a beginning ever could be made?

To me it appears that human speech and human personality are in some way bound up with each other, that the one, in some sort, implies the other, and that these two characteristics of our race present an insuperable obstacle to the acceptance by really scientific thinkers of any hypothesis of evolution which, leaving God out of nature, would account for the whole existence and progress of the universe on the principle of spontaneous development.

But again, let me be allowed to test the development hypothesis in detail at another point. This hypothesis—and any pantheistic or atheistic view of the universe which professes to be scientific—is obliged to confess that all living beings, of whatever sort, have been developed out of a single primary cell—called often a germ-cell—of protoplasm. Here they find the beginning of every kind of life. The plant, the animal, of every sort,—the lichen, the cedar, the sponge, the bird, the mammal, the minutest entozoon, the most microscopic infusorium, and man,—have been developed out of these primary cells. What then do the same men who teach us this, find to be the constitution of these same cells, when microscopically examined? They find them to be, for the most part, and indeed always, if allowance be made for very trivial exceptions, identically the same. The matter is identically the same, the appearance identically the same; no difference whatever of constitution, form, or properties, is to be detected. They cannot tell whether the nettle, or the frog, or the eagle, or the man, is to be developed out of any given cell: for anything their science can teach them, any of these might be developed, as they call it, out of any cell. But if this be so, is it scientific, is it real or true, is it not altogether misleading, to speak of *mere development* in such a case? The flower may be said to be developed out of the bud because the bud is the flower in miniature, the flower is really folded up in the bud. But surely here is no case of mere development; here is no unfolding out of the germ-cell of what is potentially contained in the cell, regarded as a merely material organism. Judged by every test of physical experiment, the primary cells are identically the same; and yet they grow into forms essentially and infinitely dissimilar. Does it not clearly appear that here is a matter in which some power above and beyond the mere physical constitution and nature of the primary cell must be admitted, on every principle of science, on every ground of pure candour and truth, to be of necessity present? Is it not evident that with each germ-cell there must be associated some individual life-power which animates the cell, which uses it as a unit to multiply, as a foundation to build upon, which does build and weave and work into it and upon it continually new material, which, for its own use in its work of weaving and fabricating, and for the completion of its own distinctive form and vehicle, takes toll of air and earth and water and heat-power—the ancient elements—selecting out of them its appropriate pabulum, in whatever chemical combinations of the primary elements known to our modern scientific analysis may be fit and needful? Surely not development, but life, the mystery of individual life, is here. And if the philosopher will deny the omnipresent creative and sustaining power of God, it appears to me that he must be prepared to animate each germ-cell with an individual intelligence which works with divine power, on a definite and most miraculous plan, and towards a distinct goal of perfection. To call such various powers and processes, such diverse and generically different operations, in every sphere of life, by the same term, appears to me to be unscientific; to speak of them all alike as processes of unfolding or development, when results the most infinitely unlike and separate are obtained from beginnings which are identically alike, appears to be not only unscientific but altogether misleading.

I do not think it arrogant or unwarranted to conclude from such considerations as I have been trying to set forth, that evolution, or development, apart from the power and guidance of the Living God, is an unphilosophical, an unscientific idea, an empty, an unmeaning word. It is a thing of naught, utterly impotent to solve the mysteries of the universe, even when expounded and reinforced by Mr. Darwin's "Natural Selection." I have not a word to say here against the views of Mr. Darwin, as defined and modified by the requirements of scientific modesty and precision. If I had any pretensions to be called a student of natural science, I should sit at the feet of Mr. Darwin when he speaks, not as a philosophic theorist, but as a scientific observer and a truly inductive naturalist. But I must say here in respect to Natural Selection, regarded as, according to Mr. Darwin's hypothesis, the handmaid of development, that, like development, it is but a name, and not a power. It describes the order and mode according to which Providence works; it is not itself a force—a working energy. Mr. Darwin himself indeed often speaks as if Natural Selection were itself a power and a providence. I find to my hand in Mr. Kingsley's fine, suggestive paper on *The Natural Theology of the Future*, recently published in *Macmillan's*

Magazine, a sentence of Mr. Darwin's in regard to Natural Selection which I will quote. "It may be metaphorically said," writes Mr. Darwin, "that natural selection is daily and hourly scrutinizing throughout the world every variation even the slightest; rejecting that which is bad, preserving and adding up that which is good, silently and necessarily working whenever and wherever opportunity offers at the improvement of every organic being." "It may be metaphorically said," are Mr. Darwin's words. But in fact he is using, not a metaphor, but a personification. The distinction Mr. Darwin does not see. He repeatedly speaks of his personifications as metaphors. But the distinction notwithstanding is most important. By personifying Natural Selection Mr. Darwin makes it appear to be a cause, attributes to it a real power, nay, wisdom and providence, as well as power. He speaks in one place of "Nature's power of selection;" contrasting this with the "powers of artificial selection exercised by feeble man," by which, however, man can do so much; and arguing that "Nature's power of selection" must be incomparably greater, and competent to produce incomparably superior effects in respect of "the beauty and infinite complexity of the co-adaptations between all organic beings, one with another, and with their physical conditions of life." Language of a similar sort he very frequently uses. He has, therefore, as a scientific man laid himself open to the reproof of M. Flourens, whom no one will deny to be a scientific critic. "Either," says M. Flourens, "Natural Selection is nothing, or it is nature, but nature endowed with the attribute of selection—nature personified, which is the last error of the last century; the nineteenth century has done with personifications." The nineteenth century ought to have done with personifications; but with the spirit of Lamarck's speculations the style of the French atheistic philosophy of the last century reappears.

Mr. Darwin, in the passage quoted by Mr. Kingsley, describes the manner in which his Natural Selection may be conceived as operating. What, if his meaning were expressed with strict scientific truth, he ought to intend to say, is that such as he describes is the result of providential working according to the mode and order which he designates by the phrase Natural Selection. "All we ask," says one of Mr. Darwin's ablest critics, "is that we may be allowed to believe in a God and a real Divine Providence, as powerful and wise and good as Mr. Darwin's Natural Selection."

But, moreover, it must not be forgotten that there is something besides the mere process of change and growth, of what our philosophers call development, to be accounted for. There is a fact on which the growth, the change, the evolution, must be held in a true sense to depend: a prior fact to be taken account of. The growth proceeds upon a plan, and fulfils an idea: protoplasm itself embodies a scientific principle. But as the seal must be before the impression, the original before the copy, so the principle must be before its embodiment, the plan and the idea must be before the growth: the end, towards which as its goal the growth or development proceeds, must have been conceived and set up as an aim before its fulfilment began. We are bound therefore, if we would exhaust the problem, nay, if we would truly conceive, and justly state it, to ask how and whence the principle, the plan, the idea, the end, had their existence? These are realities; they are the most inner and essential realities in every instance of growth or development; to deal only with the development of the physical basis, is to leave untouched the kernel of the matter, is altogether superficial and unreal. But principles, plans, types and ideas, ends contemplated in movement and progress, these at any rate are not physical, are not matters of sense and organization. They are, as I have said, prior to what is physical, they are conditions antecedent to organization and growth. Moreover, they are mental conceptions, not physical affections. They are only possible, they have no meaning, except as the thoughts of some mind. Here, then, we are brought back by an inevitable necessity to an antecedent mind, the seat and origin of all the principles, the plans the ideas, the ends, embodied in organized beings, and fulfilled in their existence, growth, and perfection. In short, from whatever side we contemplate the problems of nature, and whencesoever we take our point of departure in their investigation, we find ourselves brought face to face with creative mind. The things which are "seen and temporal" lead us always inwards to "the things which are unseen and eternal;" man and creaturely existence conduct us to the living God.

If any one would escape from the pressure of this argument by hardily denying that living organization involves principle or plan, type or idea, purpose or end, it can only follow that the living forms of the universe are an infinite congeries of accidental combinations, that in reality there are no such things as organs, that there can be no such thing as development, and that there is no such thing as law. What men call law is mere sequence that happens to follow regularly. The whole universe has been constituted and regulated by the fortuitous concourse of atoms. Against such a conclusion as this I do not need to argue. It is the naked and repulsive atheism of which I spoke in the introduction to this lecture. The line of argument which I have been pursuing seems to force us to the conclusion that there is no logical resting-place between such theism as Christianity teaches and such Democritean atheism as that of which we have now had a glimpse.

But if this be so, it follows that it is impossible to deny design and final causes in creation, and the sway and oversight of a universal Divine Providence, the providence of a living God, except by denying all law. To the Christian theist, science is living science indeed; to the pantheist, no less than the atheist, science is hardly better than a dead register. He may talk of the wisdom, the power, the order, the benevolence, of nature. But such expressions on the lips of a pantheist are utterly illusive. All the wisdom, all the marvellous adjustments of nature, are but the happy conjunctures, the exquisite chance unisons, of he knows not what. When lost in admiration of marvellous organizations, complexly apt and beautiful contrivances, of what seem like the most studied and beneficent provisions, the soul that is beginning to glow with wonder at this seeming wisdom, and to swell with thankfulness because of this seeming love, must be chilled into blank confusion and amazement by the thought that there is no Being of Wisdom and Benevolence Who is to be thanked and adored because of these His marvellous works. Surely this is enough to darken the universe to the explorer of nature's mysteries, and to fill his soul with perpetual melancholy. Nor is it easy to understand how any man of true science, any real inductive philosopher, who comes into contact with nature's living processes and hears the perpetual whisper of her living voice, can be ensnared into the acceptance of such a hard mystery of sceptical belief as this.

Surely, then, on purely scientific grounds,—the grounds not only of metaphysical but also of natural science, on every ground which can be appealed to by high and pure philosophy, we are at liberty, I should say we are bound, to reject the hypothesis which attempts to expound nature and to solve its mysteries, without the admission of a divine mind. Sense and matter and the observed order of phenomena do not constitute the whole of our science. There are some words written by a poet, too much neglected at the present time, which I cannot forbear from quoting here.

> "How should matter occupy a charge
> Dull as it is, and satisfy a law,
> So vast in its demands, unless impelled
> To ceaseless service by a ceaseless force,
> And under pressure of some conscious cause?
> The Lord of all, Himself through all diffused,
> Sustains, and is the life of all that lives.
> Nature is but a name for an effect,
> Whose cause is God. He feeds the secret fire
> By which the mighty process is maintained,
> Who sleeps not, is not weary; in whose sight
> Slow circling ages are as transient days;
> Whose work is without labour; whose designs
> No flaw deforms, no difficulty thwarts;
> And whose beneficence no charge exhausts."

Surely, if I may here quote some words of Mr. Kingsley's

in the lecture to which I have already referred, this is what men of science "are finding, more and more, below their facts, below all phenomena which the scalpel and the microscope can show, a something nameless, invisible, imponderable, yet seemingly omnipresent and omnipotent, retreating before them deeper and deeper, the deeper they delve, that which the old schoolmen called 'forma formativa,' the mystery of that unknown and truly miraculous element in nature which is always escaping them, though they cannot escape it, that of which it was written of old, 'Whither shall I go from Thy presence, or whither shall I flee from Thy Spirit?'"

The observations which I have thus far offered are directed wholly to the philosophical and scientific aspect of the argument respecting Pantheism. I cannot bring this lecture to an end without referring to the moral branch of the argument. The existence of evil in the universe is alleged as an argument against the existence of God and divine government. Doubtless, the existence of evil is a painful mystery. Many good Christians have felt it to be an oppressive and almost an overwhelming mystery. It is one of the difficulties attendant on the Christian's belief; it is, in fact, the one moral difficulty. But difficulties and mysteries cannot annul the positive necessities of thought and argument. If such arguments as I have endeavoured to state make all science to be contradictory and unintelligible which speaks, in one breath, of the laws and wisdom of nature, and, in the next, denies the existence of a God, then we are bound to accept theism with its inevitable consequences, notwithstanding the mysteries, whether metaphysical or moral, which our faith may involve. Mysteries are not contradictions, and, in whichever direction we move, we shall find it impossible to escape from them. Mysteries surround the position of the sceptic or the atheist, no less than that of the Christian theist; not only mysteries, but, as we have seen, contradictions, beset him round, in whichever direction he turns. The Christian theist, by his faith in God, accepts the mysteries which are involved in the thought of God, but, unlike the unbeliever, he escapes from contradictions and absurdities. It appears that the morality of man—his great glory—that his sense of responsibility and of voluntary moral power, that which most peculiarly constitutes him man, involves the law of moral influence as between man and man. It appears further that the power and faculty of moral influence for good must needs involve the law of moral influence for evil. From the fact of man's own moral nature and moral reponsibility, and the consequent fact of his moral influence over his fellow-men, is derived, not only the possibility of moral evil in the case of a solitary individual, but the possibility, perhaps I may say the naturalness, the probability, of a contagion of moral evil spreading throughout the race, the effect of which can only be counteracted or limited by moral arrangements and influences specially constituted for that end. So much I may perhaps say in general, although the subject is one on which I think it wiser, as a rule, to say nothing. I feel it to be a profound and perilous mystery, however gloriously it may have been made the occasion for the manifestation in Christ Jesus our Lord of the Divine superabounding wisdom, mercy, and power. But if we admit the subject to be involved in profound, even terrible mystery, is that a reason why, making shipwreck at one plunge of all that belongs to humanity, faith and hope and philosophy should commit suicide, and descend together into the gulf of everlasting darkness and despair! Reason may reel and grow dizzy while it looks too long and too absorbedly down the fearful and fathomless depths of the mystery of sin, but that is no sufficient cause why reason should cast itself headlong into the abyss.

Pantheism has only one way in which to escape from the mystery of evil, and that is to deny all distinction between right and wrong, between moral good and moral evil. Of course there can be no such thing as sin for the pantheist, because all, according to his creed, is nature and development and necessity. Holiness is a matter of taste or sentiment. Conscience is an illusive development; what we regard as divine morality is but utilitarianism sentimentalized and exalted into sacred law under the influence of unenlightened impulse and antique superstition, a mere affair of the association of ideas which science will some day explain away. The ontology and ethics of Pantheism may be summed up in one sentence, "Whatever is, is; and there is neither right nor wrong, but all is fate and nature." Pantheism—I say Pantheism just as truly and completely as atheism, for the difference between the two, as we have seen, is but one of name and phrase, and both alike deny God and conscience—Pantheism thus does cruel violence to every better instinct of our nature, outrages all the demands of religion and government, whether human or divine, and makes itself the direst foe of human progress and wellbeing. Many pantheists, doubtless, have been and are virtuous, even noble, men; some, I am prepared to believe, may even, in a certain sense, be religious men. But the direct tendency of the pantheistic philosophy is confessedly what I have now stated. When moral and pure, its pure morality can be nothing more, at least in theory, than a refined utilitarianism. Only as such can any pantheist pretend to impose morality as law.

To sum up, may I not say that Pantheism, whether in its metaphysical or its moral aspect, is the dream of men who will not admit that there is in the universe anything beyond what their senses immediately reveal to them? Its philosophy was represented in the last century in its lower and more popular form by Condorcet; the basis of whose system was laid in the principle, "penser c'est sentir,"—thought is nothing more than sense or feeling; in its higher and more intellectual form it was represented by the sceptical sense-idealism of Hume. At the present day Bain and Mill have endeavoured to develop the principle of Condorcet in harmony with the higher and more subtle philosophy of Hume. The result appears to be a sort of nihilistic sense-idealism. Matter is probably nothing different from our mental ideas—so far Berkeley, no less than Hume, is followed; our ideas, however developed, are yet essentially only the combination and interfusion of our sensations and sense-associations; meantime there is no evidence of the real and substantial existence either of the world outside us, or of ourselves as true and separate selves or persons, or of God. Such at least would seem to be the metaphysics of the distinctively *English* school of Pantheism, *i.e.*, of Pantheism rendered into philosophic system by the English mind. The German Pantheism has *infected* the *tendencies* of English thought and criticism, but, notwithstanding the influence of Hegel at Oxford, has not been reproduced in any English system of egoistic Pantheism. In their aspects and results, in relation to theism and Christian faith, the German egoistic Pantheism and the English sense-idealistic Pantheism strictly coincide.

Such then is the highest philosophy to-day of those who, refusing to be called atheists, nevertheless reject all faith in God; of those who, rejecting Christian theism, claim to be positively neither more nor less than the men of science. Men of science though they be, their philosophy is the philosophy of nescience and the philosophy of despair. We need be under no apprehension that such a philosophy will ever be generally accepted. It is too strong, too sorrowful, too nauseous a composition to suit the common taste. It not only dissolves morality and its foundations, but it precludes all hope of immortality. The race indeed may be immortal and progressively great and glorious, although how even so much can be known is more than I can see; but the individual man by man, woman by woman, child by child, perishes each one for ever. Men and women with yearning, loving hearts, with tender and passionate affections, who have buried their dead out of their sight, and who could not endure to live if they were doomed to sorrow without hope, cannot but reject with loathing and horror such doctrines as these. Men of various culture, of manifold intellectual resources, who live in the midst of refined and accomplished society, and who are not suffering from the pang of immedicable anguish and irreparable bereavement, may possibly live so merely intellectual and speculative a life, may be so wholly absorbed in mere science, may have so far separated themselves from all that belongs to the heart's affections and the trembling religious sensibilities of human nature, as to adopt the philosophy of nihilism with hardy calmness, although I confess that it passes my power to understand or conceive this; such men may be content to follow their speculative conclusions into the "blackness of darkness" for ever, and may thus, if not less, be more than the common crowd of humanity. But such a philosophy will not content those who share the ordinary wants and sensibilities of our race. The working, sorrowing, loving, hoping men and women of this human race will no more be able to satisfy themselves with any atheistic or, if any should prefer so to call it, pantheistic philosophy, than they can "feast upon the east wind." They will cleave to that Christian truth and faith which has "brought life and immortality to light," and which, in "showing" to the craving heart of needy, sorrowing, sinful man "the Father" reconciled in Christ, has blessedly "sufficed" a longing world.

Indeed, it would seem that, when it comes to the point, even distinguished leaders in the ranks of those against whose views I have been arguing, find it impossible to give up their faith, at least in immortality. Rénan is unquestionably one of the most distinguished leaders among those men of learning and culture who deny the existence of a creative will and Personal God. Yet Rénan cannot make up his mind that he has lost for ever his beloved sister; that she has passed into the night of nothingness into which he must soon follow her. In the dedication to her memory of his "Life of Jesus," he addresses an invocation to "the pure soul of his sister Henriette, who died at Byblos, Sept. 24th, 1861;" and appeals to her "to reveal to him, from the bosom of God in which she rests, those truths which are mightier than death, and take away the fear of death."

Rénan, then, after all, cannot give up his sister, nor, if it were only for her sake, his belief in immortality. And yet how utterly unscientific is such a belief, if science is to be defined and limited in accordance with the principles of the anti-theistic philosophy. Where can our men of mere sense-science find any physical basis of immortality? There is no hope, no instinct or faith, at once so indissolubly bound up with our nature, so necessary to the development of all that is best in man, and so utterly destitute of evidence and basis in merely natural science, as our assurance of immortality. If we are to retain our belief in immortality, we must maintain our faith in realities above and apart from sense, in realities which cannot be tested or investigated by any appliances of natural science. If immortality be true, Pantheism cannot be true.

What, then, have we found respecting the seductive and too fashionable illusion which has led astray so many minds, especially of speculative, restless, and daring intelligence, in the present age? We have found that Pantheism is essentially only atheism in disguise, and occupies a position in which it combines against itself the arguments which theists have to allege against atheism, and atheists against theism; that, while it dethrones the true God, it sets up in His place Development and Natural Selection as its divinities, clothing them with the attributes which it denies to deity; that its development hypothesis will not bear the test of science, of the natural science to which it professes to appeal; that the origin of protoplasm, the attributes of man, and the growth and transformation of germ-cells, alike refuse to accord with the hypothesis; that the very nature of science itself, as recognizing law and organization, is incompatible with any philosophy which denies theism; that the moral difficulties which rise up as a barrier against a denial of the Christian theism are no less insurmountable than the metaphysical and scientific difficulties; that morality, conscience, natural affection, immortal hope, every deepest, most tender and sacred, most blessed and humanising, instinct of our nature is violated by the denial of a personal and holy God and Judge; in a word, that our whole humanity revolts against it.

May I venture to hope that the views which I have now endeavoured to set forth may have some weight with young and inquiring spirits? No more terrible suffering can there be, than for an honest, loving, and virtuous nature to become involved in the meshes of pantheistic doubt and unbelief. We must make up our minds to bear with many profound and painful mysteries which are not to be solved by man; but may the good Spirit of God save us each and all from losing our childlike faith in His almighty, omnipresent, and absolutely good and holy government and providence!

POSITIVISM.

BY THE

REV. W. JACKSON, M.A., F.S.A.,

LATE FELLOW OF WORCESTER COLLEGE, OXFORD.

POSITIVISM.

Everybody in this room has, I suppose, heard of the "positive" sciences, or "Positivism" in some shape or other.

What does "Positivism" mean?

A system based on *positive* facts. But what are facts? They are (says the Positivist) observed phenomena. As for metaphysical conceptions of all sorts, these are *negatives* with nothing real, nothing positively true in them. Truth must be sought amongst cbserved phenomena.

It is worth our while to examine this last proposition. Take a "*phenomenon.*" You have all observed colour,—what is it?

A physicist, if you ask him, will tell you of a modification in a ray of light variously produced—by refraction, for example—as when sunlight breaks a dark cloud into many-tinted beauty. But how if all the world of men and animals were blind?

The physiologist will step in and speak to you of the

structure of the eye—the susceptibility of its retina for special impressions; there he says you may find colour.

Put both accounts together, and they appear as part-causes, each a factor helping to make up a result; which result physicist and physiologist would agree to call colour.

Yet again: Suppose the human and animal world were deprived of all consciousness, all which in the widest meaning we call mind—their eyes remaining like mirrors, telescopes, microscopes; perfect instruments, only every kind of intelligence, instinctive or rational, gone. Where would colour then be? The sun might play upon cloud or rain, the light of a rainbow be reflected in the eye. Were there but perceiving mind, the impression would exist. But we are supposing the impressible to be wanting; there is no sensation, no percipient; colour must remain unknown, for there is nothing capable of observing it.

Now this shows you, first, how important it is to emphasize the word *observed* added to phenomenon. It shows you, secondly, *where* the ultimate seat of every observation really lies; each observed phenomenon, each positive fact, is at last neither more nor less than a mental state. The evidence for each fact is the condition of your own mind, your consciousness as it is called. You may sift the thing witnessed, verify, examine, and cross-examine; but after all, your own consciousness is the first real evidence you have got.

It would seem, then, that the most positive of all sciences would be the science of mind; and the next most positive the sciences which enable us to draw conclusions from our positively existing mental states; the statements, we may call them, which our minds make to us. Yet, strange to say, the very first thing Positivism does is to dispense with a science of mind, as mind, altogether. Mr. Mill makes it a severe reproach against Comte, that he ignores both psychology and logic; recognizes no power in the mind, even of self-observation; accepts no theory even of the inductive process. Mr. Mill characterises Comte's want of mental science as "a grave aberration."* It is indeed so. This appears plainly enough in the example just adduced from our commonest sensation, the every-day phenomenon of colour. It was made up, you saw, of three factors, a physical antecedent, a condition of the sensitive apparatus, and a mind which received into its consciousness the impression instrumentally conveyed to it. This last, you will remember, was the *first* fact to us. It is *the* fact: the revelation of an outward world, its changes and its continuing presence, its rest and its constant motion. Without this fact of inward consciousness, nature would have possessed no more significance than pictures seen in the eyes of the newly dead.

Such being the case, it needs no argument to show the

* See Mill on Comte, p. 62, *seq.*

importance of making quite sure that our interpretation of nature is correct. If there be any unobserved illusion in our sensory instruments, or what must evidently be much worse, in our percipient mind, truth is at an end, and falsehood received in its stead. Hence the necessity of observing our own observations, subjecting our consciousness to scrutiny, and being acquainted with the criteria, not only of our perceptions, but of our judgments. It is this process of analysis and criticism which forms a large part of the method of verification,—a method the value of which did not escape the great Greek philosophers, though some recent writers seem to fancy it a modern discovery.

Inexperienced observers are often so little aware of the pre-eminent importance of this critical process, that I will detain you with an illustration of it for the benefit of my younger auditors. My example shall be taken from perception *par excellence*—our eyesight, *the* sense pronounced surest both in poetry and prose. You will remember your Horace

> Segnius irritant animos demissa per aurem,
> Quam quæ sunt oculis subjecta fidelibus, et quæ
> Ipse sibi tradit spectator.

And almost everybody else has said the same, as witness the old proverb, "Seeing is believing." Now I will mention five instances in which people believe they see something, and do not see it; in other words, the objective antecedent is wanting, and the impression is produced partly by the sensory apparatus, partly by the mind itself. As I describe these instances one by one, let my hearers ask themselves, How does this illusion come about? Is it produced by our optic instrument or by our mental activity?

First, then, Take a lighted stick, and whirl it rapidly round and round. You believe you see a circle of sparks—in reality it is no more than a simple train, and on a like illusion the Catherine-wheel is constructed. Again, put yourself in the hands of an optically inclined friend, and let him operate upon you thus. He shall place a cardboard down the middle axis of your face, quite close against your nose—one side of his board, say the right, coloured a brilliant red, the left a vivid green. After an instant or two let him suddenly substitute another board, white on both sides. Do my young friends guess what will follow? Your right eye will see green, your left red—the reverse of what they saw before; yet neither will see correctly, for both eyes are looking at uncoloured surfaces.

Thirdly, Watch the full moon rising—how large and round she looks, resting as it were upon that eastern hill, and seen amidst the tops of its forest trees! How much larger and broader than when she hangs aloft in upper sky!

Has every one here learned the true reason why? If not, look at her through a slit in a card, and her diameter will be the same. Fourthly, A schoolboy is crossing his bedroom in the deep dark night, anxiously hoping that his head may not come into collision with the bed-post. Though carefully and successfully avoiding it, he imagines of a sudden that the blow is imminent. Quick as thought he stops to save his head, and, behold, the room is as quickly filled with sparks or flames of fire. Another moment, and all becomes dark once more. I have heard many a schoolboy exclaim over this phenomenon, but never knew one who could explain it. Finally, did you ever, on opening your eyes in a morning, close them quickly again, and keep them shut, directing them as if to look straight forwards? Most persons of active nervous power, after a few trials—say a dozen, or a score—are surprised to see colours appear and flit before the sight. Some years ago, Germany's greatest poet tried, at the suggestion of her greatest physiologist, a series of experiments on these coloured images. He found that by an effort of will he could cause them to come and go, govern their movement, march, and succession. And this took place under no conditions of impaired sensation, nor any hallucination of a diseased mind. A thoroughly healthy will succeeded in impressing itself upon physical instruments, controlling their law, and creating at its own pleasure an unfailingly bright phantasmagoria.

Some here may, others may not, have apprehended the distinctions between our five cases. The first two are due to the sensory apparatus, its optical laws of continued impression and complementary colour. In the latter three, mind intervenes. The enlarged size of the moon occurs through rapid comparison, the fiery lights in a dark room through instinctive apprehension, both influences of mind on the sensory system. The fifth and most interesting of all is no bad example of interference between moral and material law. The will truly causative (you may remark) overrules the natural process of physical impression, alters it, and creates a designed effect. I wish I could induce my young friends to devise a number of experiments on similar mixed cases, and, having tried them, to dissect out their real laws. These sharpenings of the critical faculty are exceedingly useful—they cultivate clearness; and most people know that two-thirds among our mistakes in life are caused by confusion of thought.

Besides all other uses, such lessons teach at once the necessity, as we said before, of observing your own observations. And as, first, the real witness of every observation is our mind; every fact[1] which comes through our bodily senses being to us a mental impression, it seems but common sense to hear above all things what mind has to say for and about itself. Then, secondly, where would be the benefit derived from our observations, if we could not reason upon them, or could place no confidence in our own reasonings? Yet the art of reasoning is so purely a mental process, that it can be represented by symbols as abstract and free from material meaning as if they were bare algebraic signs. Thirdly, in the most accurate of sciences mind extends our knowledge far beyond the circle of observation, and gives us axiomatic assurance of its own accuracy. Who ever saw, or ever can see, all straight lines in all conceivable positions, yet who doubts that throughout the whole universe no two straight lines ever did inclose or can inclose a space? And, fourthly, can it be a matter of indifference to any of us what evidence the mind offers concerning its own moral nature, and what is the value of that evidence, and the laws deducible therefrom? How true it thus appears that "know thyself" lies at the root of all knowledge, and that the man who receives no witness from within can know nothing as he ought to know it!

Comte swept away all these and the like considerations by a neat little fiction of his own. We cannot observe ourselves observing, he said, we cannot observe ourselves reasoning. So, then, logic becomes a chimera, and psychology a word of contempt. Respecting this fallacy, Mr. Mill thinks the only wonder is that it should impose on any one. Clearly it imposed on Comte himself. But, "what organon," asks Mill, "for the study of our moral and intellectual functions does M. Comte offer in lieu of the direct mental observation which he repudiates? We are almost ashamed to say it is phrenology!" Mill regards this statement as a *reductio ad absurdum*, but the actual organon substituted is more absurd still. Comte's phrenology was not the phrenology of Gall or Spurzheim, but a funny small bantling of his own, a sort of "infant phenomenon," called into existence not without a Positive purpose. In plain words, mind was no longer to give evidence respecting itself. We must study its laws in brain. How any true correspondence of brain and mind could be known unless both were studied, does not appear. Comte overlooked the question in his anxiety to substitute for psychology and its laws a bodily function and *its* laws. Yet his motive appears to have been excellent! He regarded this dwarfed superficial phrenology, Mr. Mill tells us, "as extricating the mental study of man from the metaphysical stage, and elevating it to the positive." The chief gist of which sentence, bewildering to the uninitiated, opens up the very core and centre of the Positive system—a subject for dissection of some considerable human interest.

Each science is brought into the positive stage when it is co-ordinated according to positive laws—"systematized," Comte would say. He has a perfect mania for systematization; system is with him almost an equivalent for truth. Of course, the real value of every system turns entirely on its co-ordinating method, or principle of formation; and Comte's, we see, was one of positive laws. The nature of these laws is, therefore, the essence and turning-point of the whole matter. I cannot impress upon you too strongly the paramount importance of keeping this truth steadily in view.

But if any one inquires exactly what these laws are, he asks, I fear, a puzzling question. Puzzling, for this reason that, say what one will—employ any words, however carefully selected—one may become liable to the charge of raising a false impression. Positivist *savans* themselves do not use any uniform phraseology, and many phrases they do use are necessarily derived from philosophies most disedifying to Positive ears.

Examples showing what sort of law is really meant are therefore always welcome; and few could be more instructive than this way of making mind Positive. Comte did not falter in his purpose. Later on he explained the necessity (for his system, you understand) of bringing our intellectual and moral phenomena under the same law with other phenomena of animal life; and reduced them, not to brain action pure and simple, but to cerebral functions, controlled by the viscera and vegetative movements of our bodily existence.

Let us look at the meaning of all this. Soul used to be conceived of as different in *kind* from body. The brain, the nervous system, the body, were its organs, allies, machines. Sometimes they, especially the instruments through which the soul more immediately works, exercised reaction on their sovereign employer; they impeded or suspended her functions, and troubled her serenity. But though they might cloud the manifestation, they could not destroy the essence of a living soul. What they did was temporal and transitory; but they shall pass away and be dissolved, while soul will endure for ever.

The word mind has been much used to signify soul, as acting in and through body. There is, however, some vagueness in its employment. Yet we constantly speak of the laws of mind, because soul is in this life the partner of body; and therefore known to us as mind, and *as* mind is studied through its laws. One psychological task has always been to separate the pure activity of soul from the mixed workings of mind, by examination and cross-examination of our internal consciousness.

You will now easily understand how vast the change Comte intended by his physiological organon for the study of our moral and intellectual functions. You will see what is meant by elevating mental science to the Positive stage, and systematizing it under laws which people may variously describe as phenomenal, mechanical, or material; adjectives all roughly used to express the same general idea. What we took for a spiritual essence is only a developed animal nature, the difference between men and beasts of the field is not one of *kind*, but of degree. MANKIND is a misnomer. Humanity is (as Comte thought) a higher degree of animality. We have no right to suppose a personal immortality. Man may be said to live after death in the memory of his fellow-men, but the truly Positive philosopher believes in no other deathless existence. What we really can see and investigate is a vast moving mechanism, *our* universe. Beyond this all knowledge is a blank. We know of nothing which set this mechanism in motion; it may have moved from all eternity; it may go on moving everlastingly; or it may wear itself out. Philosophy can teach us no more than distinctions and degrees in the phenomenal law which pervades and rules a universe without a God.

Yet Comte said that he was no Atheist. He even denounced Atheism, and declared it as bad as theology. He did not wish to deny, only to ignore God. Neither did he desire to appear ungrateful; (pardon words which sound in your ears profanity;) God was a really useful hypothesis once; in the days when men had recently issued from their primæval forests. Thanking the Deity for His provisional services, Comte courteously dismissed Him from His throne.

All this will have seemed to you a most monstrous tissue of negations. But Comte held it to be a code of Positive faith; a faith firmly grounded on the self-sufficingness of human nature, read according to his version of course—void of belief in a personality which survives the grave, without knowledge of, trust in, or prayer to God. The blessings of this advanced faith he desired to extend far and wide. At the present moment his desire is realizing itself; for the like attitude of thought has become a favourite position among the *savans* of our Western world. When it penetrates the more active classes, we shall discern it easily by its *fruits!* what those fruits will be, is a qnestion for statesmen and for us all.

The chief hindrance opposing its spread amongst unsophisticated minds has been a point much dwelt upon of old by Plato, and by Cicero after him. It is the protest which that irrepressible entity called soul perseveres in alleging. We are all apt to shrink from the picture of bodily dissolution:

> "To lie in cold obstruction, and to rot;
> This sensible warm motion to become
> A kneaded clod!"

But what if the "delighted spirit" has been developed by brain, and with brain must be dissolved? Our whole distinctive human life, our mind, moral, intellectual, spiritual, rebels against a doom of subjection to that crass material law! Yet can we establish a difference? Can we show that the law of our true being differs from the law of things outside us?

This question, unspeakably interesting to every one of us, might be put in various shapes. We might ask, Can the protest of soul be set down as a mere sentiment only? If it were no more than an instinct of our nature, it would deserve consideration; for why should so high and noble an instinct be aimless and misleading? If we cannot trust our own souls, what are we to trust? Phenomena themselves are given us within. Mathematical truths, which Positivists are obliged to exempt from phenomenal law, have a subjective validity—we cannot help thinking them, and we cannot think their contradictories.

But suppose that a future state of recompence with its inferential moralities cannot be denied without denying our own consciousness—pronouncing the clearest of our intuitions a will o' the wisp—or, sadder still, a corpse light on the grave of hope—nay, more, without subverting the law which makes human society to differ from animal gregariousness, and gives to human action its spring, its liberty, its life—suppose all this true, what shall, what can we say? And such is the issue I propose to try this morning.

The plan I have devised for trying it fairly is, first, to get as clear an idea as short compass will allow of what

Positivism says on our question. Afterwards to state a case for moral law by way of antithesis. It is through the law of our moral being that we may most readily look for something to difference our souls from creatures below them. The strain I shall have to put on your attention lies in this; after grasping in brief the Positivist attitude, I must ask that you will not take my facts or arguments on trust, but will verify each severally by an appeal to your own consciousness. It is always upon the law deduced from or applied to facts that you ought to exercise your greatest vigilance. For law interprets facts to us—we might almost say that under its manipulation they bend like a nose of wax; nothing, you will remember, so flexible as figures, except facts.

Let me represent these maxims to you under a similitude. Everybody has looked (when young at least) through a kaleidoscope, and has observed the beauty of its many-coloured figures, their symmetrical shapes, and the enchantment of their succession. What magic creates this phantasmagoria? Some pretty bits of coloured glass, shining gewgaws, scraps of lace, fripperies, and other odds and ends, are put into a translucent box, and beheld through a tube fitted with mirrors which are set at an angle determined by optical law. The broken knick-knacks represent the facts of everybody's phenomenal kaleidoscope; the reflecting angle under which they are seen is its law; the coloured images are everybody's impressions of things, nature, and mankind. As long as you live, remember that whenever you are contemplating the world's phenomena—whenever you see facts of life, either great or small, you are looking at them through some optical instrument or another. If its law accords with their law, your view is truthful; but then it will be all the less pretty, the less symmetrical. There are dark spots in our real world, checks of all sorts, moral evil, anguish of heart and conscience, foresights, stern accountabilities! You have lost your childhood's magic glass, and have got a clear reflecting telescope in its stead! Pity to forego the nice kaleidoscope where all was so bright, so harmonious, and arrayed in such regular shapes. Yet the view it gave was worth what most people's views are worth—precisely nothing!

Comte had his kaleidoscope. Every systematizer who allows no mystery, no darkness anywhere, must keep the article; in point of fact, most people enjoy having one. Alas! for the 19th century! It has such a feverish viewiness, such a fashion of incessantly turning its magic tube, that life seems little else than a dreamy phantasmagoria! To construct a steady reflecting instrument for yourself requires industry, time, and thought, three things which few people care to bestow upon their beliefs. Therefore the practice is to pick up kaleidoscopes ready-made at a cheap rate, and to feel as easy as stern realities will permit on the subject of their truthfulness. Romances are the kaleidoscopes of one class, cram-books of a second, newspapers of a third, self-love the optical law of the greatest number. We are met this morning to break up a grand kaleidoscope, and to look into its construction. I shall do my endeavour to prevent you all from replacing it by any instrument of a ready-made sort. The easiest plan for all lecturers is to display a series of transparent conclusions; but I shall prefer furnishing you with facts and arguments, letting you put them together, look at them, and verify their law of true vision for yourselves.

Let us see Comte's law first. It was, strictly speaking, a law of succession and resemblance. You will guess at once that were this all we could see in the phenomenal world, our insight would be very limited. And Comte's object was to limit us. We can never know, Positively speaking, final causes; those which make up the common notion of design, purpose, intention. Nor yet any efficient causes; nothing truly productive of an effect, as men usually say. All we can know is the middle of a chain of successive phenomena. The two ends are absolutely hidden from our eyes. It was in this sense that Comte denied causation—his language was vigorous; he denounced it as metaphysical, and when Comte nicknames anything metaphysical or theological, he means, as everybody knows, Anathema maranatha.

The difficulty here is palpable. A law of averages—a statistical law, as it is often called, does not profess to account for anything; it merely generalizes crude material, and gets it ready for scientific thought to work out the true law. But a law of succession has an imposing sound, and it does in the worst sense impose. The fallacy may be shown in an instant. Day and night succeed each other regularly. Does either *account* for the other? The rotation of the earth is simultaneous with both—it accounts for both. Its effect is to expose the earth's two hemispheres alternately to the sun's rays. This rotation coincides again with other laws of our planetary system, and they account for it. It is on these laws, and not on such grounds as Hume, Comte's great Positive antecedent, alleged, that we look for sunset and sunrise. When they fail, the system of which our globe forms part will have collapsed.

Such then was the original kaleidoscope of Positivism. It was condemned for reasons which will have plainly appeared to you. Other eyes have swept the field of vision this world offers, and other instruments to aid our insight have been adopted.

You will not have failed already to remark the extreme vagueness of that word "law." There are very few English words more vague: it is applied to almost every sort of formula, force, principle, idea; besides being misused in ways almost innumerable. You must therefore, when busy with questions like the present, fix your attention upon the adjectives added to it, and the examples selected by way of illustration.

The Positive system is, according to Littré, of immeasurable extent, embracing the whole universe. Thus, whatever was conceived in dark preparatory ages, theological or metaphysical; whatsoever persons, who philosophize in either of those antiquated ways may even now dream;—if the conception cannot be reduced under Positive laws, it must be regarded as non-existent. All that really exists is included within such laws, the definition of which, therefore, becomes a subject of the greatest possible importance. They are, he says, immanent causes. The room we are in contains intelligent and educated people, but how many here could define this word "immanent"? It and its correlative, transcendent, are in truth metaphysical terms. If you will turn to Mellin's Encyclopædic Word-Book (favourably known to metaphysicians for purposes of pillage), you will find *immanent* explained, under the German *einheimisch*, into ten shades of usage. Probably, in common English Littré might have said "inherent." "The universe," he writes, "now appears to us as a whole, having its causes within itself, causes which we name its laws. The long conflict between immanence and transcendence is touching its close. Transcendence is theology or metaphysic, explaining the universe by causes outside it; immanence is science, explaining the universe by causes within itself."* Now, one stock-in-trade example is that a stone falls to the ground by virtue of an immanent cause. In plainer words, the stone belongs to universal matter of which gravity is an inherent law. Next, we find this same example Positively applied to the human will. Volition is free just as a falling stone is free; it obeys its own inherent law. Further, we read of "the rigorous fatalities which make the world what it is." Comte, Littré, and others object against calling these fatalities materialistic, because they distinguish gradations of law. Yet they limit all human knowledge within the materialistic circle, and Janet, who refuses to acquit them of Materialism, dwells on the point that, instead of defining mind as an unknown cause of thought, emotion, and will, it is said to be, "when anatomically considered, the sum of the functions of brain and spinal cord; and when considered physiologically, the sum of the functions of brain in consciously receiving impressions."† We need not wish to dis-

* Paroles de Philosophie Positive, p. 54.

† Janet refers to Nysten's Dictionnaire de Médecine, etc., by Littré and Robin.

pute about words. But suppose it had been stated in plain French or English that all known or knowable objects in the universe are placed by Positivism under the rule of laws as rigorous in their fatality as the laws of matter, would not the ultimate point in question have been more tangible, more intelligible? People might indeed have said, "Why, after all Positivism comes to the same thing as Fatalism, or Materialism;" and with certain writers this risk may very possibly be held a decisive objection.

Once more,—another explanation given by Littré is, that Positivism lies strictly within the "relative." Many here are aware how, since Kant's time, England, France, and Germany have been flooded with metaphysic, good, bad, and indifferent, on the relative and the conditioned. Pity that Littré should have plunged into these whirlpools! Ravaisson refers to Herbert Spencer and Sophie St. Germain for the point that this conception, the relative, must always imply the existence of an absolute, known or unknown.[2] I cannot follow him now, but any one interested in doing so will find the subject commenced at page 66 of his "Philosophie en France," (one of the Imperial Reports), and continued through sections 9 and 10. It is a very important discussion. Ravaisson stands out amongst Frenchmen as a consummate master of his science; and he inclines to infer that Comte tended, and that Positivism generally now tends, towards a final return to metaphysic. However this may be, I fear I have tired you, and am glad to quit this dry part of my lecture, and get away to more common-sense ground.

By way of introducing our most interesting topic, let me draw one common-sense conclusion from the difficult tract just shot over. During our passage, a thought may have flashed upon you which I remember hearing in a Bampton Lecture, somewhat to this effect—"Positivism is the most negative system of all." It appears hard to avoid this idea; for Positivism denies in express terms that human beings have any knowledge outside those generalized laws of experience which make up the Positive sciences. It denies (in a word) the most essential part of what was formerly held to be a knowledge of mind, both human and Divine.

Positive thinkers rebut the charge of negativism this way. We confine ourselves, they say, to what we know; we do not venture, like Pantheists and Atheists, into the unknowable. We do not deny God, we only ignore Him. We do not ask about the first cause of the world, or whether it has a constructural final end. Such questions as these are "disedifying." "The Positive philosophy," says Littré, "does not busy itself with the beginning of the universe, if the universe had a beginning—nor yet with what happens to living things, plants, animals, men, after their death, or at the consummation of the ages, if the ages have a consummation."* Littré's sentence, which I have rendered *verbatim*, reminds one of the prayer told to Bishop Atterbury, as offered by a soldier on the eve of battle: "O God, if there be a God, save my soul, if I have a soul!" I am sorry to repeat ill-sounding words again; but is not this really the exact religious attitude of an honest Positivist, who feels sometimes touched by visions of possible life after death,

> "Of all the nurse and all the priest have taught;"

that is, if we conceive his attitude according to the *least* negative interpretation put upon the system?

Continuing this least negative interpretation, let us view under its light the Positive cosmology or theory of the world's existence; of creation,—that is to say, if there ever was a creation. A stone falls to the ground. Trying to account for the phenomenon, we grasp a law inherent in the material world. Other phenomena lead us to other laws. We contemplate the material world with its laws in operation, a magnificent spectacle of moving forces; an organic whole, shining through its own intrinsic glory of never-ceasing development. If we turn and pursue the reverse road, and trace evolution back to its elementary principles, we may dissolve worlds into primordial force, or we may,

* Paroles de Philosophie Positive, p. 53.

as Professor Tyndall suggested at Liverpool, find the All in a fiery cloud occupying space. Then comes the complex question,[8] What beyond? What before? Whence, and How produced? a Positivist thinker may return one of two answers. He may either say, "We do not know," or he may say, "Nothing can be known." Take the least negative first, as we proposed; it surely deserves this rejoinder: If you plead ignorance, but surmise that knowledge is possible, you ought not, for reasons valid with every true lover of wisdom, to stop here. You are substituting for the ideas of creation and first cause, what you call a primordial universe, a material condition of some kind, producing phenomena regulated by inherent laws, successive, perishable, and nothing more! All once believed beyond, a blank! Even the very name of philosophy consecrated by consent of ages to the First and to the Last, admonishes you. Renounce your vocation, deny your name, or proceed. We demand a Positive result in the highest sense, not a fog of ignorance, not a slough of despond. But if the second answer be the true one, if the teaching of Positivism is that nothing more can be known, let us be told so in plain words. Let no one be charmed into the Positive circle by false allurements; for of all vices treachery and hypocrisy are the most cowardly. Are you really wiser than the pagan Lucretius? If not, why boast of 19th century discoveries in wisdom, insight, happiness? If you have examined the relics of a primæval world, explored the races of living and thinking creatures, if you have ascended to the starry firmament, and traversed its shining hosts, to come back with shame and disappointment, and tell us this is *your* all, *our* all, then indeed the wages of your science is death. While you speak your final verdict at least cover your faces,

> "And, sad as angels for a good man's sin,
> Weep to record, and blush to give it in!"

These thoughts have brought us to the most essential considerations of this lecture. Whether the Positive *savant* puts in a plea of ignorance or of blank negation, we care not. We will treat it as a challenge thrown down, and do our best to meet it. Succeed or not, we will take no refuge in ambiguities, but maintain a truly positive assertion. We say that the world we live in is not one world, but two,[4] distinguishable through the laws by which each is governed. There exists such a thing as phenomenal law; we accept the fact. But distinct, broadly distinct, apart in its working, its elements, and its final result, is moral law. An appeal lies to facts, and we shall try to justify our assertion.

The mode of proof now to be adopted is not metaphysical. I mention the circumstance because investigations into mind are apt to be confounded with metaphysic, and are then supposed too difficult to deserve attention. My argument will demand nothing beyond a hearing and a scrutiny. It will consist of just so much mental dissection as may be needful to show, first, a structural law of our inward nature, and, secondly, to illustrate its workings and effects. These two sets of facts will be placed side by side, in order that each may check the other, and that their coincidence may also (as I hope it will) furnish a fresh and sufficient proof of the contrast between moral and material law. Everybody knows how convincing are, and ought to be, facts separately ascertainable, yet converging into one and the same conclusion.

One form of speech almost unavoidable ought to be remarked beforehand. I mean the word freedom as applied to the human will and its volitions. When compelled to use it, I shall do so only in the sense of philosophic as contrasted with theological free will. By philosophic freedom I understand that sort and degree of active choice free from constraint which is required for the idea of responsibility, an idea universally agreed on by divines opposed to each other on the point of theological freewill. By this last-named idea I understand supposed powers of spiritual attainment, which go to make up a notion of self-sufficing moral strength. With it the present lecture, being purely philosophical, can have nothing whatever to do, but I should much deplore misconception, because any theory of self-sufficingness would be repugnant to my own personal convictions.

Look now at the life of an animal, with senses often more instrumentally accurate than ours. Survey the world around, which furnishes the objects of his perception and his intelligence. The mode in which that intelligence acts is held to be more or less under the absolute rule of instinct, and creatures below man are commonly described as those "that nourish a blind life within the brain." Whether this be or be not perfectly correct makes no difference to our present purpose. The point I want you to fix your thoughts upon is the *directness* of relation between the feeling or intelligent principle of mere animal life, and the object perceived, felt, or apprehended. Perhaps it may give vividness to your thought, if you figure this relation under the similitude of a right line connecting two points—object without, apprehension within. The line itself will then represent the impulsive activity of a creature, as, for example, when a hungry tiger leaps upon his prey.

Now this directness of action is *not* the thing most marked in our own proper human existence. What is really marked is the exact reverse; the more truly *human* any action appears, the farther is it away from resemblance to that animal characteristic. Suppose a man acts like a tiger, he is simply brutal;

if he be governed by his feelings, however amiable, we pronounce him weak or unreasoning.

Absolutely impulsive doings, such as the indulgence of an appetite, blows struck in passion, or even in self-defence, we separate from our volitions proper, and call them irrational and instinctive. In educating children we check displays of impulse, we bid them pause and reflect. And it is obvious that education presupposes an educable power or principle, which principle self-education (the most important training of all) will place in a clear light before you. Interrogate yourselves, then. You will see that the mental power you most wish to train and augment is distinguishable enough even in the commonest affairs of life. Take a case of feeling. Some object—no matter what—kindles an emotion within you—anger, wish affection, pursuit, dislike, avoidance—and you feel strongly impelled to take action thereupon. This would be the movement which was imaged to our minds as a simple line. But to launch along it inconsiderately you would feel neither proper *per se*—nor yet doing what is due to yourself, because it is your human prerogative to act, not according to impulse, but according to reason. And observe, to do, or to forbear doing, is a question by no means determined by finding whether another emotion be or be not stronger than the first. What reason demands is that the impulse you feel, or it may chance the strongest of a dozen impulses, shall become to you an object of careful scrutiny. You are bound in honesty to scrutinize it; not only because it exists as an incitement felt within yourself, but much, much more because it is felt to be your actual self. It is your character which gave the spring, and lives in the movement to action. Perchance this point of character is a hidden nook, an unknown depth of feeling or desire, undiscovered, unsuspected by your fellow-creatures—a secret of your inner self. Nevertheless it is amenable to the tribunal of a more inward self still, to be brought before it as an object that shall be examined and cross-examined, sentenced either to vivid freedom or present suppression—it may be even to extinction evermore! Each human being possesses this wonderful self-objectivizing power. He is able to look at himself as a NOT-self—a something partitioned off, and external; to be thought about, felt about, reasoned about; to be controlled, chastened, corrected. This power is our inalienable heritage; we cannot resign it if we would; we cannot finally suspend its exercise. Mountains could not crush, nor oceans drown it; flames of fire never burned it out from the breast of one single martyr. Whether we use our birthright for good or for evil, it still remains with us; when we act, our will is not a feeling, an appetition, travelling simply from one point to another. It is a movement of our world within, a movement of that microcosm called Man.

Suppose a person resolves to employ this power aright. Some wish or feeling, such as might drive a lower creature to instinctive action, stirs within him, and becomes the object of his contemplation. To the sessions of silent thought he summons whatever assistants he can get; the witnesses of experience, prudence, duty, the golden rules of the Gospel; whatever seems most proper to determine the question at issue,—fitness or unfitness, to act or to abstain from acting. He says to himself (as all here have done a thousand times), "This longing, thought, state of mind, is wise or foolish, good or bad, right or wrong; nay, 'tis I myself that am so!" And in thus saying he is conscious of that sort of freedom to will or not to will, which makes up responsibility. He does not deny—contrariwise, with the might of his whole essential humanity he asserts—that the act of will is thus taken out of the direct line of inevitable antecedency, away from the physico-mechanical series, and enabled to commence a series of its own. In a word, his consciousness evidences to him that functional law which makes the human soul a thing more wonderful than all the inorganic or all the animated universe besides. And the law thus evidenced is the law of moral causation.

I said that our own soul thus becomes to us more wonderful than all the known universe besides. I might have said more mysterious; so truly *sui generis* and different from all things not ensouled, as to be inexplicable by human sciences, an enigma to itself, dwelling alone in its own awful isolation. Do but think what *cause* is—nothing less than originating power; what then must it be in stern and sad reality for a soul to originate a sin! Yet we cannot deny the fact. We confess it every day, not only in our hearts and deeper utterances, but in the commonest though most tremendous of words, the word responsibility. If a man were in no true sense the cause of his own actions, he could never be held responsible either by God or Man. But as long as Justice maintains her seat, each criminal will be so held, so judged, so recompensed. And the only principle under which Justice can justify her judgments is the reality of moral causation.

If, then, this law be established, we have proved our point. Just as we recognize a material world by mechanical law—and indeed our knowledge of matter itself is only a knowledge of its laws—so in like manner, and *pari passu*, we recognize a moral world by its distinctive law. We live, therefore, not in one world, but in two:

> "Man is one world, and hath
> Another to attend him."

The point is of surpassing importance! Upon it turns

the whole issue. "Can mechanism—or, as it is vaguely called, materialism—be or be not accepted, with its attendant theories, as the truth; that is, *our* whole truth, all we have to live by and to die by?" Infinitely important issue! having much to do at this very moment with the happiness and real good of millions amongst our fellow-creatures and fellow-countrymen. It is for this reason we must not spare pains to demonstrate our moral law, for this reason also we will give some passing sentences to show how worthless in argument is the sophism most commonly circulated against it. Men speak of a "law of motives," with complete assurance, and without seeming to be aware of the twofold fallacy underlying it. Writers on the subject furnish statistics of suicide, murder, and the like; and then ask how the freedom of moral cause can be compatible with so visible a law? But what sort of a law is this? Clearly not a law upon which the results are conditioned, as sunrise on the earth's rotation; but a mere generalization, like the laws of average before mentioned. Such a law does not govern the acts, but the acts the law, or, in plain words, they *are* the law. It is an epitomized result, inferring no more consequence to our free moral causation, than a life assurance infers to the contingency of our individual life or death. The sophism would be readily detected if it were not for that unfortunate word "motive." People forget that a motive is not a power that compels us, but an object which we choose to seek. "Will," we are seriously told, "must be determined by the strongest motive." Now if, in thus speaking, the strongest motive *objectively* be meant, that is the motive essentially and in its own nature the strongest, then indeed we may exclaim, "Would that this were true!" For are not right, justice, goodness, absolutely and in themselves the strongest? Yet men in general fail to pursue them; they are chosen by those of whom the world is not worthy. But if, on the other hand, the phrase "strongest motive" is to be understood *subjectively*, and means that which on each occasion is *felt* to be the strongest; what form of sounding words has ever yielded a more barren sense, a simpler truism? "Will must be determined by the choice of will." It means this, and nothing more.

We may sum the whole matter of motive in a single sentence. Motives do not make the man, but the man his motives. To conceive it otherwise would be to imagine each man a mere bundle of instincts, such instincts as we calculate with certainty in the brute animals we wish to allure, to subdue, or to destroy.

> "Be not like dumb driven cattle,"

says the Psalm of Life, and old Herbert exhorts—

> "Not rudely, as a beast,
> To run into an action."

The beast feels an incitement, and rushes direct upon the pitfall. It is the prerogative of a true man to subsume (as logicians speak) each line of impulse into the circle of his own soul; to deliberate in the secret chambers of a being impenetrable even to his own understanding, and to put in force the result which becomes as it were the free manifestation of himself. When therefore you examine the actions of a fellow-creature, and discern his motives, you praise or blame what? not the motives, but the man.

Permit me to close this discussion by an example of the manner in which we make and unmake our own motives.

No one present is so young, or so careless, as never to have felt the pains of self-reproach. Some light or shade of life projects before us the outline of ourself. By virtue of the law described, we view and review it, as if it were the picture of another being. In contrast with it, we place our own ideal, all that our boyhood fondly fancied our manhood would become; the semblances of those we have loved and lost; of the father, who taught us to prize truth and virtue above earthly wealth and distinction; of the mother, at whose knee we knelt in prayer, and whose upraised eye imaged the serenity of that heaven to which she implored us to aspire. These beloved forms, robed in the unfading freshness of a love stronger than death, stir our heart of hearts, with accents unmistakable. They remind us of what we resolved and trusted one day to be found, in thought, in feeling, and in life. But, close to the glowing portrait of our purposed self stands the dwindled figure of what we actually are; and, oh, the shame, the anguish of that stern, disappointing comparison!

Among the lower creatures (we ask in passing) what is there to resemble this self-reforming principle? In the domesticated animal, both beast and bird, we see wounded affection, grief under a master's anger, and desire to win back his love. In the gregarious tribes we find respect for a common bond of what we almost may call utility; but has any sense of wrong as wrong, or sin as sin, ever been found educable? Man shows the mighty strength of this principle within him, even when he shows it in its most repulsive shapes. The remorseful wretch who throws himself beneath the wheel of Juggernaut, is a different *kind* of being from the horse or dog. And considering the self-interest, self-flattery, and self-indulgence arrayed against it, may we not say that the root of such passionate remorse has something sound in it, else it would long ago have been trodden out from the life and heart of mankind?

For now, as always, our honest anguish and shame sow the appointed seed of our noblest attainments. Those steps by which we climb our steep ascent are hewn in the travail of our souls. David found it so, when he heard the voice of Nathan saying, "Thou art the man!" and wrote words which have come down near three thousand years;—"The sacrifices of God are a broken spirit." "Of all acts," asks Mr. Carlyle, "is not, for a man, *repentance* the most divine? The deadliest sin, I say, were that same supercilious consciousness of no sin; that is death; the heart so conscious is divorced from sincerity, humility, and fact; is dead; it is 'pure' as dead dry sand is pure. David's life and history, as written for us in those Psalms of his, I consider to be the truest emblem ever given of a man's moral progress and warfare here below." Truest emblem indeed! In it, we see, as in a glass, how living in two worlds we cannot but have a sympathy with each; insomuch that every man feels himself to be two selves, not one; a spiritual and a psychical man. "There is," says Sir Thomas Browne, "another man within me, that's angry with me, rebukes, commands, and dastards me." A *double* consciousness which grows upon many a soul, until its truer choice and better motives are attained:

> "The life which is, and that which is to come,
> Suspended hang in such nice equipoise
> A breath disturbs the balance; and that scale
> In which we throw our hearts preponderates."

This lecture started from the question, what is a phenomenon, and how do we know of its existence? Seeing that our knowledge rests primarily on the evidence of our own mind, we drew the inference that Comte committed a fatal error when he banished the science of mind, *as* mind, from his cycle. Reviewing his various devices, and some devices of his successors, for eliminating psychology, and reducing the study of mind to a study of bodily functions, we approached the stronghold of Positivism,—law. And, after discussing the theories maintained respecting it, we boldly threw down our challenge to this effect: law phenomenal or mechanical admitted, we assert, the existence of another kind of law. We say that the freedom of human choice between evil and good is utterly unlike the freedom of a stone which falls by mechanical law, and cannot choose but fall. The inference from phenomenal law is the existence of a phenomenal world. The inference from another existent law is that there is another existent world. Man, we affirm, lives in both; has sympathies with both; and, by virtue of his double nature, is a true citizen of both. The ultimate principle of man's higher nature is to us inscrutable; for, even as the eye sees not itself, so neither does the spirit of a man discern that which makes it spirit. But, though we cannot know the soul, we can know much and many things about it; things most important—nay, all-important for us to know, since they distinguish the spirit that burns within us from matter, from mechanism, and from mere animality.

Hence we do not, with the Positivist, ignore the unknowable. Contrariwise, confessing our ignorance, where we are ignorant, we strive to observe and gather all we can.

One thing that can be thus known is the principle of moral causation; and this we have inductively investigated. We began by observing a process in our own minds, a process or law of self-objectivity. I am sorry to use such an uncouth word; but it saves a long description, and you will all remember the fact. That process carries, on the very face of it, adaptation to the purposes of moral choice, free from the material necessity which governs a falling stone, and disengaged from the control of such impulses as the incitement of ruling instincts. We next verify this law by observing its operation; *first*, in single acts of the Will accompanied, as you will recollect, by distinct consciousness of choice and responsibility. It was in respect of this conscious certainty that Dr. Johnson said, "We *know* we are free, and there ends the matter." We verified, a *second* time, the self-objectivising law, by its working and effects upon our motives, which it makes and unmakes; eliminating some, adopting others, so as to modify and alter our whole real character. Any one who is happy enough to recall the slow advances of successful self-education, or a less ordinary process by which old things passed away and all things became new, may recollect with pleasure how this law served as an instrument of change; how it placed himself before his own inward eye, even daily, in freshly instructive lights, awakening new self-questionings, emotions, aversions, desires, hopes, and stimulating to new exertions; how it opposed itself to the mastery of any single dominant passion, under which we say a man acts mechanically, because he has already surrendered himself a slave to its sway; how it became a check upon all day-dreaming or drifting with the tide, when again we are said to act mechanically because we yield to circumstances as they flow, and live a blind life, like creatures that cannot escape the chain of Instinct. For, observe: let any instinct, even the noblest, be ever so nobly developed, if we act from its impulse only, and not from a reflective choice of the prompting which it gives, we are living below the image of our true nature, because we are not striving to become a law unto ourselves.

You may verify our moral law in numberless ways among the common walks of life; and it really is a task of no great difficulty, if you take with you the truth that the whole issue is summed in one word—Responsibility. A falling stone cannot choose but fall; were a man subject to material law, he could have no choice whatever. Neither would it make any real difference, if the Will were impelled by overpowering motive, and did not make its motive to itself. The slate which slides from a roof, and kills a child, we do not accuse of murder; we do not attach moral accountability to the hungry tiger. It is because man is not impelled like stones or tigers, that we hold him responsible. And we praise or blame in the highest degree his most deliberate acts. The wrong he does with malice aforethought is a crime in the strongest sense; the good he works with considerate purpose we esteem his highest well-doing. In our time the wills of individual men have changed the destinies of nations; and any one who reads books, reviews, or newspapers sees a vigorous use of that word responsibility. No one doubts that these powerful wills are the true causes of effects felt throughout all Europe, effects which will remain when those who caused them are in the grave; nay, even when generations—perchance dynasties—shall have passed away.

In lower life, we honour the truly causative man who conquers a habit of intemperance or any evil passion: it is greater to overcome one's self than to conquer many cities. We deem every one accountable for what he allows, or disallows, in relation to his God, his fellows, or himself. In a word, we consider each man so far the true cause of his own conduct, as to load him with responsibility

Yes, responsibility! Do not shrink from the thought; it is wholesome for all. Do but practise self-control enough to look yourself with honest purpose in the face when you are about to act, you will never suppose that you act mechanically, and you will seldom act amiss. If you wish to benefit your countrymen, inculcate the grand lesson of responsibility; for what well-informed person doubts that one main root of our present social and religious ailments lies in compromise with known immoralities, indolent acquiesence in hollow words, and lifeless outside shows, where ought to be heard and seen the rigid truths of accountability, duty, consistency?—all impossible without a practical law of self-scrutiny and self-control. Yet further: Responsibility is also an undeniable witness to a world of life beyond death. Just as even Herbert Spencer himself has remarked, that the idea of relativity involves the correlative idea of an absolute; even so, in thought, responsibility involves its correlative belief, a recompence! But, in morality, the evidence is stringent beyond expression. For, the idea of responsibility is fixed in the nature of things; unchangeable, eternal. And it contains in itself the loftier idea of personality. Leading us to look for a world of righteous recompence, it leads also to belief in a personal Being, before whom we are responsible, and who will award to each of us our recompence. David travelled the same road to the same conclusion, when he looked round upon men, who lacked mercy because they lacked justice, and said, "Unto thee, O Lord, belongeth mercy: for thou renderest to every man according to his work."

Did I not feel that my strain upon your attention must now cease, I should have liked to show at length how the law by which we discover moral causation, may be verified everywhere in the whole province of mind. It is difficult, for instance, to look at the perplexing questions raised about language, without perceiving that there runs through its purely human formation the articulate results of an element resembling internal dialogue; in other words, a law of self-objectivising representation. In art, again, the perpetual efforts of ages is to present our human manifoldness of thought, feeling, and idea, before our one individual self. Hence the art formula of multeity in unity. And what is the true bond of society as distinguished from gregariousness? Is it not the Gospel's golden rule? But how can our neighbour be viewed as a second self, unless self has been already objectivised before our moral intuitions? We might follow the same thread throughout the conditions of all philosophy.

The one thing we have to remember in every research concerning man is that education, whether of self or others, implies an educable principle; a germ, of which education and attainment are the bud, the blossom, and the fruit. Therefore, if we want to know Humanity, we must look to the educated human being. The philosopher, the artist, the thinker of every sort, must have risen into clearness ere he can become a typical man. Is it not, therefore, a mistake to appeal for theories of human nature to the statistics (always statistics !) of ignorance and savagery? When modelling our physical form, Buonarotti did not seek his type in hospitals for maimed or distorted limbs, and exclaim, Behold, such is man ! Curious too, and contradictory, the way in which appeals to barbarism have worked. In the 18th century we used always to hear of that golden age,

> "When free in woods the noble savage ran,
> And man, the brother, lived the friend of man."

In the 19th, savage life is cannibalism, superstition, cruelty, terrible, revolting, loathsome; perchance, time must yet pass before we learn justice to our fellows of any age! Meanwhile, we may feel sure that our human ideal is not to be found in the frost-bitten rickety infant species; nor yet in its dwarfed and stunted adult; the cretin and the imbecile will not give its lineaments; and it may be hard to say which is least like a true man, the undeveloped or the perverted creature. For example, what superiority in moral height has the *savant*, whose self-satisfied science ignores or denies a God, over the poor pigmy barbarian, unskilled in the use of fire, and living upon berries and insects, who props himself against a tree with earthward face, and prays, saying, "*Yere*, if indeed thou art, why dost thou suffer us to be killed? Thou hast raised us up. Why dost thou cast us down?" * Better perhaps the rude stammering of our race's childhood than its half-speechless, half-paralyzed old age!

And here the argument of this lecture ends. Of causation in general, and the grand subject of design, it has not been my hint to speak. These vast topics have fallen into higher hands than mine. My aim was limited to finding the *differentia* of man—the moral characteristic which places him in contrast with physico-mechanical laws.

It occurs to me, however, that you may employ ten minutes not unpleasantly, upon what we can hardly help calling the romance of Positivism. The story, taken from first to last—part comic, part tragic—is as wild and weird as one of the Frenchman Doré's pictures,—a story too strange to be thought true, if it did not happen to have been true! It has also its stinging lessons, and they follow naturally; evolved, as it were, from the motley and mystifying commencement.

Comte's life has been written by friend and foe. For fulness of detail the right book is by his disciple and executor, Dr. Robinet, who has just figured among those who rule in the Commune of Paris. Robinet is very in-

* Harris's Highlands of Œthiopia, vol. iii. p. 63.

teresting, for he thoroughly believes in his master, and accepts the whole Comtist religion, calendar and all, which Littré and others reject. No reproach this to Comte's biographer, for that same worship is celebrated in our cooler atmosphere of England. The *Pall Mall Gazette* has, by its notices, made the celebrations widely known. There is an account of the grandest yearly solemnity which will suffice many, and excite the curiosity of more, in its number for January 7th, 1868. It is not hard to see that the worshippers differ from the recusants by a strong feeling that they cannot live upon axioms sounding like negatives. They want sentiment, emotion, excitement to sustain them. Let us observe how Comte caught the first glimpse of this requirement.

His life was sombre—a boy delicate and fractious, disliked by his masters, turned out of the Polytechnique, repudiated by his great socialist teacher St. Simon. His family relations not happy, his marriage least of all. We cannot wonder at vagaries, for he had a real fit of rampant insanity, and after release from an asylum had nearly drowned himself in the Seine. His wife found him intolerable, and left her home. Mr. Mill speaks of her respect for him;—it was oddly testified after his death, for she pleads in law that he was a madman, an atheist, and immoral; repudiates his will, and seizes the consecrated relics of his dwelling. Littré supported her against those who, like Robinet, thought her little less than blasphemous. If she had appeared in an English law court, we should have known more truth than we do.

Let us now look at such facts as we have from the more favourable side. The man lived a lonely life, as became a sort of conceptual alchemist, sustained by a belief that he was turning men's leaden thoughts into his own pure gold. One brilliant projection of his has made him the idol of Positivists. I confess it puzzles me, among many others, to imagine how a qualified critic can treat such a philosophic solvent either as true or as original. It supposes the history of all human thinking to pass necessarily through three stages, theology, metaphysics, positive truth; and that the world makes progress accordingly. We will hope that the thing called theology, a benighted belief in the government and intervention of supreme will, is not altogether extinct in this age of progress; if it be so, Mr. Froude encourages us to look for a revival. Among lesser matters, the hypothesis of metaphysical cookery is an idea one fails to realise. Was it a banquet with joints cut Laputa-like, after some fashion of concepts, or syllogistic figures? Was it a "feast of reason and a flow of soul," or, more probably, an abstraction pure and simple, as if a man could

> "Cloy the hungry edge of appetite
> By bare imagination of a feast"?

Comte's comicalities strike most people all the more because he writes on, always utterly insensible to his own comedy. If any one wishes for a serious critique in small compass, I may mention Stirling's appendix to his translation of Schwegler's Handbook; Whewell in his Philosophy of Discovery, and elsewhere.

Comte was most confiding in his own theory. Littré is not so confident, for he has another theory of his own. But, putting aside the question of its verification, we may remark that in the rough idea Comte showed himself before his age. Positive thinkers have busied themselves with physical evolution; for example, the development of a brain from an oyster or an eozoon; but Comte was intent upon mental evolution.[5] Man need not much care about the congeners of a body sprung from earth; but soul is another thing. We trust our own spirit, as carrying some image and superscription of God; we feel and conceive it to be different in kind from sensitive life; we love to think of it in its finality as a spark flowing out from Divine Light; a breath breathed into body from above. In the reverse of this belief there is doubtless an element unfavourable to happiness; it makes some men cynics, some pessimists, some simply victims. Comte's infinite self-satisfaction probably saved him from self-torture. But we judge that he felt his condition deeply, from the rapture with which he hailed a new and brilliant discovery!

Yes, it was the most wonderful of all his discoveries; he one day found an unsuspected law of life within himself; he discovered that he had a heart.

To many, this is the black spot on Comte's memory; they cannot receive his love, nay, his frantic adoration, of the lonely wife of a convict, absent in the gallies, as a piece of pure Platonism. Had Madame Comte's allegations been sifted fully, we might have known all. As it is, I for my own part like to think him innocent; he was mad from disease, and perhaps from conceit; a conceit, says Mr. Mill, too colossal to be believed without reading him up; but I trust he was not immoral. His letters are against it, the lady's face is against it, and above all, there is against it the lasting effect upon himself. After a year's happiness to Comte, she died and left him, as he thoroughly supposed, an enlightened and a religious man.

Poor Comte! His sweeter life was buried with the dead, who to him could never rise again. His religion was no more than a funereal cult; a veil thrown over it, no hope, no thought of reunion! The episode of Clotilde was, in itself, one of those touches of nature which make the whole world kin; the brief, bright, and long sad experience the solitary had of his heart; the love, the loss, the unforgetting sorrow! But, did it not prove, beyond the force of reclamation to disprove, that Comte's system ends, at last, in what is commonly called materialism? its faith (or negation of faith) being in effect this, that we look for entire human dissolution coincident with bodily death. And the end flows naturally from the beginning; all we think is phenomenal, all we know is phenomenal, first and last. Our life is only a phenomenon; and death, death joins us to the unreturning past. We are absorbed, all that is good of us, into general and generic humanity; an Eidolon, called the Great Being for our comfort; as if a name (what's in a name?) could console us! The race we may have tried to serve is to be our Euthanasia, our sepulchre, I had almost said our cenotaph!

Strange thought, not without a kind of serpent-fascination! Epidemic in England now, gaining force from its unhallowed audacity! The consistent pessimist, who rates men at the worst, thinks the worst in himself, and does the worst by all others, and by himself, if he is but fixed in this unbelief, need not fear what the world, man, or God shall do unto him. It is the old whisper, "Ye shall be as gods!" 'Tis superhuman to sit and watch the storm; to have our strong sensations, illusions they are called in France; blood-poisons which circulate in our life, working hot passion and mischief; sorrow to many a loving, many a confiding heart; passion, mischief, sorrow, what matters it? there comes an opiate by-and-by! The man of overwrought brain, used up, worn-out feelings; the distempered dreamer; the reckless worker of wrongs; the disappointed striver for an earthly crown, all shall have their common slumber at last; unconscious, impervious, unbroken. I will read you three stanzas from a longer piece written by one not unknown always where that tree of knowledge grew :—

> "Cessation is true rest,
> And sleep for them opprest;
> And not to be,—were blest.
>
> Annihilation is
> A better state than this;
> Better than woe or bliss.
>
> The name is dread ;—the thing
> Is death without its sting;
> An overshadowing."

If such be the thought to them whose natural heritage stands strong, fringed with luxurious hope to live beloved, to die regretted; what will the "overshadowing" be when it passes, like a plague breath, over the children of toil and anxiety, over them whose life is at best hard, and their lot depressed and without "illusions"? Will they not want their strong sensations? Will they respect any law, human or divine, which stands between them and their enjoyments? Will they not crush all who bar their pleasures, aye, choke them in their own blood? Why not? The opiate comes to all at last. 'Tis an act of oblivion! The overshadowing will cover all.

And this is the coming creed of the 19th century. To return to Comte, about whom I might say much, but must not;—of course, he had no foresight of anything worse than an immediate realization of his crowning ideas—sociality, fraternity, Positivism. Europe split into small states; women made incapable of property, but held objects of religious worship; men worked on a communistic principle; an oligarchy of rich; a spirituality of Positive believers, with a supreme infallible pontiff at their head; Paris the seat of infallibility and of order. Clotilde had shown Comte a principle antagonistic to, and predominating over, all egoism; Altruism was to burn out of men all selfish aims, nay, the ordinary feelings of a man! A rigorous rule of life was to aid, and a religion without a God to enforce, this new law. Two hours a day, divided into three private services, were to be spent in the adoration of Humanity under the form of a living or dead woman. The image of the fair idol, dress, posture, everything was to be brought distinctly to mind; and the whole soul to be prostrated in her honour. Comte, it has been said, gave woman everything except justice.

There is a grave moral in this tale. Theology was extinguished; but the desire to worship burned on—a fire unquenchable. Is that desire, or is it not, a broad reality, an inalienable truth of our nature? Comte accepted it for himself, and not for himself alone, but for our whole human race. Along with it he accepted the only principle which could bestow universal validity. Our moral intuitions were acknowledged safe guides, and something more; the rulers of an intellectual world, the revealers of truth higher than all beside. Often and often he asserted the dominion of heart over mind. Probably, if Comte had lived longer he would have acknowledged other revelations of our moral nature. Moral causation, for example. That strange phrase of his—"a modifiable fatality," self-contradiction in words, suicide in sense, what did it portend? Was it the first sound of a marriage-bell, freedom and duty once again united? A change of his system wonderful to contemplate, yet not more wonderful than the state in which he left it.

One cannot help here asking how matters would have stood if Comte had died without knowing his Clotilde. How incomplete according to his own account his philosophy! how wanting in that which perfected the whole! A notable fact this, throwing great light on the value of suchlike systematization which, after all, much resembles secretion from that interesting viscus, the system-maker's own particular brain. And there is another fact quite as notable. How curious that Comte should have lived so long without discovering whatever truth his own heart and a strong human affection disclosed to him! Hence we might illustrate and confirm a previous remark, that any one not living a truly human life—call him undeveloped, uneducated, dwarfed, or immature—is no typical man; and if we believe ancient maxims, scarcely a learner in philosophy, certainly not a judge of its highest and widest problems.

The most notable fact and greatest surprise of all is, that Comte's prayer without petition, his passionate self-mesmerizing adoration, his religion without a God, should have taken any hold on men. No one can transfer to others his private sorrow or his private joy; it is hard for a man to get his thought understood, harder still to make common pasture of his heart. But Comte devised extraordinary propagandist expedients; those who consider his developments mere madness, should explain why sane people have accepted them. Comte set no value on Protestantism in any shape. The religion of his own country he carried back to mediæval forms, and then travestied it. There were many festivals, a calendar of saints, nine sacraments, and a horrible caricature of the Christian Trinity. This idea crowned his sociology, which I need hardly say was communistic socialism, enfolding (as socialism always must enfold) and scarcely veiling the most iron of despotisms, both temporal and spiritual. His mind delighted in contemplating a synthesis of the great Fetish, Earth, with the great Being Humanity; which last somehow assumes on occasion a feminine gender.

To Clotilde, symbolizing that supreme object, Clotilde, his noble and tender patroness, he transferred Dante's homage of Beatrice: addresses to the mother of our Lord; and stranger than all, the prayer of Thomas à Kempis to Almighty God, "Amem te plusquam me, nec me nisi propter te"—"May I love Thee more than self, nor self at all except for Thee." Now consider: when Comte died, sixty-four years had not quite elapsed since goddesses of Reason were worshipped in the cathedral and other churches of Paris. Upon each high altar a fair woman, chosen for her faultless beauty, sate enthroned, her feet resting upon the consecrated slab. Gaily clothed in tunic and Greek mantle, she was so displayed by a torch behind her throne, so elevated above her worshippers, as to attract from Phrygian cap to Italic shoe their passionate gaze and adoration. Low down beneath her footstool lay the broken symbols of a faith then declared effete and passed away; just as half a century afterwards Comte declared theology passed away. Music sounded, incense smoked, Bishop Gobel, who assisted at a parody of sacred rites, wept tears of shame, but in fear and trembling he assisted. The object of this mad mockery of religion, this empire of heart over mind, this woman-worship, was to proclaim afresh Fraternity, Progress, Sociality. Sociality, for the supposed law of which final development Comte worshipped humanity and Clotilde—but disowned immortality and God.

These two madnesses, how near akin, how far apart were they? The world is not really made young by destroying old things; yet the path of 18th century madness lay through fire and blood. Its deeds are sometimes spoken of, even now, as great crimes; but no great crime is criminal in the sight of men whose life is godless, dark, and unsubstantial. Horrors pass before them like unrealities. "The world," writes Mercier on the trial of Louis XVI,—"The world is all an optical shadow." In our 19th century life, 'tis a skilfully prepared overshadowing, beneath which men beat their brows till their blood-shot eyes see red. "I see red," exclaimed Eugene Sue's ruffian, "and then I strike with the knife."*

* While these sheets were passing through the press, I read in the *Pall Mall Gazette* for April 24th, as follows: One of the Communist papers, the *Montagne*, writes: "Education has made sceptics of us; the Revolution of 1871 is atheistic; our Republic wears a bouquet of immortelles in her bosom. We take our dead to their homes, and our wives to our hearts without a prayer. Priests! throw aside your frocks, turn up your sleeves, lay your hands upon the plough, for a song to the lark in the morning air is better than a mumbling of psalms, and an ode to sparkling wine is preferable to a chanting of hymns. Our dogs that used only to growl when a bishop passed will bite him now, and not a voice will be raised to curse the day which dawns for the sacrifice of the Archbishop of Paris. We owe it to ourselves, we owe it to the world.

Let me end by telling you a dream, which is not all a dream.

A company of *savans* were seen in the visions of the night, busy with a new scientific invention. Earth, they argued, earth has her volcanoes, her burning exhalations; men have electric lights, fires, gas lamps, furnaces. These make up the world's proper illumination. The effect intended was, therefore, to darken the air we breathe, so that no rays from the upper sky should pass through it. The inventors hoped that a district, a country, nay, even a world, might thus be overshadowed by a gloom impervious to moon and stars by night, to sun by day; and the human eye see no changes, save those which the earth's activity, or human power and skill, might produce. Terrestrial and artificial alternations excepted, all was to be changeless as winter midnight—deep impenetrable darkness! It was seen slowly, very slowly, to descend. In thirty years the men of science hoped and purposed its perfection.

Did those who had previously known the beautiful light of heaven, who had bathed and basked in the life-giving sunbeam, feel happy, or even calm, when they saw their

The Commune has promised us an eye for an eye, and has given us Monseigneur Darboy as a hostage. The justice of the tribunals shall commence, said Danton, when the wrath of the people is appeased; and he was right. Darboy! tremble in your cell, for your day is past, your end is close at hand."

children and children's children robbed of celestial glory and gladness?

Yet there is one thing worse than a world without a sun—you know what I mean—Humanity without a GOD.

Postscript.

The Lecturer purposely abstained from reading Professor Huxley's acute critique on Positivism until this Lecture had gone to press. He now strongly recommends his auditors to read No. viii. of the Lay Sermons.

Should any reader find difficulties in pages 23—25 of the foregoing Lecture, he will do well to peruse Littré's "Auguste Comte et la Philosophie Positive," chapter iii., particularly pp. 42, 43.

SCIENCE AND REVELATION.

BY THE VERY REVEREND

R. PAYNE SMITH, D.D.,

DEAN OF CANTERBURY; LATE REGIUS PROFESSOR OF DIVINITY, OXFORD.

SCIENCE AND REVELATION.

THE duty which has been imposed upon me to-day by the Christian Evidence Society is, I conceive, to state as clearly as I can, what is our ground for believing that a revelation is not only possible, but is a necessary part of the system of this world. As the programme further joins science and revelation, I conceive that I am debarred from any but a strictly scientific proof. We may reasonably infer the probability of a revelation from God's necessary attribute of love. We may ourselves feel morally sure that a creature, approaching so nearly to the spiritual world, and capable of so much good as is man, would not be left by his Maker in that miserable state of vice and misery in which we find ourselves. There are many good and weighty reasons for believing that God would give us a revelation, and that the Christian religion is God's revelation—reasons drawn from the nature of God, from the actual condition in which man is placed, and from the direct teachings of Holy Scripture—all these, like a cord of many threads that cannot easily be broken, serve to confirm the faith of the believer, but I must forego their use. In confining myself to what I conceive to be the strictly scientific basis of a revelation, I would, nevertheless, beg you to remember that the evidences of Christianity are cumulative. They cover a vast field, and it is in their united force that their strength lies. The very vastness of the field often invites attack. Some outlying work seems capable of overthrow. Some discovery in the domains of history, of philology, or of physical science, seems to provide new weapons for the assault. Possibly not all the arguments used in defence of Christianity will endure the test of close and accurate examination. Possibly, too, in our views of the nature of Christianity, and in our exegesis of the Scriptures, we have arrived only at partial truth, and do not distinguish with sufficient accuracy between what is certainly revealed, and what is nothing more that a possible explanation of the Divine word. There are, moreover, I will candidly confess, difficulties in the way of faith. However new may be the form of the attack, and however modern the materials which it uses, yet the strength of the attack lies in real difficulties, which are no new matter, but have ever lain deep in the minds of thoughtful men. I do not believe that belief is a thing easy of attainment, any more than virtue is. I believe that both are victories, gained by a struggle—gained over opposing forces.[6] But as certain as I am that this present state of things was intended to train man to virtue, though I cannot answer all the objections brought against the system of the world being exactly what it is, nor solve all the doubts and difficulties, moral and metaphysical, which surround us: so I am convinced, in spite of similar difficulties in the way of religion, that belief, and not unbelief, is the end at which man ought to aim. I believe that man was intended to attain to a higher and more perfect state than that in which he now finds himself, and that he can only attain to it by virtue and faith; but as the very value of these lies apparently in their being won by an effort, long and earnestly maintained, I am not surprised at the existence of difficulties, least of all of such difficulties as arise from our ignorance. Still belief would be unnecessarily * difficult,[7] and we may even say, morally impossible, if the sum of the arguments in defence of a revelation did not largely exceed the sum of the arguments against one. With these arguments I have to-day nothing to do. The evidences of Christianity, external and internal, will be treated

* I use this word because if the value of faith and virtue consists in their being a discipline, while this implies the existence of difficulty, it also limits the degree of the difficulty.

of by others. My business is to show that a revelation was to be expected; that it was probable, or at all events possible, and, therefore, that the evidences of Christianity have a claim upon the consideration of every right thinking man. In showing that a revelation was to be expected, I shall at the same time show what is the exact position which it holds, and in what way revealed knowledge differs from all other knowledge, scientific and unscientific.

Now the argument which I shall use as my proof of the possibility of a revelation is simply this, that in the present system of things we find no being endowed with any faculties without there being also provided a proper field for their exercise, and a necessity imposed upon that being of using those faculties. In this statement I assume nothing. I do not assume that there is a God who made these beings. I do not assume that they were made or created; still less do I assume that they were intended to use their faculties. I put aside all theories of design and causation, not because I do not believe that they possess force, but because the actual facts which I see around me, or which I am taught by scientific men, are enough for my proof. The only thing which I assume is, that the laws of nature are universal; and I assume this simply because it will be readily granted me. The universality of nature's laws compels us to admit that a law which holds good in all known cases, will necessarily hold good in all cases whatsoever.

Our whole language is so essentially based upon religious ideas that it would be very difficult for me to use only neutral words. But in using religious words, I wish them to be understood in a neutral sense, If I speak of creatures, I mean only beings, things which exist now, or have existed. If I speak of them as endowed with faculties, I merely mean that they possess them. By nature, I mean simply the present state of things, whether designed by an intelligent mind, or a mere come-by-chance. I look simply around me at what is—or at all events appears to be—and I find myself in a world in which there is a very exact correspondence between the endowments and faculties of every existent being, and the state of things in which it happens to be.

So exact is this correspondence, that if you give Professor Owen a bone, he will tell you to what order of animals its owner belonged, what were its habits, the nature of its food, of its habitat, and mode of life. Nature works out this correspondence even to the most minute detail. By looking at the bone of a quadruped we can tell, not merely great things about it, but such trifles as which leg it used first in getting up from the ground. For nature is so undeviating that the outward habits, even in things of no apparent moment, correspond to the internal conformation.

Now, possibly, it will readily be granted that such is the present state of things. Whatever may have been the stages through which we have, or have not, passed, we now find ourselves in a world of apparent cause and effect—full of infinitely varied forms of life, but of which none are purposeless. I cannot upon this point bring forward a better witness than Professor Huxley, who, in his most interesting essay on Geological Contemporaneity (Lay Sermons, p. 236) speaks as follows :—" All who are competent to express an opinion upon the subject are, at present, agreed that the manifold varieties of animal and vegetable form have not either come into existence by chance, nor result from *capricious exertions of creative power;* but that they have taken place in a definite order, the statement of which order is what men of science term a natural law." The whole chain of animal and vegetable life seems to this great authority so perfect and complete, that even the variations which have taken place in it, have been governed, he considers, by a law, that is, a regular and orderly succession. These variations have been the result, apparently, of certain changes in the external state of things, to which the external conformation of the animal has somehow or other been made to correspond. But as Professor Huxley points out, these variations have been confined to very narrow limits. When people speak of the enormous changes which have taken place in the living population of the globe during geological eras, they refer, he says, to the presence in the later rocks of fossil remains of a vast number of animals not discoverable in the earlier rocks; but the fossils which you do find in the early rocks differ but little from existing species. (See p. 238.) He thus negatives on sure grounds the idea that a state of things ever existed on this globe essentially unlike what exists now.

What then exists now? I answer, first of all a vast chain of vegetable life, fitted in every portion of it to find its own subsistence, and to propagate its species. Its main function is to "manufacture out of mineral substances that protoplasm, upon which, in the long run, all animal life depends." (Lay Sermons, p. 138.) I need not detain you by enumerating the many various contrivances by which plants are enabled to manufacture food for us out of carbon, hydrogen, oxygen, and nitrogen—substances upon which, in their original state, animals cannot feed—nor the still more curious and elaborate processes by which their fecundation, and the propagation of each species is provided for —processes which seem often to require the intervention of animal life. I need not detain you upon this point: you will readily grant that this correspondence does exist. If a plant is not suited to its habitat, and cannot use its natural powers, nature imposes upon it the severe penalties—first, of degradation, and then of death.

Upon the animal world she imposes just the same penalties. There is neither excess nor defect in her operations.* Whatever she gives must be used, but animals, being governed in the main by instincts, have no choice. They necessarily employ all their living powers, and apparently have no powers beyond those indispensable for their existence. This point, however, I will not press, though it seems to follow from the fact asserted by Professor Huxley, that no important difference can be observed between the fossil remains found in the earliest strata, and animals of the same species and order existent now. (See pp. 241, 242, and for vegetables, p. 240.) For, as he tells you, facts establish a scientific law—law in the mouths of scientific men, meaning an established order of facts. Well then! I will put this fact of absence of progress aside, and with it the corollary of the absence of latent

* "Rudiments," so far from disproving, prove this. A rudiment shows that nature might have given more, but has not done so. Why? Because the further gift would have been useless, for instance, man would not have been benefited by being able to feel with his eye-brows. (See Darwin, "Descent of Man," i. 25.)

powers.* But of actual powers it is evident that animals do use them all, and have to use them all. So close, too, is the agreement between the powers and the external position of every animal, that a change in its external relations will modify its powers to a certain extent. But only to a certain extent; there are fixed limits to the adaptability of those living powers. If the changes are suc ash to occasion a more active exercise of its living powers, the animal increases in strength, size, and beauty; if unfavourable, but still permitting some use of its powers, it dwindles and decays. But pass the appointed bounds and the animal dies. Nature is exacting the penalty of the non-use of what it has given. Nature exacts a severe penalty for the mis-use, and the last and final penalty for the violation of her laws. I do not know that an ascidian jelly-bag has any other faculties than those of sucking in water, and of sticking to a stone.† But this I know, that if it does not use all the powers it possesses and suck in

* Professor Huxley's words are, "In these groups there is abundant evidence of variation—none of what is ordinarily understood as progression; and if the known geological record is to be regarded as even any considerable fragment of the whole, it is inconceivable that any theory of a necessarily progressive development can stand, for the numerous orders and families cited afford no trace of such a process." (p. 245.)

† Darwin, "Descent of Man," i. 205. 8

its water, and stick to its stone, no process of natural selection will ever develop it into a monkey: it will go to the limbo of nonentity.* But what an alarming thought, that at a period separated from us by such vast geologic ages, that, according to the nebular hypothesis, held by so many of our leading astronmeors as a probable theory, this whole universe was a mass of heated vapour; what an alarming thought that the very existence of man should have depended upon a jelly bag sticking to a stone and sucking up water! Alas! there was then no water, no stones, no jelly bags, and therefore there are now no men! Man escapes, poor thing, from his humble parentage: he need not feel his ears to find the proof there of his monkeyhood:† but his escape costs him dear. What with astronomy and biology, men of science between them have cleared us out of existence. Scientifically, man is no more.

My argument, fortunately, depends upon matters of fact: facts for which the believer accounts by holding

* It is a curious fact that these Ascidians possess a heart and a circulation, but that after the heart has beaten a certain number of times it stops, and then beats the opposite way, so as to reverse the circulation. (Lay Sermons, p. 95.) In what stage of its progress did it so degenerate as to lose this remarkable power?

† Darwin, "Descent of Man," i. 22.[9]

that this world is the work of a Being possessed of infinite wisdom and power, and who therefore has endowed all His creatures with those faculties which they needed, and with no others; because to give useless faculties would be a violation of God's attribute of wisdom. The student of natural science may take another view. It is no part of his business to do so. His office is to discover and tabulate the order of facts, of phenomena, and this order he calls a natural law. Well and good. But teleology, the science of ends, which gives the reason why a thing is what it is —teleology belongs to the metaphysician. It is his business to inquire into causes and effects. Still, as a matter of fact, scientific men do try their hand at accounting for the present state of things, and they say, perhaps, that there is a struggle, a competition in nature,[10] so sharp and close that no creature can continue to exist save by the vigorous exercise of all its necessary faculties, while all useless qualities will be cast away as mere overweight and incumbrance. I need no decision upon this point; the fact is all I want. I do not want you to decide whether mind preceded matter, and consequently that there is a God: or whether matter and mind came into existence contemporaneously, in which case there is no room for the theory of development, but abundant room for impossibilities, metaphysical and actual; or, lastly, whether matter preceded mind, the latter being simply the result of a high corporeal organisation, slowly attained to by the processes of selection, natural and sexual. Whether this present state of things was worked out intelligently, by a Being possessed of will and understanding, or is the result of blind and unintelligent powers, working fortuitously, this, to my argument, matters not. All I want is the admitted fact—that every living organisation fully possesses all those faculties which it needs, and must use all its faculties under penalty, first of degradation, and, finally, in the long run, of extinction.

But man is a living organization, and must, therefore, come under this law. Let us see whether the fact confirms this deduction. Now, in all the long line, from the ascidian upwards to man, nature had supplied none but physical wants. Her children need food; she gives them each those senses and that conformation which enables them to get each their own food. They need safety: she uses much ingenuity in providing for their safety. She is, moreover, liberal. Their food is, in general, gained so easily, and their safety so well provided for, that their lives are full of enjoyment. Her care, however, is taken in the main for the species, and not for the individual. He enjoys his food because nature has taken loving care for the whole family to which he belongs; and she further takes care that that family shall continue to exist. If it perish, it is because by some change in temperature, or the like, the correspondence is destroyed between its faculties and its external position. Short of this, the ingenuity employed by nature in providing for the continued existence of every species of insect and animal is as wonderful as that employed by her in continuing vegetable life; and, as a rule, the lower the creature is in the scale of being, the more curious the contrivances used for its preservation.

Well, when we come to man we find these three leading necessities equally well provided for. Man is provided with the means for obtaining food, for providing for his safety, and for propagating his species. But, though nature's ends are the same, and reached with equal certainty, her means are, in the main, different. The animals are moved to gain their existence by their senses working upon their instincts. This is a great advance upon vegetable life. You had there neither senses nor instincts, but simply powers. But man rises above the animals as much as they transcend vegetables. He attains to these same ends of food, safety, and continued existence by the use of his reason.

Now, I wish you to notice this. Nature is not limited in her resources, nor confined to one method. She is not obliged to plant animals in the ground that they may suck up food through their legs; she can and does give them instincts by which they can get their food in a very different way. But perfect as these instincts are, nature can do still better. She can produce an animal capable of reasoning upon causes and effects, and who, therefore, provides for everything which he imagines to be good for him by setting those causes in motion which produce the desired effect.*

But with the possession of reason there also goes the possession of what we call mental faculties. Not only can man by the use of his reason obtain food, provide for his safety, and continue his race, but higher ends are made possible for him, to be attained to by the use of this higher endowment. Man has the power of articulate speech, and upon this follows the power of learning to read, to write, and to cypher; and upon the power of doing these three things follows a plenitude of other powers. Now, I shall not stop to enquire how man gained these powers, whether by natural and sexual selection or not; but I venture to point out that there is

* There is something of this in animals just as, on the other hand, man is not altogether devoid of instincts. I should have expected this from the teaching of the first chapter of Genesis, which represents men not as a distinct creation but as the last act of creation.

a vast chasm between physical and intellectual powers. The most sensible monkey is a parody rather than an imitation of man, and the difference between the two is enormous.* The points of agreement serve rather to enable us to measure this interval, and see how wide it is, than to bridge it over. Now, let us suppose ourselves philosophers come, we will say, from the planet Jupiter, on a mission intrusted to us by the Jovians, to examine and report upon the nature of the creatures which people the four inferior planets, Terra, Venus, Mercury, and Mars. Of course, we should look upon the inhabitants of such small communities with contempt, but, being philosophers, we should not neglect anything because it was trifling. Well, when we came to Terra we should report that it was a very curious region, inhabited by a long scale of beings, each one fitted to its place, and that at their head there was a rather noxious, troublesome, and uppish creature

* Physically the monkey is man's superior. Anatomists assure us that they can find no very great difference between his brain and ours. His larynx also is as well fitted as ours to produce articulate sounds. So far we are equal. But he has four hands, and we have but two. Read Sir C. Bell's "Bridgewater Treatise upon the Hand," and you will see at once that a vast superiority is implied in this. I can never believe that when, by natural and sexual selection, a creature had been attained possessed of four hands, nature could so degradate in her work as to fall back upon two. No well-bred monkey would have mated with one so deformed.[11]

called man, whose examination had caused us an infinity of trouble.

In examining this creature we should find that it shared in all the wants of those beneath him, but that it supplied its wants, not by the use of instincts, but of reason. Over and above, however, man's physical wants, we should find that he had mental wants; and with these wants faculties also, by which he could supply them. Supply all the physical wants of an animal, and having none besides, it will lie still for hours or days until hunger stirs it to renewed exertion. Supply all man's physical wants, and his mental wants then develop into full activity. Give him the lowest and basest drudgery; make him work morning, noon, and night in the meanest occupations, for the supply of merely physical necessities, and, though you can infinitely degrade, you cannot destroy his mental powers. He still thinks, still connects causes and effects. But our purpose will be best answered by taking the case of those whose faculties are most highly cultivated. Has nature supplied a proper field for the exercise of the mental powers, not merely of Fuegians, but of the most highly developed man? You know that she has. Take the senses which he has in common with the animals, but see what vast means have been provided by which he can make an intellectual use of them. What arts and sciences, painting, music, harmony, numbers, eloquence, have grown out of their use. As for our mental powers, think only of the vast number of ologies which are claiming admission into our very normal schools. Think only of all our learned Associations. our Royal Societies, our Social Congresses, our British Museums full of books, which have been written, and are waiting only to be read, and you must own that men do use their mental powers, and have means enough for a more ample use of them. Nature makes us use our mental powers to some extent. She encourages us to use them thoroughly and earnestly.

Use them we must. Man is placed is such a position that he must study what passes round him. Man learns by experience. Instincts are but slightly progressive. Unless brought into contact with man, the animals learn little—perhaps nothing. I do not doubt but that those huge monsters, whose remains we behold in geological museums, were the most dull and stupid creatures possible. I think this simply because I suppose that man did not then exist, and, therefore, that these monsters had nothing to waken them up out of their sluggish torpor. But scientific men* tell me that existing mammals actually have larger brains than their ancient tertiary prototypes of the same

* Lartet, quoted by Darwin, "Descent," i. 51.

order. Let man enter the stage, and the instincts of animals are quickened. Nature did not create man without taking care to guard the inferior animals from his destructive powers. But man in himself, essentially, is at once progressive and retrogressive. Bound up with him is an infinite possibility of advance and decay. He is never stationary. Both individuals and communities are perpetually either ascending or descending in the scale, morally and intellectually. But this law of nature obliges man to perpetual mental effort under the usual penalty of degradation. We have not merely to advance, to win new ground. If this were all, at length we should have nothing to do. We have to win back lost ground. Our gains are, I hope, greater than our losses; but the progress of no community will ever be fast enough, continued enough, and assured enough, to justify the members of it in living in a fool's paradise. This, then, was our second point. The first was, that nature has provided us with a proper field for the exercise of our mental faculties; the second, that she imposes upon us the necessity of using them.

We may add, that the law of scientific progress also makes it certain that no advance of science will ever deliver us from the necessity of using our faculties. The valuable part of every science is its theory—the mental part. Facts and fossils are of no value, except as being the materials for thought. No geologist would care much for a discovery of fossils in agreement with an established theory, but if the theory were still debated, then every discovery that tended to prove or disprove it, would be canvassed with intelligent interest. The pure sciences can grow, I am well aware, only by additions. But then they are simply instrumental. They are to the mixed sciences what arithmetic is to the ordinary business of life. Logarithms, algebra, the integral and differential calculuses, are simply easy ways of doing difficult sums. It is a great thing, no doubt, for science to perfect its instruments and processes, but scientific progress lies in the mixed sciences themselves, and these are constantly undergoing modification. The spectrum analysis is largely modifying the science of astronomy. Deep sea dredging, and other fresh means of information, have so modified geology, that no one holds now that similar strata are necessarily of the same date. A vast cretaceous formation is probably going on at this very day in the bed of the Atlantic. (Huxley, "Lay Sermons," p. 206.) The law, then, of scientific progress is constant modification; fresh facts are discovered, new theories started, old theories revived, existing theories altered, recast, newly shaped. Should a science become, practically, complete and perfect, scientific men would care for it no longer. The manufacturer and merchant would then seize upon it. In this way what was once a problem in the mind of the student, becomes an article of use, comfort, and enjoyment in our daily lives. Meanwhile, new sciences spring up, and old sciences take new shape, and, as a matter of fact, so large has become the scientific domain, that no one man can master it. Division of labour has become as necessary here as in the manual crafts. We are no longer encyclopædists, but each one must stick to his own page in the great book of learning.

Many of these sciences relate to our social condition. And of these the importance and value every day rapidly increases. Good government largely depends upon knowledge of all those natural laws upon which moral and physical well-being depends. Upon good government follow increased wealth, active trade, higher wages, and larger consumption of commodities. Upon these follows increased population, and that population concentrated upon spots favourable for all this activity. And upon this follow new social difficulties; fresh problems arise to be solved, and new questions to occupy the mind both of the student and of the statesman. Unless solved, society will retrograde; it will suffer in health, in wealth, and morality; turbulence will take the place of quiet industry; and that community will decay. Here again nature provides a field for the employment of our faculties, and compels us to use them. If not there is the same penalty, degradation. I do not know how many geological periods it would take before, by the neglect of our powers, we could retrograde back to our ascidian progenitor; but I see everywhere around me the proofs that retrogression is as much a law of man's nature as progress. We can only continue what we are by using all our powers.*

But I may have lingered over this part of my subject too long. No one perhaps will deny that man both can and must use his mental powers as thoroughly as an animal must use its instincts, and a plant its vegetative powers, or it will suffer for its neglect. Only remember that my argument has nothing to do with individuals; I am treating of man as a species, and investigating the general laws which regulate his well being. Well, now, has man any other powers than

* The body politic is in fact very much like the natural body. There is a constant waste and a constant repair. The waste may be greater than the repair—and in that case the body dwindles—but the repair may be greater than the waste, in which case there is growth, progress. In both alike real growth can only be by assimilation. The new must be taken up into the old, and become part with it. That which is losing vitality must be put away; but that which is to take its place must become one with the old. After a certain time, however, natural bodies lose their powers of assimilation, and old age and death are the result: I cannot enter into the question how far this is also the case with political bodies.[12]

those already described? Has he merely physical powers to enable him to get food, and other bodily necessaries; and mental powers to enable him to read, write, and cypher? Is this all? You know that it is not all. There is another broad distinction between man and all the other inhabitants of this earth. He alone distinguishes between right and wrong.*

Now if man possesses this faculty, however acquired, and by whatever name called, then if nature's laws are universal, he is both bound to use it, will suffer from not using it, and will have a proper field provided for its use. Nature gives no faculty without imposing an obligation of exercising it: an obligation, however, which rests in its full force upon the species, and upon the individual only as belonging to the species. Some powers every individual must use or he would die; there are other powers which, if he does not use, nature will be content with a lighter penalty. Far be it from me to affirm that every one here uses his reasoning powers. I hope he does; but if he does not use them, I am quite sure that nature will exact of him the penalty of stupidity. But the species must use them; if not, upon degradation

* Animals brought into contact with man attain some small share in this power. The influence of man over domesticated animals is most remarkable. I should doubt whether a wild animal was at all capable of making such a distinction.

would soon follow extinction. Nature, for instance, would not let man exist as a mere animal. If he did not use his reason, the instincts of other animals are so superior to his, that while they found food he would be unable to do so. Even if necessity quickened his instincts, he would yet have ceased to be a man, and would be retrograding back to the ascidian. To continue to be a man he must make some low use at all events of his mental powers. Now, can you establish any such difference between man's intellectual and moral powers, as will justify you, while acknowledging that you must use the one, in neglecting the other? Can you give any reason why you need not use the faculty which undoubtedly you possess of distinguishing between right and wrong, and the faculty, let us say, of "using the imagination in matters of science." I am sure you cannot. By not using your mental powers you will be in an inferior mental position; by not using your moral powers you will hold an inferior moral position.

But you may say the penalty is slight, and we will pay it. We will use our physical powers, and become grand animals and we will use our mental powers, and become grand intellectual men. Not men I answer. Add intellectuality to animality, and you merely get an intellectual animal. Your moral powers are an essential part of yourselves. Confessedly too, there is ample field for using them. The whole world is so constituted that morning, noon, and night, the question perpetually arises of right and wrong. You cannot take a step in life without conscience intervening. It is so inseparably a part of yourselves that constantly it acts as a mere instinct, and approves or condemns your conduct as spontaneously as your palate distinguishes between sweet and bitter. You may render your palate dull, so that you cannot taste what you eat and drink; you may render your conscience dull, but it has a strong recuperative force, and, after years of dullness, will awaken, and exercise again its judicial functions with stern and decisive energy. Struggle as much as you like, but the conclusion cannot be evaded, that you can distinguish between right and wrong, that you ought to do so, and that you must do so.

If so, what follows? I answer, the necessity of religion, and therefore of revelation. Resist as men will and do, they have but a choice between two alternatives. Either all this present state of things, in which every faculty has its appropriate field of exercise, and every external possibility has opposite to it an internal faculty; either all this is an illusion and deceit, a purposeless and objectless piece of jugglery;* or if it be a reality, then the existence in man

I have taken these words from the "Vedanta Philosophy." It teaches that the apparent reality of this world is *māyā*, i.e., deceit, illusion, of faculties, obliging him to distinguish between right and wrong, constitute him a *responsible* agent. If he is responsible, he is responsible to some one : and certain penalties are necessarily attached to the neglect, the misuse, and the violation of his moral powers. The person to whom man is responsible must be capable of forming an equitable judgment, and therefore must know the motives as well as the outward acts, and for this nothing less than omniscience will suffice. He must have the power of apportioning adequate rewards and punishments to human actions, which will need little less than omnipotence. And as no adequate reward or punishment follows in this life, there must be some other state in which men will be dealt with according to their true deserts. If not, then there exists in man a whole class of faculties, moral faculties, which seem to find in this present state of things an appropriate field for their exercise, but which man is under no necessity of using. A man who lives in the habitual violation of every moral obligation, but does so with discretion, may have a very large enjoyment of the things of this world : while generally a man whose conscience is tender, and whose life is regu-

jugglery :" "naught besides *the One* exists :" the world was made out of nothing and is nothing. "All that is real in this visible, is the God who is invisible." See Ballantyne's "Christianity compared with Hindu Philosophy," pp. xxxi—xxxvii, 43—50.

lated by the highest motives, necessarily and voluntarily abandons much, both of pleasure and prosperity. Nature cannot have so bungled her work. The highest possible exercise of the powers which she has given us must necessarily lead to the highest possible good. It does not matter to the argument whether conscience and your other moral faculties be natural or acquired. If nature endowed an ascidian with the power of acquiring moral faculties, it was bound to use them as soon as it had got them. The question whether you are bound to use your mental faculties does not depend in the least upon the question whether man is an improved monkey. You are bound to use them simply because you have them. So you are bound to live as a responsible being simply because you have the faculty of distinguishing between right and wrong. You know, too, that you act yourselves upon this principle. If any one were to push one of you out of your seat and take it himself, not only would you be angry, but our chairman would call in a policeman to expel the disturber, and give you your seat back again. Why? Because the man would have been doing wrong, and need not have done it; and because it was wrong you are angry and punish him. But can you stop there? There are things which we know to be wrong, but which hurt none but ourselves; things we know to be wrong, but which benefit society. A man may liberally support useful institutions from motives of ostentation, or as a bribe, if he is a candidate, let us say, for a seat in parliament. An act may be apparently right, but the inner motive wrong. Now, conscience judges of things absolutely; it condemns or approves of things, not as they seem, but as they really are: not by results, but by their intrinsic character. What is there which answers to this outside of man? Must there not be a judge who also judges men absolutely? You can find no such judge but God. Either, then, nature is a sham, and her laws not universal, and this present state of things a delusion, or there is a universal judge, and a future state in which reward and punishment will be meted out in strict accordance with the rightness and wrongness of human action. A being omniscient and almighty can alone judge actions absolutely in the same way as conscience judges us, both for our thoughts, words, and deeds.

I have chiefly spoken of conscience, but the argument takes in all man's moral and spiritual powers.* No man

* It is the examination of these moral and spiritual faculties which makes it so probable that man possesses something more than a highly organised body and mental powers, which, though superior in degree, are still of the same kind as those possessed by the animals. And it should be remembered that the proof that man possesses a soul, and that the soul is immortal, is entirely independent of revelation. It is based upon the intelligent study of the facts of psychology. If, how-

can doubt but that man has within him powers which exactly answer to religion outside of him. The power of faith is as much a faculty as that of sight; and so also is that instinct, I had almost called it, which makes a man ever turn away in discontent from the present to struggle for the future. And what is more, man's moral and religious faculties develop with advancing civilization just as his mental faculties do. The mental questions which agitate our minds would be entirely void of interest to a savage; the social difficulties which occupy the attention of our political economists and statesmen would be mere trash to a peasant: so, too, with religion. I do not see any reason why a race may not sink so low as to lose the very idea of a God; but I am sure that such a race would hold the very lowest place in the scale of humanity. Whatever round in the ladder of human progress you like to examine, I will make bold to say that you will find the religious and moral state of mankind there holding a very close relation to the degree of mental culture and civilization to which it has attained.

Now, the only thing that acts powerfully upon man's

ever, it is said that man does not really possess, but only seems to possess these faculties, I answer that then nature is a mere deceiver, and its works a sham: and that, consequently, all physical science would be the study of the illusive.

moral faculties is religion. I do not say that this ought or ought not to be so; all I assert is that it is so. Call, if you like, the great mass of your fellow men Philistines, and despise their low culture, but you will find nothing that acts powerfully upon these Philistines to give them culture, to raise, refine, and purify them, except religion. Conscience, too, holds a most direct and evident relation to religion. You will not find conscience amenable to reasoning. When virtue begins to reason, the proverb tells you it is lost. When conscience condemns, it is because the thing condemned is a sin against God; when it approves, it is because the thing done is absolutely right, and as God commanded. Conscience never asks whether a thing is a sin against society; it never troubles about consequences, knows nothing about political economy, or political morality either. It judges by a higher and absolute rule. By so doing it makes man a responsible agent absolutely, brings him into direct relation with God as the absolute judge, and renders necessary a more exact apportionment of rewards and punishments than exists at present. There must be some other state of existence in which man will be judged in the same way as now he judges himself, and in which the natural effects of this judgment will be fully carried out.

But, if there is thus a future judgment, and a state in which happiness and misery will follow as the natural* results of our actions here, man will require a certain amount of knowledge concerning this judgment. By the possession of conscience and other religious faculties, man holds a definite relation towards God. Plainly the most tremendous results may follow from this relation, and man ought to have some sure knowledge of these results. Now it is conceivably possible that God might have given us this knowledge by means of the light of nature, as we call it. But He has not. Confessedly natural religion is neither clear enough nor certain enough to affect powerfully the masses. Man is not a quiet, orderly, neutral sort of being; he bears about with him a nature fraught and fully charged with the most dangerous passions. Reason, with its prudential maxims, has never done much to restrain these passions. To take, then, the lowest possible ground. As nature has given us moral qualities, I suppose that moral excellence is a thing as necessarily to be attained to as physical and mental excellence. But while nature has provided ample means for attaining to the two last, she will not, without a revelation, have provided sufficient means for the attainment of the first. By the aid of religion, about

* Though we draw a distinction between the natural and the supernatural, this distinction is tenable only when we look at things from below, and not when we look at them from above. We call those processes natural of which we know or might know the secondary causes.

as many men probably attain to moral excellence, as by other natural means attain to physical and mental excellence.* Without religion nature will have broken down. You would have universally a state of things like that in ancient Greece —one Plato, surrounded by the mass leading the most grossly sensual life.

Nature cannot develop any being higher than herself, nor endow it with wants which she cannot supply. If nature develops intellect, morality, religion, then that power which developed these faculties must also be intellectual, moral, religious. What, then, can this power in nature be but the working of God? Out of nothing comes nothing. The effect cannot be greater than the cause. The existence of man, with his mental, moral, and religious powers, forbids us to believe that that which caused man to exist can be less possessed of these powers than he is.

* It is no argument against revelation that it does not make us all holy and devout. It is not the law of this present state of things that all men attain to the highest possible physical and mental excellence. All that we can say is, that they ought to aim at nothing less. So neither do all men attain to moral and religious excellence. Equally it ought to be their aim; but why they so often fail in attaining to it is more than any one can answer. The failure of individuals to attain to the highest good possible for the species is one of nature's universal laws. Why this present state of things is so constituted is a mystery, which cannot be solved here; but which will certainly be solved when we have the perfect knowledge promised us in 1 Cor. xiii. 12.

Infinitely higher he may be, lower he cannot be. And as surely as man's physical and mental wants are provided for by that power which called these wants into being, so surely will man's moral and religious wants be supplied.

They are not supplied by the light of nature; nothing then remains but revelation. Into the formal proof of revelation I must not enter; all that devolved upon me was to show the *à priori* probability, or at least possibility, of a revelation. I have endeavoured to show this by a consideration of what man is, viewed simply as a natural being, and by the consideration of his natural wants. I have not taken into consideration any of the additional knowledge given us in the Bible concerning man. I have treated him in much the same way as I might one of the creatures in the Zoological Gardens, if I had been asked to study it in order that I might see what its wants were, and tell the keeper what to give it to maintain it in the full possession of its powers. No doubt it would have helped me if I had been told what and where the creature had been before. I should then have had no difficulty in explaining and accounting for everything. Such knowledge, however, even revelation does not give us, because it is not indispensable. It gives us that only which is necessary for the supply of our wants.

Even with this knowledge my argument is not concerned; but certain general principles about revelation follow from what I have laid down. And first, revelation has nothing to do with our physical state. Reason is quite sufficient to teach us all those sanitary laws by which our bodies will be maintained in healthful vigour. If the Bible condemns drunkenness, gluttony, and the like, it does so not for sanitary reasons, but for moral reasons, because they are sins. So revelation has nothing to do with our mental powers; whatever we can attain to by our mental powers we are to attain to by them. Physical and metaphysical science alike lie remote from the object-matter of revelation. Because God has, in the Bible, given us revelation in an informal way, in order, perhaps, to commend it to our entire nature, people often forget that its proper object-matter is simply the moral relation in which man stands to God, especially with reference to a future state of being. Religious men forget this. They often take up an antagonistic position to science, and try to make out systems of geology and astronomy and anthropology from the Bible, and by these judge all that scientific men say. Really the Bible never gives us any scientific knowledge in a scientific way. If it did, it would be leaving its own proper domain. When it does seem to give us any such knowledge, as in the first chapter of Genesis, there is a very important differentia about it. What it says has always reference to man. The first chapter of Genesis does not tell us how the earth was formed absolutely ; geology ought to tell us that. It tells us how it was prepared and fitted for man. Look at the work of the fourth day. Does any man suppose that the stars were set in the expanse of heaven absolutely that men might know what time of year it was ? But that is their special service, and in old time a most important service for man. To the geologist man is just as much and just as little as a trilobite or a megatherium. To the student of the Bible man is everything, and the first chapter of Genesis teaches him that man was the cause of all other terrestrial creation, the sum and crown of the Creator's work.[13]

But if believers mix up science and revelation, so do the students of physical science. No sooner is a theory started, than it is immediately compared with what the Bible says, or is supposed to say. Now, no doubt, the comparison between the teachings of revelation and science is inevitable. Whatever is mixed up with revelation, owing to the manner in which God has been pleased to bestow it, must, at least, be true. It would be impossible for us to accept the authority of the Bible upon those points in which we cannot judge of its truth, if in those points in which we are competent judges we found it erroneous. The teachings, therefore, of science and of revelation must be compared ; but in this comparison not only must we remember that it is not the object of the Bible to teach science, and that, as it speaks to all people at all times, it must use popular language, but also that the comparison must be made, not with the floating theories of the hour, but only with established truths. If the wisest geologist of our days could show that there was an exact agreement between geology and the Bible, it would rather disprove than prove its truth. For, as geology is a growing science, it would prove the agreement of the Bible with that which is receiving daily additions, and is constantly undergoing modification, and ten years hence the two would be at hopeless variance. At the same time there is a good side to the discussion, and the theologian especially is the gainer. In the present day the attack upon revelation draws its weapons from our increased knowledge of physical science, of philology, and of history, and the theologian can no longer neglect these studies. I have no scruple in saying that I look with pride upon what my countrymen have done, and are doing, in enlarging the bounds of our scientific knowledge, even if I do not always approve of their spirit, or accept their conclusions; and I am quite sure theologians must study, intelligently and dispassionately, all those branches of knowledge which are brought into contact with revelation, or they will lose their influence over the intellect of the country. It is no use treating physical science as a bugbear. Let our theologians master it, and they will find it a manly study, which will give their minds breadth, will teach them what are the difficulties which press heavily on many thoughtful minds, and which must be fairly met. An opposition between an old science like theology and new sciences there must be: but let both sides remember that revelation was never intended to teach us anything that we could learn by the use of our natural faculties, and that what the Bible teaches must be compared not with floating and probable theories, but with proved theories. These proved theories will, I believe, fall into their place in due course of time, as easily as Galileo's theory about the revolution of the earth round the sun. If not, I do not see how the claims of the Bible to be the Word of God can be maintained: for I cannot believe that there is any chasm between the teachings of God in nature and in revelation. But I think it perfectly possible that men may misinterpret and misunderstand both one and the other.

I have detained you too long. But I must make one more remark. If the proper object matter of revelation is that knowledge, which being necessary for us as moral agents, was yet unattainable by our natural powers, then reason is no judge of what revelation teaches. There may be in our relations to God, things which we never should have expected: deep truths opening onwards into mysteries past our present finite comprehension. If everything had been plain, easy, commonplace, revelation would not have been needed. Nevertheless, reason holds a very high office with respect to revelation. In a matter of so high consequence, as whether God has spoken to us or not, we are bound to examine most scrupulously the evidence upon which the fact of the revelation rests. And this examination involves an enquiry into the teachings of revelation. The existence of mysteries in a revelation is reasonable: the existence of immorality in it would be fatal to its claims. For if the scientific basis for my belief in the gift of a revelation is the existence in me of conscience, and of moral faculties which make me a responsible being, I am left absolutely without a basis for a revelation which makes me violate my conscience. A revelation which degrades my moral and spiritual powers is as much against nature as anything that degraded my physical or mental powers. If religion be true, it must ennoble, elevate, purify, and perfect me, here as far as the present condition of my existence permits, entirely in that other state to which our present responsibility points, provided, of course, that I submit myself to its teachings. I know of no way by which I can make this examination except by reason and experience. And I hold this further, because I hold that a true religion must be commensurate with the whole of man. It must make him better physically, mentally, morally, and spiritually, and consecrate all his powers to God.

I am only too well aware that much which I have said has been put in a feeble and confused manner. Much also necessary for the support and elucidation of the argument had to be omitted because of the necessity of compressing it into so short an essay; but I trust that the main line of thought is clear, namely, that religion outside of us stands in so plain a relation to what we are internally, that either it is real, or this whole state of things is a delusion. Man, without a revelation, and therefore without religion, is the only one thing of all that exist upon the face of the earth that is a bungle,* a failure, and a mistake.

* Professor Huxley considers that man is a bungle. At all events he would be glad to be "turned into a sort of clock, and wound up every morning before he got out of bed," on condition that he should always "think what is true, and do what is right." (Lay Sermons, p. 373.) I suppose this means that we should like to be governed by very perfect instincts, but I question whether he would not find his new kind of life dull. At present both right thinking and right doing require of him an effort, which, from the spirit of his writings, I should think he enjoys. But, after all, what he says has a true foundation. Sin is not a necessary part of man's lot. It cleaves to him because he is fallen; and this world apparently offers us a state of moral and religious discipline, by the aid of which, in a future state, we shall be free from sin. But those who do not wish to retrograde would prefer to have this freedom by the force of perfected habits than by the force of instinct.

THE

NATURE AND VALUE

OF THE

MIRACULOUS TESTIMONY TO CHRISTIANITY.

BY

JOHN STOUGHTON, D.D.,

KENSINGTON.

MIRACLES.

One of the most touching narratives in the New Testament relates to a want of faith in miracles. It is said that when Thomas was told of his Master's resurrection, he replied, "Except I shall see in His hands the print of the nails, and put my finger into the print of the nails, and thrust my hand into His side, I will not believe." He was not denounced for this. No word of withering scorn, or cutting ridicule, or threatening anger, fell on the ear of the doubting disciple. But evidence was offered. "Reach hither thy finger, and behold my hands; and reach hither thy hand, and thrust it into my side; and be not faithless, but believing." As far as rebuke appeared, it was only by implication, in words respecting those whose faith is of keener eye, and swifter foot: "Blessed are they that have not seen, and yet have believed."

I think that every one who speaks of miracles to doubting minds should from this narrative take a lesson. Surely the gist and purpose of it is, that we should distinguish between intellectual difficulty and moral prejudice, and deal patiently and convincingly with honest seekers after truth. Sometimes the subject before us has been so handled as to drive the unbeliever into deeper unbelieving—I would rather strive to work upon a little faith, and make it more.

I.

I am to speak to you respecting the *nature* of the miraculous testimony to Christianity. My business is with mighty works, recorded in the New Testament as having been wrought for the purpose of testifying to a Divine mission. No definition of their character in relation to physical law can anywhere be found in this ancient record. They are not spoken of as *violations* of law, or as *suspensions* of law, or as *interferences* with law, or as *contradictions* to law. They are described, not on the side of their physical nature, but on the side of their moral signification. They are depicted, not in their connection with the obvious order of the material universe, or with any hidden powers and principles of a higher and harmonious description; but in their connection with Him who claimed to be the Redeemer of mankind, who came, according to His own words, to seek and save that which was lost. They are denominated "*wonders*," startling occurrences, things contrary to common experience; and "*signs*,"—not mere marvels bursting idly on the public gaze, and exciting in a multitude of spectators a barren curiosity, but *signs*,—replete with an ulterior meaning, and testifying to the character and work of Him through whom they were accomplished.

There is no necessity, then, for us at the outset to define a miracle on the physical side of it—to call it a violation of law, or a suspension of law—an interference with it, or a contradiction to it. In other words, there is no need imposed by the conditions of our argument, to inquire into the mode in which such a phenomenon can be produced. It is enough to show that it did occur, and to dwell upon the religious significancy of its occurrence first to the witnesses, and next to ourselves. What is the exact position which miracles may be thought to occupy as wonders in the universe, whether, through breaking in upon common experience, they are referable to the operation of occult laws, known and controlled at a fitting moment by the mysterious touch of the wonder-worker; or whether they are to be considered as resulting simply from the immediate fiat of the Supreme will, are questions which may with advantage be relegated for consideration elsewhere.

1. But, at the very threshold of our inquiry we are met by the assertion, that a miracle, however defined, is in itself simply impossible. Impossible! In what sense impossible?

Does it mean impossible to man, or impossible to God? Impossible to man, of course, it is. That impossibility enters into the popular idea of a miracle. Man has no such control over nature as to be able to produce one. But if it be said a miracle is impossible to God, such an impossibility involves the extension of human inability to God Himself. It involves either the idea, that nature has ever been independent of God, or the idea, that if produced by Him, He is no longer Lord of His own works—this Lordship having been surrendered by His will, or having escaped from His hands. Summarily disposing of this gross anthropomorphism, we find behind it the dogma of Spinoza, that there is nothing transcendental anywhere, no transcendental beginnings, no transcendental interpositions; for God and nature are one through the eternities. In the wake of Spinoza's philosophy follows the modern axiom—"to recognise the impossibility even of any two material atoms subsisting together without a determinate relation—of any action of the one on the other, whether of equilibrium or of motion, without reference to a physical cause—of any modification whatsoever in the existing conditions of material agents, unless *through the invariable operation of a series of eternally impressed consequences, following in some necessary chain of orderly connexion.*"*

* "Essays and Reviews" (Baden Powell), p. 133. The italics are mine, simply to call attention to the point of the quotation.

Here, *in limine*, before examining this principle, let me observe, once for all, that miracles do by no means cast any slur upon the settled order of nature, as if it were faulty and imperfect, and required correction or supplement for effectuating its proper ends—as frail constructions in engineering departments of human contrivance need subsequent repairs. Nature is perfect enough for her own ends; miracles are introduced for other and higher purposes. This requires to be borne in mind throughout our entire discussion.

But to come to the antagonist principle, that there is a development in nature through the agency of physical laws, apart from an original Creator and an everlasting Lord. I do not say—far from it—that the principle denies the existence of such a Creator and Lord, but it supposes at least that the physical order of the universe is fixed in such a sense, as to have ever excluded from it the action, directly or indirectly, of a Divine will, beyond the inflexible maintenance of ordinary operations. It is said, "The enlarged critical and inductive study of the natural world cannot but tend powerfully to evince the inconceivableness of imagined interruptions of natural order, or supposed suspensions of the laws of matter, and of that vast series of dependent causation which constitutes the legitimate field for the investigation of science, whose constancy is the sole warrant for its generalization." In reply to this it may be fairly urged that science, whilst she maintains the invariable sequence of causes and effects, and the uninterrupted order of physical events, is a prophetess of truth and wisdom. She enunciates lessons bound up with the welfare of the race. Thus far there is no antagonism between her and religion. She can, without abandonment of her principles, nay, in the act of carrying them out, officiate as a priestess at the altar of God; nor is there anything in the position for which she stipulates contrary to the claims of Revelation. For Revelation, in appealing to miracles, supposes the ordinary course of physical phenomena to be inviolable, and no book more than the Bible exhibits the normal constancy of natural agencies. But when science pronounces as impossible all such signs and wonders as are recorded in Scripture, she steps out of her province. In her own province she may justly affirm there are no signs of miracles; she may sweep her telescope over the fields of the sky, and ply her microscope amidst the growths of the earth, and say, I can see no traces anywhere but of inflexible law. These realms of existence are full of order. It is the perfection of their beauty, that they are free from violations, suspensions, disturbances, and interferences. But to say this—and I fully concur in it—is not to demonstrate that the Scriptures relate impossibilities. To do so, philosophy must pass beyond the range of physical observation, since *there* no place can be found for working out the desired demonstration. Philosophers do not always remember how difficult it is to prove a negative. Showing that certain things are, they are apt to slide into a belief that *therefore* certain other things cannot be, the conclusion proving on logical examination a simple *non sequitur.* Doubtless it is a fact, that we can detect nowhere in nature a provision made for producing miracles such as come under our review in this lecture, that no prophecy nor hint of them can be discerned throughout her measured realms; but this is a very different thing from saying, that nature teaches the belief of them to be absurd. So far from its being absurd, there may, after all, be found in nature something analogous to a miracle. In nature there are distinct worlds, worlds between which there are gaps and gulfs. I do not dispute that there are striking approximations in the phenomena of some realms to the phenomena of others; but there are also broad deep spaces, here and there, never bridged over by the discoveries of science. Hence, "an animal," as you have been told already, in the words of Hegel, "is a miracle for the vegetable world." It is a new creation in some way, and a new creation in any way is a miracle. After wandering amongst rocks, we find in plants a new world. Organized life is so; so also, compared with animal instinct, is the mind of man, with its spiritual reason, and its moral consciousness.

Not only do Coleridge, Kant, and Plato regard man's highest faculty as essentially different from the mere adaptive understanding of an animal nature; but what is still more remarkable, Aristotle himself, whose turn of mind was so different from theirs, differentiates man from other creatures on the ground of his being endowed with the faculty ot reason. In his work on the Generation of Animals, he says that there is no resource except to believe, that the reason has no affinity with the material elements out of which the human embryo is formed, but that it comes from without, and that it alone, of all the component parts of man, is divine.* Thus, in the opinion of one of the greatest philosophers the world has ever known, the line of demarcation between man and all lower creatures is broad and clear, a line which in the simple order and development of nature they could never cross. The superior attributes of humanity, according to him, come *from without;* here, then, amongst the component parts of humanity is something divine. In other words, we have a new world; a new creation. I do not say there is a strict parallel between any new race or species in nature and the occurrence of individual miracles

* De Gen. An. II. iii. 10. See article by Sir Alexander Grant in the *Contemporary*, May, 1871, p. 277.

on rare occasions, but I do say that there is enough of resemblance between these two descriptions of change to exempt a believer in both of them from the charge of being absurd.

Furthermore, there are in human minds varieties of power of an astonishing description: although there be faculties common to all men, the vigour of those faculties in some cases is such as perfectly to eclipse the vigour of them in others. The superiority of individual minds, whose works have filled the world with wonder, is such as to leave behind, at an unapproachable distance, the ordinary measure of human endowment. Certain intellects (I need not name them) have long exercised a formative power upon the civilized portions of our race. They have been as crystals inserted in a solution, and other crystals have received shape from them. Whence have come these typical energies in the intellectual world? No law of development will account for a resplendent genius now and then flashing on the world; for the appearance of a master mind, after humanity has kept on a low level through generation after generation; for the ascent again of gifted spirits into the highest heaven of invention, after another lapse into mere mediocrity. No known laws of causality account for such facts in the realms of intellectual existence. If, in the case of man, as compared with other animals, the difference, as Aristotle says, is something which comes *from without*, the same may be said with respect to the difference between ordinary mortals and William Shakespere or John Milton. There is forced upon us the conviction, that these stars which dwell apart are kindled by fires burning in superhuman spheres. I do not say, in this case, any more than in the others I have cited, that we find an exact parallel to a miracle; but I do maintain, that we discover here a kind of inspiration which, like the miraculous, transcends all known laws, and brings to mind what was said by the first of those just named:

> "There are more things in heaven and earth, Horatio,
> Than are dreamt of in your philosophy."

What is called physical science must change her name, and renounce her office, and assume functions of another order, before she can pronounce a peremptory negative upon the point in controversy.* Physical science needs to

* Since writing the above, I have lighted on the following passage in an able university sermon by one of the lecturers in the present course. I am glad to confirm what had struck my own mind, by quoting the words of so careful a reasoner. In reference to philosophic doubts directed against the idea of design, and the analogy between human and natural productions, he remarks: "This is evidently a very hard question, and if it properly belonged to the province of physical inquiry I should shrink from hazarding any investigation of its merits. But the question has overstepped the boundary of such sciences, and become a branch of philosophy. I may seem obscure in making this assertion, but you will see its truth if you consider for a moment the limit which

become metaphysical, and to pass into fields of abstract reasoning in order to the utterance of a universal dictum. To this kind of mental employment in itself I make no objection; for the science of merely physical nature, without any outlook into higher regions, keeps the soul in humiliating imprisonment. The excursions of thought, however, now before us are regarded in some quarters under the singular delusion of being strictly scientific, whilst employed in devising a theory of the universe which excludes the constant control of a personal God, an Almighty will. The assaults on what is miraculous can be carried on only with metaphysical weapons. The facts of physical nature do not supply them; only from theories of physical nature, taking a metaphysical form, can they be gathered. Even Positivism, with all its doubtfulness and denial—strange contradiction that—must, in order to deny the possibility of miracles, build up a wall

divides science from philosophy. Sciences are often content to accept their principles, the lower from the higher (as Aristotle puts the case) in an ascending scale up to metaphysic, which, if it is anything at all, is the philosophy of first grounds so far as they are discoverable. While the various kinds of inquiry assume their several grounds as postulates, each keeps its separate and subordinate place. But one prime impulse of the human mind is unification, and thus, in every science, there springs up a tendency to ground itself. The moment this attempt is made, a science becomes a philosophy, and must be tested by the ordinary criteria of philosophic procedure."—*Right and Wrong*, by the Rev. W. Jackson, M.A.

to shut them out, by trenching first on ground beyond its own domain. Pure Positivism, consistently with itself, is not competent to contradict the existence of the supernatural; it can but leave it an open question. The common method of distinctly denying miracles is one involving either some atheistic or pantheistic principle. Assume—and it is but an assumption—that matter is eternal and self-sufficient; that natural laws have not originated in, or are not administered by, a personal will; and thus assuming what prepares for, if it does not necessitate, some atheistic or pantheistic hypothesis, you can plausibly maintain that the wonders of which we speak are utterly inconceivable. But, as you see, it is not physical science simply considered which brings out this result; the result comes through adding to physical science what is really a metaphysical element.

At what a tremendous cost, it may be observed by the way, is such a result achieved. The philosophy of universal necessity places man in the same predicament as it does simple matter. If all nature excludes voluntary control, and is subject only to an iron rule of invariable succession, then man also must himself be incapable of voluntary control, whether it comes from a supreme will or from his own. Thus the warfare which assails miracles, threatens to destroy all ideas of freedom and moral responsibility. And this dark foreshadowing is not concealed. "Step by step," we are confidently and calmly told, "the notion of evolution by law is transforming the whole field of our knowledge and opinion. Not the physical world alone is now the domain of inductive (?) science, but the moral, the intellectual, and the spiritual are being added to the empire. It is the crown of philosophy to see the immutable even in the complex action of human life."*

But when all assumptions are denied, the whole question presents another aspect. Given the fundamental distinction between things physical and things moral; given the higher nature of man, the personal existence of God, a moral element in the Divine rule, the immortality of the human soul, and the present vicinity of invisible spiritual realms; and, immediately, miracles wrought by the Divine will for men's moral welfare are completely removed out of the sphere of the impossible.

Positivism, Atheism, and Pantheism are considered in other lectures of this course, and therefore it is not my office to examine them. To what has been said by the Archbishop of York and the Rev. Mr. Jackson, and to what may be said by the Rev. Dr. Rigg, I must refer my hearers.

I would only observe in passing, what, indeed, I have hinted at already, that it puzzles me beyond description to conceive how, by any course of natural evolution, inde-

* *Westminster Review*, Oct., 1860. Art. on New Christianity.

pendent of the introduction of a new force by an overruling power, the phenomena of the human will with its morally creative energy for good and evil could have been produced. To solve, on the principle of pure development, the problem of the genesis of that mysterious faculty, is an insuperable task. If we may speak of what is inconceivable—and scientific men set us the example—we should say the existence of volition in man, with its moral accompaniments, is utterly inconceivable, apart from belief in a Divine will, of which ours is the offspring.

It appears, then, that science really presents no antecedent grounds for rejecting miracles, and that if we believe in a personal God, the presumed impossibility melts away. This point has been conceded by one of the masters of modern reasoning. "A miracle," as was justly remarked by Brown, "is no contradiction to the law of cause and effect; it is a new effect, supposed to be produced by the introduction of a new cause. Of the adequacy of that cause, if present, there can be no doubt, and the only antecedent improbability which can be ascribed to the miracle, is the improbability that any such cause existed."*

2. When we have disposed of the preliminary objection which, in some way or other, says miracles are impossible, we are met by another objection, namely, that they are

* Mill's "System of Logic," ii., 160.

immensely *improbable.* Hume's ingenious position,*—that miracles are contrary to human experience, that no amount of human testimony is sufficient to establish them, and that it is far more likely men should be deceived or mistaken, than that such events as miracles must be, could ever take place,—has been made to do abundant service in this controversy; very little, if anything, has been added by those who have persistently used the argument, to improve its form or to increase its plausibility. One of its latest modifications is, that incidents out of the common course of things, said to happen in the present day, are by all of us sceptically regarded, that supernatural pretensions are felt by us to be inadmissible, and that where we are compelled to allow the honesty of witnesses, if they affirm anything involving a miraculous nature, we at once dispose of the whole matter by saying 'there must be a mistake somewhere.' Undoubtedly it is true that miracles are contrary to common experience. They must be so, or they would not be what they are. If they were of frequent occurrence,

* "The argument in Hume's celebrated Essay on Miracles was very far from being a new one. It had, as Mr. Coleridge has pointed out, been distinctly indicated by South in his sermon on the incredulity of St. Thomas; and there is a remarkable statement of much the same argument put into the mouth of Woolston's Advocate, in Sherlock's Trial of the Witnesses."—Art. on Miracles in Smith's "Dictionary of the Bible."

if they had happened in the history of the world so often as to become familiar to mankind, they would change their character completely. Their nature and purpose, in the view of those who receive them, is such as to render it necessary that we should bear this in mind. But to allege that they are contrary to human experience, taken in the widest point of view, is to beg the question at issue, a fact remarked a thousand times. That they are not contrary to the experience of certain persons who lived eighteen hundred years ago, is what Christians affirm; to say that they are, is illogically to cut the controversy short, and, by a general denial of everything of the kind, to put out of court the very case about to be tried, in support of which there are credible witnesses waiting to give evidence. The question of probability must be looked at all round. The circumstances under which any alleged wonders may have happened must be taken into account, before we pronounce upon their probability or improbability. When extraordinary things, coloured with a supernatural tinge, are related to us as having occurred without any assignable purpose, or only for some sectarian or party end, in connection with beliefs long cherished and avowed, of course we look on them suspiciously; giving to the authorities relating the narratives, credit for integrity and truthfulness, we naturally say 'there must be a mistake somewhere.' And, no doubt, the general culture of the present age, however superficial that culture may be, makes us far less ready than our fathers were, to endorse popular tales of wonder. There is a salutary scepticism which grows out of extensive knowledge. Truth is of such immense value, that we should not be indifferent to it in the smallest communications and concernments of life. Most assuredly any wayward, eccentric, unmeaning, and useless departure from the common course of things, tending only to shake our faith in nature,—as if men might gather grapes of thorns, or figs of thistles, as if barley being sown, wheat should spring up, or an apple tree by a sudden freak should bear oranges,—would deserve to be stigmatized as unworthy of belief. But the wonders in question come under another category. They are represented in the history which has recorded them, not only as being exceptional incidents in themselves, but as having been accomplished under exceptional circumstances. They are not waifs and strays on the stream of time, floating no one knows why and whither; but growths rooted in what appears as a unique system of moral instruction and improvement, designed by the loving Father of spirits for His lost children. They do not produce what may be called a disturbance of nature—that is, a throwing things in the physical world out of gear, so that men are thereby puzzled to make out what nature is, and how far it may be trusted. The documents which contain our miraculous chronicles attest the immutability of Him who is the King of nature, and the unchangeable foundation of His government and law, with a pre-eminent luminousness and with an unparalleled force.

The wonders chronicled were avowedly wrought for purposes of the highest order; and here, again, we fall back upon the distinction between what is physical and what is moral. Those purposes of the highest order to which we refer are moral. They bear on the noblest destinies of humanity, and they link themselves with the principles of natural religion, with the being and sway of a mighty, wise, and gracious God, with our conscience and responsibility, and with the future existence of the soul. Natural religion, though it speaks not a word of miracles, though it gives no prophecies of their advent, yet prepares for their appearance so far, that its teachings, fairly considered, cut off all antecedent unlikelihood of their occurrence. For natural religion suggests the desirableness of revealed religion, and revealed religion is only another name for supernatural interposition.

In a lecture upon Science and Revelation, by the Dean of Canterbury, it has been shown that man's moral nature, man's religious susceptibilities, render religion a necessity for the supply of his deepest wants; but that what is called natural religion is not clear enough, nor certain enough, to affect the generality of our race. Revelation, then, it may be fairly argued, looking at man, is a desideratum, looking at God, is a probability; and Revelation, being obviously a supernatural bestowment, seems to imply some authentication of itself, in part at least, by means of evidence corresponding with its own supernatural origin and character.

The conditions under which Scripture miracles are said to have been performed must be kept in view when we are told they are improbable. They were not performed in one continued series by a succession of Thaumaturgists; but they are found grouped together in certain clusters. As science indicates particular epochs of the energizing power of nature, so the Bible records particular epochs of an energizing power above nature.

The first great cluster of Bible wonders we find gathered round the Lawgiver of Israel; the second round the great Reformer of God's ancient Church; the third round Him who is spoken of as The Word made flesh, who dwelt among us, and who imparted to His apostles miraculous powers akin to His own. Miracles, for the most part, are halos of divine light encircling three grand names—Moses, Elijah, Jesus,—the last the greatest of the three.

Physical wonders we meet with in company with spiritual ones—wonders in outward nature in company with wonders in the great soul-world, of which sensible things are the types and shadows. In other words, miracles occur in connection with inspiration, and, whilst marvels startle the eye, new truths or new applications of truth are addressed to the mind. In harmony with facts in the intellectual universe already noticed, resembling the exceptional illuminations of genius which at intervals have flashed on the rest of mankind,—like the lightning that lighteneth out of the one part under heaven, and shineth unto the other part under heaven,—souls inspired with a grand moral message have come forth from the secret place of the Most High; and it has been in the pathway of these inspired souls that physical miracles have started up; rather, it has been by their hands that physical miracles have been wrought.

There have been surprising coincidences in modern times between the wonderful in nature and the wonderful in history; for example, between the sailing of the invincible Spanish Armada, and the storm which strewed the shores of Great Britain with its ponderous wrecks—between the march of Napoleon's army and the winter's snow which blinded, benumbed, and destroyed so many thousands. The connection is unexplained except on the principle of a Divine providence.* And so in ancient times there were coincidences between the lightning and thunder of Sinai,

* See Martensen's "Christian Dogmatics," 222.

and the legislative wisdom of Moses—between the fire that fell on Carmel, and the reforming zeal of Elijah. The connection is explicable only on the principle of these men having been the internunciators of the Divine will. This explication is strengthened by what they did with their own fingers or their own lips.

It may be considered as entrenching too much on the domain of doctrine to speak in this lecture of the Incarnation; but I would venture to say thus much, that Jesus appears on the face of the evangelical narratives, as the Son of God, in a sense in which no other being can be rightly called so; that in the opinions of early Christendom, the lowest as well as the highest, He was esteemed as a supernatural Person;* and that, by common consent, amidst diversities of theological sentiment, it is acknowledged, never man spake like this man, or lived like this man, or died like this man, or was like this man. And being, by the perfection of His moral character, and by the purpose of His benevolent mission, a truly exceptional person, it is only in keeping with the first blush, and with the deeper study of His wondrous life, to believe in signs and wonders attending His earthly career, showing whence He came, and illustrating what He came to do. Christ Himself is the

* I must here refer to Dorner's "Doctrine of the Person of Christ," where evidence is afforded of what I say.

greatest of wonders in the history of the world. No other approaches Him in wisdom, love, beautifulness, and glory. In more senses than one His name is "above every name." Taking the four Gospels together, the Incarnation of the Word is associated with a supernatural birth. The miracle in the spiritual world of the manifestation of God in Jesus Christ, is coupled with the miracle in the physical world of the Virgin's conception. If Christianity be more than the republication of natural religion, if it be the revelation of God's redeeming love, it involves a miracle as the very starting-point of the process; and the unfolding of the idea in the New Testament includes a divine manifestation, which is a miracle in history, and a divine birth, which is a miracle in nature.*

His advent in the world comes out in the four Gospels as a central sunlike marvel, and therefore it seems no improbability, but rather the clearest of all probabilities, that around Him there should revolve a planetary circle of miracles.

Difficulties are needlessly created by forgetfulness of the character ascribed to this extraordinary Person. To argue as to what He did, or as to what He did not do, without a recognition of the actual *One* painted in the Gospels, is really to argue about another Christ, not the one whom Christians follow.

* See again Martensen's "Christian Dogmatics," 220.

In accordance with the view I have taken, is the manner in which the New Testament miracles are narrated. It seems assumed that such things might be expected in the wake of such a personage as the Son of God. They are not introduced as a procession of facts challenging supreme admiration. No flourish of trumpets heralds their march; but they follow as the fitting and humble retinue of Him who walked the earth its undisputed Master. The Evangelists write as men who were not astounded at what their Master did, because they were so filled with reverence and admiration, at the thought of what their Master was.

Having considered the antecedent objections made to miracles, we are now prepared to look at what is really the *nature* of the miraculous testimony afforded to Christianity. And here, for the sake of simplifying the argument, I shall confine myself to the miracles ascribed to Christ. Faith in His miracles will lead to faith in the miracles of His apostles. If it be granted, as we contend from what has been said it ought to be, that this is a case in which historical proof is admissible, then it is impossible to find stronger historical proof than comes to hand in support of the truth of the evangelical narratives. The historical proof, as such, has of late been comparatively little impugned; the assaults made on the prior credibility of supernatural facts being the main opposition with which believers in

Christianity have to contend. That opposition overcome, and the validity of competent witnesses, as to the question at issue, established, the course is free for an accumulation of evidence, such as Dr. Lardner, with rare erudition, has piled up in his volumes on the Credibility of the Gospel History: such as Archdeacon Paley, with unique ingenuity, and with singular felicity of arrangement and illustration, has condensed in his view of the Evidences of Christianity.* The works now mentioned do not, it must be confessed, supply all that is wanted for the settlement of the question, according to the phase it assumes at present. But when scientific and metaphysical difficulties of modern creation have been grappled with and removed, the array of pagan and Christian testimonies in support of the original credibility of the Evangelists, as collected by these and other writers, comes to render service of immense value. It is more than any one has yet attempted, to overturn, by citation against citation, criticism against criticism, argument against argument, the bulwarks of historical defence built up by the researches of learned advocates. Indeed, the early historical evidence all goes one way. It is evidence without counter-evidence.

And to pass for a moment to foreign literature. After the

* I would also mention "The Divine Origin of Christianity," by John Sheppard. A work less known than it deserves to be.

endeavours of Strauss and others to resolve much of the Gospel story into myths of a later age, and of Rénan, to construct out of the original documents a French philosophical romance, we are provided with the works of Ebrard and Pressensé, who have vindicated the truth of the New Testament story.

It would be idle to attempt, within the compass of this lecture, any outline of the mass of matter brought together in this service. But I may be allowed to indicate that it may be arranged in three divisions. *First*, the concessions of the Jews. Talmudical writings imply that Jesus of Nazareth did many mighty works. The *Toldoth Jeschu* relates a number of things, such as raising the dead, healing lepers, and restoring the lame. It represents people as falling down before Him, exclaiming, "Truly Thou art the Son of God."* The Christian miracles are allowed, but they are attributed to magic. "There can be no doubt," says Whately, "that this must have been (as our sacred writers tell us it was) what the adversaries of Jesus maintained from the first. For if those who lived on the spot in His time had denied or doubted the facts of the miracles, and had declared that the accounts of them were false tales, and that no miracles had ever really been wrought, we may

* Wagenseil's Confutation of the Toldoth Jeschu: Sheppard's "Divine Origin of Christianity," ii. 205, *et seq.*

be sure that the same would have been said ever after by their descendants."* *Secondly*, the admissions of heathens. The extracts from Celsus in Origen afford an abridged history of Jesus Christ, and acknowledge that He did many marvellous things. Celsus explains the fact by saying, Jesus went into Egypt, and having made trial of powers practised there, returned highly elated, and pronounced Himself a God.† Porphry speaks of Christian miracles as wrought by poor rustics through magical arts.‡ Julian does not contradict them when he contemptuously affirms, that Jesus did nothing in His lifetime worthy of remembrance, unless any one thinks it a mighty matter to heal lame and blind people, and exorcise demons in the villages of Bethsaida and Bethany.§ To these heathen admissions, which are of considerable value, are to be added, *thirdly*, the affirmations of Christians. Miracles are asserted by them in manifold forms and in manifold writings. The Fathers follow in the wake of Apostles and Evangelists; and, be it remembered, each New Testament author who testifies to these superhuman achievements is an independent witness, so that their statements bear the value of as many concurrent proofs: and

* Lessons on Christian Evidence, 33.

† Celsus in Orig., L. i., § 28.

‡ Hieron, T. ii. 334.

§ Cyril contra Jul., L. vi., p. 191. See, respecting these and similar passages, Lardner's Credibility, vii. 225, 442, 627.

if it should be said that, because they were Christians, they are partial witnesses, on the other hand it can be said that some of the Fathers, and all the New Testament writers, had become so, contrary to former habits and prejudices, in part, at least, through the very force of miracles, and that too at the cost of extraordinary self-sacrifice and suffering.

I have not sufficient space to exhibit adequately the argument for the credibility of the New Testament witnesses. I must, however, observe that the force has not departed from the old-fashioned method of stating the case, namely, that you must accept them as competent and satisfactory; or you must believe either that they were dishonest men, intending to deceive, or that they were dupes of their own or of other people's fancies. I am disposed to extend the dilemma, and to say, that there is a third supposition, growing out of the junction of these two, the supposition (according to a not uncommon occurrence in the mysteries of human nature) that the witnesses might be partly the victims of delusion, and partly the inventors of fiction, that credulity and imagination might be both at work, the result being a fabrication of miracles, having no basis, or but an exceedingly slender one, in facts occurring before men's eyes. With these alternatives under our view, the inquiry is, Which shall we apply to the witnesses of the miracles of Christ? Rénan has applied the composite supposition to the witnesses of the resurrection. "On the Sunday morning, Mary Magdalene first came very early to the tomb. The stone was displaced from the opening, and the body was no longer in the place where they had laid it. At the same time the strangest rumours were spread in the Christian community. The cry, 'He is risen,' quickly spread amongst the disciples. Love caused it to find ready credence everywhere." "Such was the impression He had left in the hearts of His disciples, and of a few devoted women, that during some weeks more, it was as if He were living and consoling them. Had His body been taken away, or did enthusiasm, always credulous, create afterwards the group of narratives by which it was sought to establish faith in the resurrection? In the absence of opposing documents this can never be ascertained. Let us say, however, that the strong imagination of Mary Magdalene played an important part in this circumstance. Divine power of love! Sacred moments in which the passion of one possessed gave to the world a resuscitated God!" No one is more ready than I am to do justice to the extraordinary literary merits of the "*Vie de Jésus*," its lucid style, its descriptive power, its manifold charms; but I cannot conceal my amazement that the author, with his exquisite genius, should adopt such a travestied rendering of the noblest of Bible stories. There are no documents, as he confesses, to work upon but the four Gospels; and from these Gospels it distinctly appears that, so far from the witnesses produced being of the character he indicates, so far from their love snatching at anything within reach, however airy, out of which to weave a web of wonders, there were men amongst them slow of heart to believe what the prophets had written, and what Jesus had said about the resurrection; men who counted the report of that resurrection, when they first heard of it, as an idle tale,—one of whom even would not yield to sight itself, but demanded to touch the nail-prints in the holy palms, and to thrust his hand into the sacred side. And as to the women, when they came to the sepulchre on the third day, it was not to hail a risen Jesus, but to anoint a buried one. That persons represented by the historians as burdened with doubts, and fears, and unbelief, and demanding demonstrative evidence, should have been finally convinced, and should have staked their all upon that conviction, removes them for ever utterly beyond all reasonable suspicion of dreaming strangely coloured dreams of their Lord's risen life,—to say nothing of collusion and fraud,—and places them at once amongst witnesses, who well knew what they said, and whereof they affirmed.

The credibility of the witness borne to another resurrection is also well established. For evidence of the authenticity of the Gospel of St. John, I refer to Professor Lightfoot's lecture, and would only remark upon the narrative in this Gospel—a narrative so full of pathetic beauty—that it is impossible to explain away its details by possibilities of misapprehension, and pardonable exaggerations of extraordinary incidents. Thus much is indisputable, Lazarus was sick unto death. To all human appearance he died. He died, and was buried, and remained so long in the grave that it was believed the corruption of his corpse had commenced. Coincident with the utterance by Jesus, at the door of the tomb, of the words, "Lazarus, come forth!" the body moved, arose, came forth, bound hand and foot with grave-clothes; in consequence of which, "many of the Jews which came to Mary, and had seen the things which Jesus did, believed on Him." Here were presented to the senses of witnesses phenomena involving the performance of a miracle. A distinction has been justly drawn between testimony to phenomena cognizable by the senses, and miracles completely considered on their invisible and divine side, as well as their visible and human one. "Testimony," it is said, "can apply only to apparent sensible facts; testimony can only prove an extraordinary and perhaps inexplicable occurrence or phenomenon; that it is due to supernatural causes is entirely dependent on the previous belief and assumption of the parties."* With the omission of the words "previous belief and assumption," and the substitution of the words "reflection and conviction,"—whether exercised and experienced at the time or afterwards,—I accept the statement. Phenomena are immediately apprehensible; the cause is not so. A persuasion that the cause is miraculous arises in the mind as an inference from what is directly witnessed. But what is directly witnessed may be of such a nature as to compel the witness, as a reasonable person, to believe that what has taken place results from a supernatural interposition. This conviction implies, indeed, that the person believes in the existence of supernatural power —in other words, believes in the existence and agency of God—which belief may be described as a "previous belief:" but a conviction that particular phenomena are the result of a supernatural cause, depends on the exercise of reason in regard to the phenomena themselves. "No testimony," I admit, "can reach to the supernatural," directly, but it may reach it by implication.

Keeping in view the distinction laid down, we say of the narrative of the resurrection of Lazarus, that no natural solution of the event recorded is within reach. Fraud, collusion, trickery,† are excluded by the character of Christ

* "Essays and Reviews" (Baden Powell), 107.

† That Rénan should treat the Resurrection of Lazarus as a pious

and of Lazarus : no reference to accidental coincidences, or to mesmerism, or to electric influences, or to any known physical agencies, meets the case. Nor is there room for the anticipation that the advancement of science will ever solve this problem. If a solution be attainable, we are shut up to the one solution accepted by Christians. To leave it unsolved, to refer it to the class of unaccountable phenomena, through a persistent determination not to believe in anything supernatural, in the face of all which can be said in reply to antecedent objections, is most unphilosophical.

Let me here add, in reference to narratives of the miraculous, that it is easy to marshal a number of general reflections together, casting a slur upon evidence, and to invest with some plausibility its denial or non-acceptance. But, when we think how fallaciously, yet plausibly, general reflections may be emplcyed for the contradiction of evidence,—how, by reference to the proverbial exaggerations of travellers' stories, accounts of other countries, of their customs and productions, may be discredited; how, by insisting upon men's liability to illusion, the observations of scientific inquirers may be set aside; how, by dwelling on credulity and passion, party spirit, and the like, historic

fraud, and the one moral blot in the story of Christ, is the greatest literary, as well as moral, blot in his "Vie de Jésus." See Hutton's Essays, i., 297.

doubts may be conjectured respecting the existence of Napoleon I., and how, in the same way, historic doubts may be hereafter raised respecting a large part of the career of Napoleon III.; we see how little such general reflections are to be trusted, how much more they may do to hinder the interests of truth than to help them.* The absurdity of the conclusions in such cases discredits the process by which they are reached.

Let us not pass from this part of the subject without saying one word as to the presumption in favour of the New Testament narratives of miracles, when compared with narratives of miracles found elsewhere. Place side by side with the Scripture narratives the miraculous stories in the Apocryphal Gospels, in the writings of the Fathers, in mediæval chronicles, in modern legends of Saints, and one sees the force of a remark by an eminent German theologian: "The critical acumen of Niebuhr was, as is admitted, inferior to that of no man, and he has done away with only too much of the ancient history of Rome. Yet he acknowledged, 'with respect to a miracle, in the strictest sense of the word, it needs but an unprejudiced and searching investigation of nature to perceive, that the miracles related are anything but absurd, and a comparison of them with the legends or so-called miracles of other religions, to recognize what a different

* See Art. on Miracles in Smith's Dic.

spirit dwells in them.'"* To take only one step farther in this direction, when it is asked, "What, if so many apparently competent witnesses were to assure you, that they had seen such and such a miracle—mentioning the most monstrous absurd, fantastic, and ludicrous confusion of nature—would you believe them?" We answer in the words of a modern Writer: "We are only concerned with the miraculous under that form and those conditions under which it has actually by trustworthy report taken place, as subordinated to what has been called 'a general law of wisdom,' *i.e.* to a wise plan and design in the Divine mind under which check the course of miracles has, so to speak, kept near to nature, just diverging enough for the purpose, and no more."†

II.

It is time to attend to the second part of our subject, the *value* of the miraculous testimony to Christianity.

1. The miracles must not be taken alone; they form a part of Christianity; and therefore, to be rightly understood, they should hold in the mind an inseparable relation to the rest of Christianity. Christianity is its own evidence. Each portion harmonizes with the other portions. They yield mutual support. Miracles, therefore, are concurrent with

* Niebuhr's "Lebensnachrichten," quoted in Luthardt's "Apologetic Lectures," 200.

† Mozley's "Lectures on Miracles," 120.

other proofs. "External" and "internal" are convenient words, but they are liable to mischievous application. One objection to the word "external," as designating the evidence of miracles, is that it assumes them to be outside the Gospel—only bulwarks for defence, not pillars identical with the inner structure. It is curious that opposite classes of persons have attributed to miracles an externality which their place in Scripture will not allow. By one class, consisting of advocates for the evidence, miracles are presented as the chief part of the evidence, as marks indispensable for the authentication of Divine truth, yet quite *ab extra* things, placed round about the temple to ward off evil-disposed persons who would dare to violate the shrine. By another class, consisting of those who take exception to the miracles, they are also treated as things *ab extra*, things which may well be cut off from Christianity—burdens which there is no necessity it should be made to bear—a dress which disfigures it rather than otherwise, and which, for the sake of its progress in the world, had better be stripped off and cast away. These two modes of assuming one and the same thing, are as objectionable in themselves, as they are curious in their coincidence.

The miracles really run into and intersect the lines of New Testament teaching from end to end. They are not seals externally attached, but contents deposited inside—

not post-marks showing simply whence the letter comes, but paragraphs written in the folded sheet. The "*internal*" and the "*external*"—if we may use the words in their popular currency—must occupy our attention together. Miracles cannot be torn from the life of Christ. His nature, character, teaching, wonders, constitute an unparalleled spiritual unity. Criticism here, of course, has its own department of duty to fulfil. What really constitute the synoptical Gospels and the Gospel of St. John, is its province to determine. Readings of MSS. require to be examined with an honest desire to render the *textus receptus* as perfect as possible—a desire which a reverential regard for the genuine contents of the record must serve to stimulate. When all that labour has been accomplished, the miracles of the genuine rolls of Scripture are to be regarded as integral elements of faith. "The facts of Christianity," says Archdeacon Lee, "are represented by some as forming no part of its essential doctrines; they rank, it is argued, no higher than its external accessories. It is impossible to maintain this distinction. In the Christian Revelation the fact of the Resurrection is the cardinal doctrine, the doctrine of the Incarnation is the fundamental fact. Christianity exhibits its most momentous truths as actual realities, by founding them upon an historical basis, and by interweaving them with transactions and events which rest upon the evidence of sense."*

* "Lectures on Miracles," 5.

2. Miracles are reasonable attestations of a Divine mission. As such our Lord appeals to them, they "bear witness of me, that the Father hath sent me." As such Nicodemus received them: "We know that Thou art a teacher come from God: for no man can do these miracles that Thou doest, except God be with him." As such the poor blind man regarded them in that exquisite piece of *naïveté*, in which he says, "Why herein is a marvellous thing, that ye know not from whence He is, and yet He hath opened mine eyes." As it is reasonable, in the case of an ambassador, to refer to his credentials in proof of his legitimate authority; so it is reasonable, in the case of a professedly Divine teacher, to refer to signs and wonders he is capable of working, in proof of his Divine commission.

Of vast importance is it that we should note precisely the point touched by the finger of miraculous evidence. It may be said, not only are miracles incapable of enforcing a train of argument, but they are incapable of establishing any moral or religious proposition. No physical demonstration, it may be alleged, can ever link itself on to a spiritual truth, because the two things belong to totally different spheres. We should get involved in metaphysical subtleties, were I to inquire thoroughly into this position. It is enough to say, that, admitting it, the exact point touched by miraculous evidence, is, according to the teaching of Scripture itself, the *office* sustained and the *commission* borne by a person. "The works which the Father hath given me to finish, the same works that I do, bear witness of *me*." "Jesus of Nazareth, a man approved of God among you, by miracles, and wonders, and signs, which God did by *Him*." In these passages, the witness of miracles is attached to a person. "My works bear witness of *me*," says Jesus. They are the approval of "*a man*," says Peter. The evidential force of them bears on Christ Himself, the sent of God. Thus considered, miracles free themselves from objections made to their competency to serve as direct proofs of spiritual truths.

The miracles of Moses afford evidence of his Divine legation: in like manner the miracles of Jesus afford evidence of His Divine Messiahship. It is said of Him that "He taught them as one having authority, and not as the scribes." Authoritativeness is characteristic of His mode of teaching. "Verily, verily, I say unto you." He claimed a right to speak, as one who had power to command men that they should obey. There is in His utterance little of argument, but much of law. Miracles can add no force to a chain of reasoning, and you may say they cannot immediately demonstrate spiritual truth, but they afford a basis for the enunciation of a Divine message, a mandate of the Divine will.

Miracles, no doubt, come within relations to spiritual truth, through the medium of the miraculously demonstrated authority of its utterer; but spiritual truth has other distinct and appropriate marks of its Divine origin and character. It contains an inward witness—it shines by its own light. It commends itself to men's consciences in the sight of God, and when believed, vindicates the justness and wisdom of such belief.

It cannot be too much insisted on, that miraculous evidence comes not out in Scripture *by itself.* The works of Jesus include more than His miracles. The whole beneficent influence of His life is covered by the words, "who went about doing good." With the thought of what He did, stands associated the thought of what He was; and with the character of His matchless life is interwoven the character of His matchless teaching. Miracles form but one strand in the cable which binds the Church's faith to Him who is the Anchor of her hope; and *they* expose the ship to peril who untwist the rope, and lay upon that single strand the whole amount of strain—the entire stress of tension. Holy Writ warrants no such course; but warns against it. "If there arise among you a prophet, or a dreamer of dreams, and giveth thee a sign or a wonder, and the sign or the wonder come to pass, whereof he spake unto thee, saying, 'Let us go after other gods which thou hast not known, and let us serve them;' thou shalt not hearken unto the words of that prophet, or that dreamer of dreams." Moses, himself a worker of miracles, appeals to something beyond miracles as essential to the final establishment of religious authority. The moral proof is put in the foremost place, and no mere physical achievement can exercise exclusive force apart from that. And, as if to remind us of these words in Deuteronomy, we read in the last chapters of Revelation of men being deceived by the miracles of the beast, of the spirits of devils working miracles, and of the false prophet that wrought miracles. Thus the New Testament teaches us to bind the evidence of Christian miracles to that which shows how utterly different they are from all the pretensions of deceivers, from all the delusions of fanatics. To dwell on extraordinary incidents, apart from other considerations, is to open a door to superstition, and even revolting credulity. In this way, a belief in witchcraft, sanctioning most unrighteous and cruel laws, maintained its ground in England to the end of the seventeenth century. From anything like the unreasonableness of staking religious faith upon physical events or historical circumstances, *simply because* they are unaccountable upon any ordinary hypothesis of human affairs, the Gospel is perfectly free. He who appeals to His own mighty works, appeals also to His own self-evidencing words, and to the moral disposition of His disciples. "To this end was I born, and for this cause came I into the world, that I should bear witness unto the truth. Every one that is of the truth heareth my voice." "My doctrine is not mine, but His that sent me. If any man will do His will, he shall know of the doctrine whether it be of God, or whether I speak of myself. He that speaketh of himself, seeketh his own glory; but he that seeketh his glory that sent him, the same is true, and no unrighteousness is in him."

The solitary position assigned to the evidence of miracles in the controversies of the last century was mischievous to the interests of religion. I believe with Coleridge, "how little of divine, how little fitting to our nature a miracle is, when insulated from spiritual truths, and disconnected from religion as its end:"—and I would ask with him, "What then can we think of a theological theory, which, adopting a scheme of prudential legality, common to it with 'the sty of Epicurus,' as far at least as the springs of moral action are concerned, makes its whole religion consist in the belief of miracles!" There is some room for this severe censure of theologians in the last century, who failed to insist "on the creating of a new heart, which collects the energies of a man's whole being in the focus of the conscience—the one essential miracle, the same, and of the same evidence to the ignorant and the learned, which no superior skill can counterfeit, human or demoniacal." I should assign a higher place to the physical miracle than Coleridge did,—but there is to my mind a true and deep sense in what he asks respecting the moral one :—" Is it not that implication of doctrine in the miracle, and of miracle in the doctrine, which is the bridge of communication between the senses and the soul ?"* Christianity as a whole, at the present time, establishes its claims by the new spiritual creation which it effects in its sincere disciples. And here, let me add: looking at the position of our inquiry at the present day, it appears of great importance, not to lay down as a principle, that miracles are indispensable in the authorization of a Divine message. To do so hampers our argument. To do so contradicts Scripture,—" John did no miracle." If one eminent servant of the Most High could make good his authority without effecting any physical marvel, so might another. Regarding Jesus simply as a Divine Teacher, there would, then, be no absolute necessity for His working wonders in the fields of material nature. His moral acts, His freedom from moral defects, and the whole moral tenor of His life, would evince the holiness of His character, and the oneness of His own spirit with that of the Father of spirits, the fountain of love and truth ; for what He said of men applied to Himself, "By their fruits ye shall know them." Yet, though I cannot see that miracles, as some think, were essential to the proof of

* Coleridge's "Friend," iii., 104-6.

what He said respecting Himself, they are, as indicated already, what might be expected in one who was all that Jesus of Nazareth claimed to be; they also corroborate claims to spiritual authority, resting on other grounds; and, still further, the manner in which some of them were performed, points to the higher nature which tabernacled in His humanity.

The place in the sphere of evidence occupied by the miracles of Jesus, is not exactly the same to us that it was to the multitudes who witnessed them. I fully agree in the remark, "We do not ask any one to begin with the miracles,—to regard power, and still more the record of power, centuries afterwards, as the one irresistible proof of the truth and Divine origin of a Revelation. This has been done—done perhaps too long—done certainly in this age without conviction."* A miracle never was *the one* irresistible proof. It never was more than one amongst others. But at first it had a power of awakening attention, which it does not possess now. *Seen*, it irresistibly produced excitement, which led to inquiry. *Recorded*, it fails of that effect. It is wise, at this time of day, to begin the exposition of Christian evidence by insisting on Christianity as a fact—as a moral spiritual power in the world; and then, examining its principles, and tracing its achievements to the beginning,

* Dr. Vaughan's "Christ the Light of the World," 172.

to bring out the evidential worth of Christ's miracles as a crown on the head of other proofs. At the same, time it should be observed, that their pertinency as proofs remains unaltered. They are not less true for being old. They are as good witnesses now as they were eighteen centuries ago. What was done by Julius Cæsar, what was done by Alexander the Great, as it appears on record, is still as valid an indication as ever, of the genius and prowess which the men possessed. So, what Jesus did, as we find it recorded in His fourfold memoirs, produces undiminished assurance of His superhuman character. If any one asks for miracles now, I reply, they are not wanted, they could not be used as credentials of one who left the world ages since. His own miracles, ascertained by history, will, to the end of time, in connection with His whole life, avail as guarantees for faith in His Divine might and goodness.

3. And, finally, the miracles promote the acceptance of Christian truths by the illustrations of them which they afford. Christ's miracles are of the same description as the principles and precepts in Christ's teaching. They are animated with benevolence, instinct with love. The Gospel perpetually offers to men a spiritual salvation; Miracles at the beginning brought them salvation of a lower kind, which nevertheless pointed to a higher. Of the author of Christianity it might be said literally, "He is the Saviour of the

body." His wondrous works of healing sparkled with a tenderness, compassion, and help, like those with which His main mission to mankind was filled. And, as they were eminently beneficial to human beings, and so were of the same class as the other bestowments the Christ of God came to confer, they exhibited types of the nobler blessings themselves. They are mirrors reflecting larger and better gifts. Signs they are as well as wonders; parables as well as proofs. In cures of the blind, there are parables of spiritual illumination; in the cleansing of lepers, parables of spiritual purification; and in exorcisms, parables of spiritual disenthralment.

The benevolent animus, and the didactic form of the miracles of Jesus seized the attention of early Christian writers, and were employed by them for the purpose of establishing and recommending the Christian religion. They used them much more under their illustrative than under their strictly evidential aspect. Arnobius (A.D. 306), in ten chapters of his seven books, "*Adversus Gentes*," lays special stress upon their kind and beneficent tendency.* Lactantius, his contemporary in his "Institutions," whilst regarding Christ's miracles as proofs of His higher nature, manifests particular delight in searching out their ethical significance. He goes through the mighty works of our

* Ad. Gen. l. i. c. 42, *et seq.*

Lord in order, and points out, how they demonstrated the renewal of the human soul, the opening of its eyes, the unstopping of its ears, the loosening of its tongue.* And Athanasius (A.D. 326) takes special pains to show that the miracles of Jesus were revelations—self-representations of His Person as Divine Creator, not mere credentials of His doctrine, but veritable victories over nature, so that no one can doubt who Christ is, when once he beholds His works :—and moreover, that by the manner of His working miracles, He at once proved his Divinity, and His humanity, His Godhead and His incarnation.† And Augustine insists much on their design as symbolical of redemption, as instructive acts, charged with prophetical import, and calculated to inspire delight more than wonder.‡

These remarks and quotations bear chiefly on the relation of miracles to the spiritual blessings of the Gospel at the beginning. But miracles also sustain a very interesting relation to the like blessings as bestowed in after, and in present times. When the spring is over, and its produce of blossoms has passed away, it is found, that though the ground is covered with leaves of white and pink, the

* Inst. L. iv. c. 25.

† Dorner, in his *Person of Christ* (Clark's Trans.), ii. 254, dwells upon this subject as unfolded by Athanasius. See also Athanasius' third discourse against the Arians, § 32.

‡ In Johan. Evan. Tract, 16, 24, 49.

blossoms have set into precious fruit. They have bequeathed more than blossoms. Each folded up a promise of what is richer than itself. The peach flower, the peach —the pear flower, the pear. We read in the Apocalypse, of the Tree of Life. Is not the Gospel the Tree of Life? Is not Christ the Tree of Life? It is not fanciful to speak of the miracles as early blossoms. Long since they burst out profusely. Long since they fell. To some eyes, they may seem to lie in the paths of history, as withered leaves. But if the spring-time is past, the autumn-time has long since come. Christianity can tell of spiritual blessings which it has conferred on the children of men down to this day, and is conferring still. A tranquil conscience, a pure heart, a holy life, a hope that maketh not ashamed,—these are the clustering felicities, the manifold beatitudes, of the Gospel of Love. Thank God! abundant has been the ingathering. Thank God! abundant is the harvest, still waiting to be gathered. In nature the bloom is more plentiful than the fruit, but here the fruit is more plentiful than the bloom.

THE GRADUAL DEVELOPMENT OF REVELATION.

BY THE RIGHT REVEREND

THE LORD BISHOP OF CARLISLE.

THE GRADUAL DEVELOPMENT OF REVELATION.

When I undertook, at the request of the Christian Evidence Society, to deliver a lecture having for its title *The Gradual Development of Revelation*, I confess that I did not perceive that the title was open to criticism. I thought that I understood the terms employed, and I still trust that this is so; but a little consideration showed me that the language was not used very strictly, and that there was in it a confusion of metaphors, which might possibly be connected with a confusion of thought.

This being so, I propose to introduce what I have to say by a short examination of the words which express the subject of my lecture: and I do so, as I need hardly say, not for the purpose of finding fault, but because it seems to me that I shall in this manner most easily explain the nature of the subject which I conceive to be committed to me, and indicate the manner in which I purpose to treat it.

Now the word *development*, which like many other long words has become very common, is also, like many other words, not unfrequently used somewhat loosely. The root of it, the word *velop*, is unknown in any other form than the two words *envelope* and *develope*.* In mathematics, the word *develope* is used, as all words are, with the utmost precision. We speak of *developing a function*, that is, putting it into a new and unfolded form, which, however, shall be essentially equivalent to the original. So also we speak of *developable surfaces*, that is, surfaces such as cones and cylinders, which can be unfolded and laid flat upon a plane without tearing. It will be seen that in these applications of the word the essential thought is that of a change, by a process of unfolding, in the condition of something which you already possess; and this I take to be the true definition of development.

From this, however, we easily pass to a cognate meaning of the term. Thus we speak of the development of an idea, that is, the unfolding and applying of the results of an original thought, a discovery or principle, which were truly contained in it from the first, but were not from the first perceived to be so contained. For example, we say that railways are only a development of the original idea of

* See Brachet's "Dictionnaire Etymologique," sub voc: *Developper*.

turning to account the expansive force of steam; or that Newton's "Principia" and Laplace's "Mecanique Celeste," and, in fact, the whole of modern physical astronomy, are developments of the idea, or fact, call it which you will, of the universal gravitation of matter; or that the British constitution of this century is a development of *Magna Charta;* and so forth. What we mean by this language is that the essential principles of the development were implicitly contained in the original idea, and that one has been derived from the other somewhat in the same way as that in which the bird comes from the egg and the plant from the seed.

Dr. Newman, in his Essay "On the Development of Christian Doctrine," takes a somewhat different view. He speaks of the development of an idea as follows: "When some great enunciation, whether true or false, about human nature, or present good, or government, or duty, or religion, is carried forward into the public throng and draws attention, then it is not only passively admitted in this or that form into the minds of men, but it becomes a living principle within them, leading them to an ever-new contemplation of itself, an acting upon it, and a propagation of it. Such is the doctrine of the natural bondage of the will, or of individual responsibility, or of the immortality of the soul, or of the rights of man, or of the divine right of kings, or of the hypocrisy and tyranny of priestcraft, or of the lawfulness of self-indulgence. . . . . Let one such idea get possession of the popular mind, or the mind of any set of persons, and it is not difficult to understand the effects which will ensue."* Taking this view, there is manifestly a difficulty in determining whether an idea has been rightly or wrongly developed, whether the growth be wholly from the root or partly parasitical; and the prime intention of Dr. Newman's book is to supply tests of genuine development, and to apply them in one particular case; but I wish it to be perceived that whether we take this wider view, or the stricter one which I endeavoured to present to you just now, it is essentially necessary to regard development as the exhibition in a new unfolded form of that which already existed in another.

When therefore we speak of development with reference to God, we must regard Him as the developer, and His eternal purposes as the thing developed: the point which I have to bring before you with reference to its bearing upon the faith of Christians, and the unbelief of those who scruple to be regarded as disciples of Christ, is the gradual character of the process by which God has developed His purposes.

And this being the meaning of development, I think it is

* "Essay on Development," page 35.

manifest that it is a confusion of figures to speak of the *development* of a *revelation.* To *reveal* is to *draw back a veil,* and so to uncover something which was concealed before. Hence we can properly speak of God as *revealing* to us His person, His character, His will. His person is eternal and unchangeable; so is His character; so is His will; but He uncovers and shows these to us; it may be by Holy Scripture, it may be by the living voice, or the life, or the person of the Lord Jesus Christ; but however it be, the conception appropriate to the word revelation is that of something which exists independently of our minds, and which is uncovered, so that our minds can perceive it. Revelation, therefore, cannot be developed; if we use the word as meaning the process of revealing, then this is a different process from that of developing; and if we use the word as meaning objectively the knowledge which has been revealed, the knowledge which we obtain of God by revelation, then this knowledge comes to us in an already developed form: it is not an idea to be developed, but a truth to be received.

On the whole, I regard as the most important word in the title of my lecture, the word *gradual:* whether we speak of the development of His eternal purposes and intentions, or the revelation of His person and character, the process appears to have been a gradual one, and in a certain sense a slow one: and this gradualness of operation may be variously estimated according to the turn of mind and habits of thought of him who considers it: some will be content simply to bow their heads and worship as being in the presence of Him whose ways are past finding out: some will say that that which Christians believe to be the development of His purposes and the revelation of His person is inconsistent with their conceptions of God, and so will reject it: others will hesitate to reject on *à priori* grounds that which, to say the least, admits of a strong argument in its favour, but will confess that they feel the difficulties which have been urged against the creed of Christendom; and with regard to that particular phase of difficulty with which I am professing to deal in this lecture, they will say, and perhaps say with sadness, that the revelation which the volume of Holy Scripture purports to contain, does not commend itself to their minds, as corresponding to their highest thoughts of that which God might be expected to do in making Himself known to man. Now it is to minds in this condition that considerations concerning the doings of God may be hopefully offered. I do not see how it is possible to treat such a subject as mine, if I consider myself as speaking to persons who deny the impossibility of revelation as distinct from human knowledge: if a revelation be impossible, *per se*, it is useless to discuss the qualities of that particular form of revelation which Christians profess to have received; but if a man is willing to receive a revelation, and has something of the spirit indicated by the words, "Oh, that I knew where I might find Him," then it does seem to be possible to offer some suggestions which shall tend to show that the manner of revelation which Holy Scripture exhibits is in harmony with all that we know of our Creator from other sources, and that the gradual character of the Divine operations, as exhibited in that history which culminates in the Lord Jesus Christ, is wonderfully analogous to the character of every other operation which we can rightly call divine.

Let us then observe what the revelation of God purports to be; and for the special end which I have in view, I think we may suitably divide it into the following principal steps :—

1. That made to Adam and Eve;
2. That made to Abraham;
3. That made to Moses;
4. That made in and by Jesus Christ our Lord.

Let us look at each of these for a moment.

The revelation to Adam and Eve is represented as being of the simplest kind possible. In fact it is difficult to conceive how anything beyond a very simple and partial revelation could be possible in the very infancy of humanity. It amounts to little more than the revelation of God as a personal governor, whose will must be obeyed: a command is given; that command is broken, and a punishment is inflicted; and then mankind is represented as cast out of Eden into the wild, uncultivated world. It is necessary to realize the extreme simplicity of this history, and the imperfect character of the revelation: the more so, because there is some temptation to imagine Adam and Eve as being in the possession of more knowledge than Scripture attributes to them; Scripture in reality attributes no knowledge to them, but rather represents the tree of knowledge as having been the cause of their fall. Philosophically speaking, we may describe the condition of things which existed in Eden as being the dawn of man's religious consciousness; he has no responsibility, and no sin; but a law is imposed upon him, and thus comes responsibility, and thus by the breach of law comes sin: man "was alive without the law once, but when the commandment came sin revived," and man "died."

The sacred history represents the world as engaged, so to speak, in working out the results of this primitive revelation till the time of Abraham. God is represented as punishing the evil and rewarding the good, the punishment of the evil being the more conspicuous conduct of the two; thus Cain is punished, the people in the days of Noah are punished, the builders of the tower of Babel are punished: but I do not think it can be said that the being and character of God are any further revealed till the time of Abraham. Then we have the new fact of God calling out a family; granting to that family special promises and special privileges, and making it (as it were) the depository of the fortunes of the world. Probably this is a step which we should not have expected; possibly it may even be argued that it is no real step in advance; but, be this as it may, it is represented in Scripture as the next step in the process of revelation; whether it strike us as strange or not, we are compelled, on the hypothesis that Scripture contains the history of revelation, to regard Abraham and his family as a point, a station, in the process.

And so we come to Moses. I am disposed, however, to regard the Mosaic revelation as differing in degree rather than in kind from that made to Abraham. A family was called in Abraham, a nation in Moses; but in the one case as in the other, the fortunes of the whole world were bound up with the history and conduct of a chosen few; the family of Abraham was a peculiar and chosen family, the Israelites whom Moses made into a nation were a peculiar and chosen people: the principle was the same, namely that of selection, and whatever difficulty belongs to one case, belongs equally to the other.

It would be a long task, and for my purpose an unnecessary one, to trace the gradual progress of the revelation made "in sundry times and in divers manners" to the Israelitish church and people; beginning with the grand announcement of the Name of God from the Burning Bush, and continued by the declaration of the law in the wilderness, rendered visible, so to speak, by the sacrificial ritual, and expounded by priests and prophets, it gradually became clearer and clearer, until "the fulness of time" came, and "God sent forth His Son made of a woman." I need not say that to Christians this is emphatically *the* revelation of God—"he who has seen the Son has seen the Father." All previous revelations are only preparatory for this; and when we have received this, all others seem to be lost, just as the moon and stars which shine so brightly at night are absolutely extinguished as soon as the sun is risen. Assuming all this, however, it may be worth while to remark, first, that Jesus Christ expressly connected Himself with all that had gone before, saying that He "came not to destroy, but to fulfil;" and secondly, that He, like Moses and Abraham before Him, founded an *ἐκκλησία*, or church, as a depository of the fortunes of mankind, only with this difference or extension of principle, that whereas the church of Abraham was a family, and the church of Moses was a nation, the church of Christ was catholic, knowing no distinction of family or nation, but embracing all who were willing to take Him as their Captain, and His Cross as their banner.

This sketch, slight as it is, of the progress of revelation, as presented to us in Holy Scripture, will be abundantly sufficient for my present purpose. In considering its claims to be received by mankind, I think it should be at once candidly owned, as seems indeed to be conceded in Holy Scripture, that the method of revelation is probably different from anything which we should have expected on general grounds of reason. Perhaps it is difficult, it may be impossible, to say very precisely what we should have expected; but certainly I think we should *not* have expected to have found the principal revelations of God made, as they are alleged to have been made, to a selected family, a selected nation, a selected corporate body. It is only candid to acknowledge that, from a philosophical point of view, we may here see a great difficulty; and the difficulty becomes more salient when we look out of the narrow groove of sacred history into the wide history of the world at large. There we find a remarkable growth of knowledge, and an exhibition of the highest powers and gifts of humanity, quite separated from that region which is asserted to have been specially illuminated with light from heaven. The progress of our knowledge of the literature of ancient nations, and a greater familiarity with the thoughts and feelings of people outside the Christian pale, have tended to throw this difficulty into stronger relief: our old acquaintance with Greece and Rome, our more recent acquaintance with such countries as India and China, have made us aware that, somehow or other, great light did shine upon these countries in olden days, and it is harsh to say that the light did not come from heaven. Let, therefore, the difficulty be frankly acknowledged; while at the same time it is also acknowledged that in a matter so much beyond the scope of our faculties as that of saying in what manner God can best reveal Himself to mankind, all difficulties depending upon the strangeness or unexpectedness of a method alleged to have been adopted, must in the nature of things be of less than first-rate magnitude, and must give way to sufficient evidence.

Acknowledging, however, as frankly as can be desired, the difficulty here stated, I observe that there is anyhow a remarkable consistency in the scheme of revelation which Scripture contains. One step leads naturally to another; and looking at the whole course of Scripture history, from the first verse of the Book of Genesis to the last verse of the Book of Revelation, it is wonderful (perhaps upon any infidel hypothesis, more than wonderful) how the various parts hang together, and how the beginning, the middle, and the end seem to dovetail themselves together into one connected and consistent whole. I do not know that I have ever been more struck with this, than when reading the recent work on "The History and Literature of the Israelites," by C. and A. de Rothschild. In this work we have the advantage of seeing the Old Testament exhibited in a reverent and loving spirit without the New, and as it might have appeared if Jesus Christ had not been born. Any one reading the book would be impelled to say that the influence of the literature of the Israelites must be for the improvement and enlightenment of mankind; but the questions press upon the mind of the reader—at least they did upon mine—"What does all this lead to? What has become of these Israelites? and what is the meaning of the language of their prophets?" In fact, the book seems to put the reader very much in the position of the Ethiopian nobleman in the Book of the Acts of the Apostles, who was prepared by reading some of the "literature of the Israelites" to receive from Philip the evangelist the preaching of the name of Jesus. The New Testament seems exactly to *fit* upon the Old; and that gradual progress of revelation which we notice in the Old Testament, seems to lead up to, and find its completion and explanation in, the history which is contained in the New.

On the whole, looking at the scheme of revelation as it appears in Scripture, and as it has been illustrated by history, both profane and sacred, I believe that I discern these features. I see the knowledge of God emerging from very obscure beginnings, and imparted in very unexpected ways; I see, however, that this knowledge does somehow or another not merely remain with mankind, but increase and become clearer and more influential; I see a particular family and nation selected for the reception and spread of this knowledge, and the family and nation so selected, after going through much education and many vicissitudes, producing at length One in whom the whole history appears to culminate, and then disappearing from all position of influence upon the fortunes of the world except through this one pre-eminent member. Still further, I perceive, and it is absolutely impossible for the most sceptical to deny, that the name of this remarkable member of the selected family and nation has been the most potent that has ever been named, and that His influence in the world has been and is far greater, more extended, and more intense in its action, than any other influence which has ever been brought to bear upon the human heart and mind. Even in the work to which I referred just now, in which the Old Testament alone comes under consideration, the dates of the history are given by reference to the birth of Jesus Christ; and whatever view men may be disposed to take of the more mysterious and transcendental allegations concerning the life of Jesus of Nazareth, it is impossible to deny that the civilization and improvement of the world, and the purification of human society and the like, are more connected with His Name than with that of any other philosopher or teacher or leader of mankind. When I say that it is impossible to deny this, I am of course aware that it has been denied, and that there are and have been persons who have asserted that Christianity has not only not been that which Christians believe it to have been, but has been positively detrimental to human progress; but what I mean is, that to make the denial to which I refer, is so contrary to the general verdict of mankind that it is hard for any one to make it, and impossible for any one who is at all likely to be influenced by anything that I can say. For those who are at all likely to be influenced are persons who are *sceptical*, not those who are *antagonistic*; a man may doubt—who has not doubted?—and a man may be tortured by his doubts, and it may be possible to relieve him; but I see no probability of helping that man who has come to the conclusion that the influence of Jesus Christ has been a mischievous and obstructive influence in the history of human progress; with such a man, I, at least, as a Christian apologist, do not feel that I have any common ground.

Taking then the view of revelation to which I have referred as being that contained in Holy Scripture, and acknowledging that such a view presents difficulties to thoughtful and inquiring minds, I wish to examine and see whether we cannot find some help towards a right appreciation of God's method of revelation by examining the course of nature, or that which is supposed to be its course.

And when we look to nature with this purpose, it is impossible not to be struck by this general fact, namely, that gradualness of development appears to be a universal law. The manner in which the original design of the Creator (for I assume that there was an original design) has been carried out, so far from being sudden, has been very slow;* and more than this, the method of operation has been frequently such as we should scarcely have expected, and greatly opposed to those notions of creative majesty which most of us are very

* I will here quote the words of a great man, who has for many years been one of the chief scientific ornaments of this country, and whose departure from this life, at the ripe age of seventy-nine years, I see, with much sorrow, recorded in the *Times* of this day.

Speaking of the manner in which the universe has come into its present condition, and is preserved in that condition, and of the possibility of collision amongst the constituent bodies, Sir John Herschel says: "Ages, which to us may well appear indefinite, may easily be conceived to pass without a single instance of collision, in the nature of a catastrophe. Such may have gradually become rarer as the system has emerged from what must be considered as its chaotic state, till at length, in the fulness of time, and under the pre-arranging guidance of that DESIGN which pervades universal nature, each individual may have taken up such a course as to annul the possibility of further destructive interference."—*Outlines of Astronomy*, p. 600.

I quote these words for the sake of the phrase which they contain, and the importance of which it is impossible to exaggerate, "The pre-arranging guidance of that DESIGN which pervades universal nature."

much disposed to preconceive. In order to put this clearly before you, let me call your attention to the very picturesque and poetical view of creation, contained in Chateaubriand's "Genie du Christianisme." That work appeared after the explosion of the volcano of the first great French revolution, and was intended to reconcile the minds of men, weary with the infidelity and atheism which had so long been rampant, to the views of God contained in Holy Scripture, and maintained by Christians. Writing with this purpose, M. Chateaubriand tells us that we may conceive of the Creator as having called the world into existence in a condition as complete, and having as many marks of antiquity, as we now see about us: when this earth was created there would be already ancient forests, and abundance of animals, some in their maturity, others dancing about in the friskiness of youth; the trees would be furnished with birds' nests, and the crows and pigeons would be hatching their eggs, or tending their young; the butterflies and moths would be sporting on the plants; the bees would be making honey from the new-formed flowers; the sheep would be followed by their lambs; and the nightingales would be astonishing themselves with their first, yet perfect songs, in all the groves. Finally, Adam would be a man of thirty, and Eve a girl of sixteen. "Without this original antiquity," says our author, "there would have been neither pomp nor majesty in the work of the Eternal; and, which could not well be, nature in her innocence would have been less fair than she is now in her corruption. An insipid infancy of plants, animals, elements, would have crowned a world devoid of poetry."* No doubt this description is anything but devoid of poetry; it is perhaps the only way in which a poet would be disposed to conceive of creation; it is difficult to imagine the music of Haydn set to any other description of the creative work; but undoubtedly it is not scientific, and, what is more, it is not Scriptural. Chateaubriand no more got his picture of creation from the Book of Genesis than Ernest Renan got his picture of Jesus Christ from the four Gospels; and that there may be no mistake about this latter point, let me ask you to observe that the most marked and salient feature of the Bible picture of creation is the gradualness of the creative work. I do not say that the picture is not poetical; I believe it to be quite as poetical as that which Chateaubriand would substitute for it, and I quite admit that it ought to be regarded from a poetical rather than a scientific point of view; still gradualness of development is the most marked and salient of its features: first, a chaos of matter without life; then vegetable life; then the lower forms of animal life; then mammals; and lastly, man. No one can deny that these and other

* "Le Genie du Christianisme," Bk. iv., chap. v.

steps, spread over the time which is indicated by the mysterious creative days, do together make up the Bible history of physical creation; and no one can fail to perceive that the order of proceeding is as different as possible from that described by the French apologist. According to this latter view, creation starts forth, Minerva-like, from the mind of God; according to Scripture, the work is expressly gradual and presumably slow. We are so accustomed to the first chapter of Genesis, that I think we sometimes scarcely perceive its peculiarities; but suppose that the reverse order of arrangement had been adopted, and that man in deference to his dignity had been represented as coming in first, and that other creatures had been represented as being made afterwards for his use and pleasure, would not this have made a radical change, and introduced an enormous scientific difficulty? I remember once being told by a person, who held strong views with regard to the dangerous character of the conclusions of geology, that it seemed to him absolutely incredible that a period should have existed when the earth was inhabited by nothing but fishes, reptiles, and the like; yet this is precisely what Scripture affirms to have been the fact; and if the creative work had been concluded with the fifth day, there would have been no mammals upon the earth, and no man.

Gradualness in creative work, therefore, is so far from

being contrary to the indications of God's method given in Scripture, that it is one of the few things which stand out from the scriptural account with undeniable prominence. That this same feature is not less prominent in the results of all the physical sciences, it would take more time and more ability to demonstrate than are at my command; nevertheless it is necessary that I should ask you kindly to accompany me, while I endeavour to show you that the conclusions of science, and even the guesses of scientific men, point to this conclusion, and tend to make untenable any objections to the revelation of God contained in Scripture, on the ground of the gradual manner in which that revelation is alleged to have been made.

The general evidence of geology is familiar probably to most of us, and it is only the general evidence with which I can desire to deal on such an occasion as this; but pray observe that while the particular conclusions of geology, like those of other physical sciences, are liable to continued modification and amendment, the general drift of the conclusions is sufficiently clear and certain. No one can doubt, for instance, the great antiquity of our globe, and the fact that it has gone through successive changes with regard to the character of its surface, the nature of its inhabitants, and the like. Undoubtedly there was a time when civilized men did not dwell upon it; undoubtedly there was a still more distant period when men did not dwell upon it in any form, civilized or uncivilized; perhaps there was a period even more distant, when life was not to be found upon the earth's surface at all. And physical astronomy will take us even beyond geology, and will make it probable that the earth was originally in a fluid condition, in which from the excessive temperature no form of life could have existed. Few problems are more curious than that which deduces the present figure of our globe from the hypothesis of original fluidity. Take a mass of fluid, and set it revolving slowly about an axis, as our earth revolves, and it can be shown that it will assume such a form as that which our earth has. I do not lay stress upon the remarkable numerical coincidence of the ellipticity of the earth, as derived by Laplace from theory, with that which is discovered by observation, because this involves certain arbitrary hypotheses; but taking those results which involve nothing arbitrary at all, it is almost impossible not to believe that the earth was at one time a hot fluid mass, and that it has gradually cooled down and hardened into its present permanent condition.

Look upon the earth then as being once in this hot fluid condition. It turns slowly round upon its axis and cools. I cannot trace the whole of the process, but before it arrived at its present condition there must have been crackings and burstings and eruptions; and so continents and islands and mountains would be formed; but upon the whole, even in the wildest times, the process would be very gentle, for the highest mountains on the earth's surface are but as the down upon the surface of a peach. Then upon this globe appear creatures suited to its condition; and the eye which could have watched the world in its progress would have seen animals of successively higher types occupying the earth's surface, till at length that surface was spotted with cities built by the hand of man, and the ocean studded with his ships. It is impossible to guess the time which must have elapsed between the epoch when the earth was a hot revolving mass of fluid, and the epoch in which we live; neither is it very possible to say, though it is possible to guess, what would have been the successive scenes presented by the earth to the eye which should have witnessed the whole of the changes; but whatever may have been the nature of the changes, this conclusion is inevitable, namely, that there has been a progression of some kind from the fluidity of the primæval dead revolving mass to the inhabited world of this nineteenth century; it matters not for my argument whether the progression, so far as animal life is concerned, has been due to natural selection, or to such a process as that advocated by the author of

"Vestiges of Creation," or to successive and distinct creative acts; the fact holds good, upon any hypothesis, that the Almighty Creator has produced that universe which we see, not by one act, but by a gradual and apparently very slow creative process, whether continuous or discontinuous it matters not for my purpose to inquire.

Now this course of nature is strikingly analogous to that gradual mode of proceeding which is alleged to belong to revelation; and any difficulty which belongs to one appears to attach equally to the other. Nay, if we are to give any weight to the most recent physical speculations, it may be fairly argued that the difficulties connected with revelation are but as trifles compared with those which nature presents. I refer to those views of which the latest exposition is to be found in Mr. Darwin's "Descent of Man." Let me touch upon those views for a moment.

It seems that "the early progenitors of man were once covered with hair, both sexes having beards; their ears were pointed and capable of movement; and their bodies were provided with a tail, having the proper muscles. . . . The males were provided with great canine teeth, which served them as formidable weapons. . . . At a still earlier period, the progenitors of man must have been aquatic in their habits." And lastly, "the most ancient progenitors in the kingdom of the Vertebrata, at which we are able to obtain an obscure glance, apparently consisted of a group of marine animals resembling the larvæ of existing ascidians." This is certainly a somewhat alarming conclusion; looking however to the *ascent* (for so I think it ought to be called) rather than the *descent*, it would seem to be the view of some of our advanced natural investigators, that the marine animals in question produced certain lowly organized fishes; these produced ganoids and the like; these produced amphibians;—here there seems to be a difficulty—"No one," writes Mr. Darwin, "can at present say by what line of descent the three higher and related classes, namely, mammals, birds, and reptiles, were derived from either of the two lower vertebrate classes, namely, amphibians and fishes." However, once get to the mammals, and all difficulty ceases: the Monotremata produced the Marsupials; these the placental Mammals: thus we come to the Lemuridæ, and from them the interval is not great to the Simiadæ; the Simiadæ branched off into two great stems,—the New World and Old World Monkeys; and "from the latter at a remote period, *Man*, the wonder and glory of the universe, proceeded."*

Of this pedigree, which, "if not of noble quality," is "of prodigious length," Mr. Darwin tells us "we need not feel ashamed." Perhaps not; though certainly the nerves of any one unaccustomed to anthropological investigations may

* "Descent of Man," p. 208.

be excused for trembling slightly as he hears it recited; but the point which I wish to press is this, that supposing (for argument's sake) this view of man's origin, or anything like it, to be true, it is impossible to imagine a more thorough case of gradual development; there is nothing in the religious history of mankind as expounded in Holy Scripture so amazingly marvellous as that which is contained in this physical history; and certainly those who are prepared to receive the Darwinian view of the development of man's body, ought not to find anything to offend them on the ground of improbability in the Scriptural account of the revelation made by God to the human soul.

I do not know to what extent Mr. Darwin's views are likely to be permanent; but supposing that they, or any view of the same class, should eventually overcome all existing difficulties, and be generally regarded as representing the process by which it has pleased God to bring about man's physical and mental supremacy, then it can hardly seem strange that the same God should have adopted a course of progress and development in the spiritual and religious world. I say, emphatically, "if it has pleased God" to act thus; because if I accept the hypothesis of the nebular origin of planetary systems, or the supposition of the earth being a fluid globe gradually cooled, or even the assertion that our most ancient progenitors were marine animals, I must do so with the underlying assumption that it has pleased God so to work. I do not find fault with scientific men for not putting their theories in this form; but looking at the question from a religious, or even from a philosophical, point of view, I cannot consent to lose sight of God, as the intelligent maker of the whole. If this earth was originally a fluid mass, then I believe that that was the best, or, for anything I know to the contrary, the only way of making a world; if the marine animals, which Mr. Darwin sees through his scientific telescope, did become fish, and those fish eventually became men, then I believe that that was the best, or, for anything I know to the contrary, the only way of making men; and this being so, why may I not deal in the same manner with the alleged course of man's spiritual history? I have in my hands something which purports to be a revelation to my intellect, and to my soul, of the God who made me: that revelation is contained in a history which tells me that God spake at sundry times and in divers manners to the people of olden time, and that finally He spake by One who is called His Son. Now I do not say that this revelation is or is not a real one; but I do say that there is nothing to render us suspicious of its reality in the fact that it has been communicated gradually, that it has grown as the human race has grown, and that some of the steps in the process of revelation appear strange, or even, at first sight, unworthy of the grand scheme of which they form a part. No one has a right to find fault on this ground who has read the lessons of natural science, and observed how it points to gradual progression as a characteristic of the doings of God. Least of all can they find fault on this ground, who receive in whole, or even in part, the recent theories concerning the origin of man. I will not undertake to answer for those students who have gone deeply into these physical questions; but I do assert, without fear of contradiction, that to men of ordinary education, and ordinary habits of thought, the difficulties of accepting Scripture as the revelation of God to the human soul, however much those difficulties may be expounded or even exaggerated, are absolutely nothing as compared with the difficulty of accepting recent views of man's prodigious pedigree.

The fact is, that it is not so much the process by which a result has been brought about, as the result itself, which is the all-important thing. Whatever may have been the history of our earth in the dark dim distance of incalculable ages, we know that its present condition is very beautiful, and that it answers admirably well the purpose for which it seems to have been originally designed, namely, that of serving for the residence of intelligent man; and whatever may have been the process by which that creative work was consummated, which is described in Scripture as the making of man out of the dust, and breathing into his nostrils the breath of life, we know that man is high above all the rest of creation, and worthy of being spoken of as being made in the image of God. And so in the case of man's spiritual history, we need not be over-careful to criticize the several steps when we are able to see the result; the question is, not so much whether the steps of God which we trace in Old Testament history be such steps as we should imagine that the Most High would have left, as whether the mystery of the Incarnation, and the truth that God has spoken to us by His own Son, be not worthy of all acceptation. If Christ be worthy of our adoration and love, then, though the way may have been long, and strange, and dark, and sometimes even weary, yet we may be sure that it is the right way, because it has led us to Him.

For there is this further analogy between nature and revelation, namely, that in each the progress is not indefinite, but tends to a limit. Whatever theory be adopted with regard to the history of the earth, we seem to see in its present settled condition the limit towards which everything has been moving in past geological ages; and even if man has been a progressive animal, and has only gradually attained his present physical perfection, I presume it is not anticipated that the process of natural selection, or any other process, will carry him beyond the point which he has now reached. Or, if we take the divine picture of creation, we see the creative work tending from the limit of chaos to the limit of man; then physics cease and religion begins, and we hear utterances of the voice of God beginning with whispers, and becoming more and more distinct, until we are permitted to listen to divine oracles uttered by human lips. Beyond this the dreams of philosophy, and the aspirations of the human heart, and the longings of the weary and heavy-laden cannot carry our thoughts or raise our desires.

Those who are acquainted with Bishop Butler's great work will perceive that I have now been endeavouring—how imperfectly no one knows better than myself—to apply to the question of "the gradual development of revelation," those principles of reasoning which Bishop Butler has taught us to use. I was very sorry to see it stated in the evidence taken before the select committee of the House of Lords on University Tests, that Bishop Butler's *Analogy* was "out of fashion" in Oxford.* I trust that the witness only intended to assert

* Report of Evidence, 1870:—

Q. 376. I thought you said Bishop Butler had been excluded?—It is not excluded, but being an optional subject it is one that has been discouraged.

Q. 377. Why?—He is gone out of fashion; I do not know why.

Q. 378. Who makes the fashion?—I suppose the particular set of examiners at one time.

Q. 379. What are the works of Bishop Butler which have so gone out of fashion?—The Analogy and the Sermons were the books which we used to take up.

that the *Analogy* was not now so commonly chosen for examinations as formerly, for it will be an evil day for us all when the method of reasoning which Bishop Butler taught us shall be "out of fashion" with thinking people. In truth, the advantage of the method is that, properly speaking, it never can be out of fashion; it is like the method of Euclid, or that of the Differential Calculus; it is an *organum*, an instrument, a machine, which may be applied in all the varying circumstances of theological controversy, and to almost all religious difficulties. For the principle of the method is this. You find certain difficulties in that which professes to be a revelation of God; you think to get rid of these difficulties by denying the revelation; will you succeed in doing so? Not if you find precisely analogous difficulties in the course of nature; unless you go further, and deny not only that there is a God of revelation, but a God of nature too. Nay, the argument carries you beyond this point, and suggests to you that if there be difficulties in God's natural world, and if He be pleased to reveal the spiritual world to us, then we ought to expect to find the same general method of proceeding in matters spiritual which we have been able to observe in the natural world. I quite admit that this reasoning has no force for the man who says "There is no God;" he must be dealt with in another way; but it has force and it has comfort for the doubting inquiring soul, by assuring it that it can find a logical resting-place, and that the refuge from the misery of blank and hopeless atheism is to be found in simple faith in the Lord Jesus Christ.*

With the atheist, I honestly confess, that I have little or no sympathy; certainly I should not think it worth while to compose a lecture intended for his special behoof. I should feel disposed rather to send him for his answer to the fourteenth and fifty-third Psalms. The difficulty of supposing the framework of the universe to have had no architect, appears to me to be so great, so absolutely immeasurable, that the man who can fancy that he has got over it must, as I believe, either not have understood the difficulty, or else have deceived himself as to his power of

* The subject of this Lecture is touched upon, but not expanded, in the following pregnant passage of Butler's *Analogy:* "The thing objected against this scheme of the Gospel is, that it seems to suppose God was reduced to the necessity of a long series of intricate means in order to accomplish His ends, the recovery and salvation of the world: in like sort as men, for want of understanding or power, not being able to come to their ends readily, are forced to go roundabout ways, and make use of many perplexed contrivances to arrive at them. Now, everything which we see shows the folly of this, considered as an objection against the truth of Christianity. For, according to our manner of conception, God makes use of a variety of means, what we often think tedious ones, in the natural course of providence, for the accomplishment of all His ends. Indeed, it is certain there is somewhat in this matter quite beyond our comprehension: but the mystery is as great in nature as in Christianity."—*Analogy*, Part II., chap. iv.

solving it; anyhow, I feel that he has cut away all ground of argument, as between him and me. Not so the man whose mind is sceptically inclined. Be it ever remembered that the word *sceptic* is derived from a word which means to *look* or to *see*—it is the same word which forms the root of the word *bishop* or *overseer;* and accordingly there is nothing radically reproachful in the name of *sceptic.* It implies that a man is determined to look into matters for himself, not to trust every assertion, not to repeat a parrot creed; and so far as this determination is concerned, it is high and noble, and is in fact the very root and spring of all human knowledge; but who can wonder if looking should lead to doubting, and that so the name of sceptic should popularly imply, not the man who looks and believes, but the man who looks and doubts? And I am not ashamed to confess that I have much sympathy with this sceptical frame of mind. Not only is it closely connected with a noble instinct of inquiry and search for truth which God has implanted in the human mind, but also, as I believe, it is well-nigh impossible that an inquiring mind should deal seriously with religious subjects and remain entirely free from doubt. In my opinion, the amount of scepticism which has, during some period of his life, occupied the mind of each thoughtful earnest man, will be merely a question of degree; while, at the same time, I most sincerely believe that scepticism ought not to be, and need not be the lasting condition of the human soul, and that all doubts may be made to vanish in the light which God has given to "lighten every man who is born into the world."

I know not what may be the condition of mind of those to whom I have been speaking to-day. I presume the hope of the Christian Evidence Society is that some persons who feel practically the pressure of doubt and unbelief, will come and see whether any of their difficulties can be resolved by this course of Lectures. If there be such in this company, I beg them, in concluding this Lecture, to believe that they have been listening to one who does not wish to treat their speculative difficulties as trifles, but who would consider it as an unspeakable privilege to be able to help a doubting brother to get rid of his doubts, and to exchange them for the steady assurance of faith in the Lord Jesus Christ.

THE ALLEGED HISTORICAL DIFFICULTIES

OF THE

OLD AND NEW TESTAMENTS,

AND THE

LIGHT THROWN ON THEM BY MODERN DISCOVERIES.

BY THE

REV. GEORGE RAWLINSON, M.A.,

CAMDEN PROFESSOR OF ANCIENT HISTORY, OXFORD.

THE

ALLEGED HISTORICAL DIFFICULTIES

OF THE

OLD AND NEW TESTAMENTS.

IN addressing you on the historical difficulties of the Old and New Testaments—a large subject, which it will be hard to treat adequately within the time allowed to me—I must in the first place premise, that with difficulties which lie on the verge or outskirts of the historic field, on the debatable ground between Science and History, I do not on the present occasion profess to deal. Questions as to the origin of man, whether by development or by direct creation, whether from one pair or from more; questions as to his primæval condition, his possession from the first of the faculty of speech, his original savagery or civilisation, and the like, lie (I think) beyond the domain of history proper, belonging to what has been properly termed the "*pre-historic* period" of our race, and so not coming within the terms of the subject on which I have undertaken to speak to-day. History deals with man from the time to which written records reach back. Historical difficulties arise from divergence, real or apparent, between the different accounts contained in those records. Now the profane records, to which any modern critical school would attribute an historical value, do not reach back within many ages of the origin of man, and thus no "historical difficulty" can arise with respect to these primitive times. It is only when we descend to an age of records, when the apparently authentic accounts of ancient countries preserved to our day can be compared with the Scriptural narrative that difficulty arises and that either agreement or disagreement can be shown.

The first difficulty, really historical, which meets us when we open the volume of Scripture, is the shortness of the time into which all history is (or at any rate appears to be) compressed, by the chronological statements, especially those of Genesis. The exodus of the Jews is fixed by many considerations to about the fifteenth or sixteenth century before our era. The period between the Flood and the Exodus, according to the numbers of our English version, but a very little exceeds a thousand years. Consequently, it has been usual to regard Scripture as authoritatively laying it down that all mankind sprang from a single pair within twenty-five or twenty-six centuries of the Christian era, and therefore that all history, and not only so, but all the changes by which the various races of men were formed, by which languages developed into their numerous and diverse types, by which civilization and art emerged and gradually perfected themselves, are shut up within the narrow space of 2,500 or 2,600 years before the birth of our Lord. Now this time is said with reason to be quite insufficient. Egypt and Babylonia have histories, as settled kingdoms, which reach back (according to the most moderate of modern critical historians) to about the time at which the numbers of our English Bible place the Deluge. Considerable diversities of language can be proved to have existed at that date; markedly different physical types appear not much subsequently; civilization in Egypt has, about the Pyramid period, which few now place later than B.C. 2,450, an advanced character; the arts exist nearly in the shape in which they were known in the country at its most flourishing period. Clearly, a considerable space is wanted anterior to the pyramid age for the gradual development of Egyptian life into the condition which the monuments show to have been then reached. This space the numbers of our English Bible do not allow.

Such is the difficulty. Now how is it to be met? In the first place, candour should (I think) induce all those who urge it to let their readers, or hearers, know that a special uncertainty attaches to the numbers in question, from the fact that they are given differently in the different ancient versions. We possess the Pentateuch in three very ancient forms, in Hebrew, in the Greek version known as the Septuagint, and in Samaritan. Our English numbers represent those of the Hebrew text. The numbers of the Septuagint and the Samaritan version are different. Those of the Samaritan version extend the period between the Deluge and the birth of Abraham from the 292 years of the Hebrew text to 942 years,—an addition of six centuries and a half—while those of the Septuagint, according to some copies, give 1,072 years as the interval, according to others 1,172 years, thus increasing the period between the Deluge and Abraham by a space of nearly eight, or nearly nine centuries. Now if the Greek, or even if the Samaritan, numbers are the right ones, if they represent, that is, the original text, it may be questioned whether anything more is wanted. It may be questioned whether a term of from six to eight centuries is not enough for the production of that state of things which we find existing in Babylonia and in Egypt when the light of history first dawns upon them, whether within that space might not have been produced such a state of civilization, so much progress in art, such differences of physical type, and such diversities of language as appear to have existed at that period.

If, however, the ultimate verdict of calm reason, and

rigid scientific inquiry should be against this view, if more time seem to be absolutely wanted for the development of settled government, of art, science, language, ethnical diversities, varieties of physical type, and the like, than even the enlarged chronology of the Septuagint allows, then I should not be afraid to grant that the original record of Scripture on this point may have been lost, and that, as it is certain that we cannot possess the actual chronological scheme of Moses in more than one of the three extant versions of his words which have come to us with almost equal authority, so it is quite possible that we may not posses his real scheme in any. Nothing in ancient MSS. is so liable to corruption from the mistakes of copyists as the numbers; the original mode of writing them appears in all countries of which we have any knowledge to have been by signs, not very different from one another; the absence of any context determining in favour of one number rather than another, where the copy is blotted or faded, increases the chance of error, and thus it happens that in almost all ancient works the numbers are found to be deserving of very little reliance. Where they to any extent check one another, they are generally self-contradictory; where they do not, they are frequently in the highest degree improbable.

A second historical difficulty connected with Genesis was much insisted upon by the late Baron Bunsen. The primitive Babylonian kingdom is declared in the tenth chapter of Genesis to have been Cushite. Baron Bunsen held that there were no Cushites out of Africa, and that "an Asiatic Cush existed only in the imagination of Biblical interpreters, and was the child of their despair."* But an analysis of the earliest documents recovered from Babylonia has shown that the primitive Babylonian people, that which raised the first structures whereof any trace remains, in the country, and whose buildings had gone to ruin in the days of Nebuchadnezzar, was (at any rate to a large extent) Cushite, its vocabulary being "undoubtedly Cushite or Ethiopian," and presenting numerous analogies with those of the non-Semitic races of modern Abyssinia. Hence, modern historical science, in the person of one of its best representatives, M. Lenormant, commences now the history of the East with a "First Cushite Empire," which it regards as dominant in Babylonia for several centuries before the earliest Semitic Empire arose.†

A difficulty less noticed, yet one which was, in the state of our historical knowledge a few years since, more real, may be found in the narrative contained in the 14th chapter of Genesis with respect to the invasion of Palestine in the time of Abraham by a number of kings from the vicinity of the

* Philos. of Univ. Hist. i. p. 191.

† Manuel d'Histoire, tom. ii. p. 16.

Persian Gulf. These kings act under the presidency of a monarch, called Chedorlaomer (or Chedor-lagomer), who is stated to be "king of Elam." Now till very recently there was no profane evidence that Elam—which is not Persia, as many have supposed, but Elymaïs or Susiana, the country between Babylonia and Persia—had ever been an independent state, much less a powerful kingdom, and still less one that at so remote a date could have exercised suzerainty over so many and such important nations. But the Assyrian cuneiform inscriptions have shown that throughout almost the whole of the Assyrian period Elam maintained herself as an independent state and one of considerable military strength on the south-eastern borders of the empire; and very recently* it has further been discovered that, according to the Assyrian belief, an Elamitic king was strong enough to invade and plunder Babylonia at a date, which expressed in our ordinary manner would be B.C. 2,286, or somewhat earlier than the time commonly assigned to Abraham. Further, the primitive Babylonian remains bear traces of the extension of Elamitic influence into Babylonia at a remote era; and the possibility of such distant military expeditions at this far-off period of the world's history, receives illustration at once from the epithet "Ravager of Syria," which is borne by a Babylonian monarch of about this date, and also from the numerous expedi-

* Zeitschrift f. Œgypt. Sp. Nov. 1868.

tions conducted not very much later by the Egyptian princes from the valley of the Nile into Mesopotamia.

No other historical difficulties, so far as I know, present themselves in the narrative of Genesis. Some attempts were made in Germany, about thirty or forty years ago, to prove that the description of Egypt contained in the latter portion of the book exhibited numerous "mistakes and inaccuracies;" but the "mistakes and inaccuracies" alleged were scarcely of an historical character, and the writers who alleged them have been so triumphantly refuted by Hengstenberg, and others, that the sceptical school has ceased to urge the point, and now allows the entire truthfulness and accuracy of the whole account. Few things are in truth more remarkable than the *complete* harmony and accordance which exist between the picture of ancient Egypt and the ancient Egyptians, as drawn for us by Moses, and that portraiture of them which is now obtainable from their own contemporary writings and monuments.

With regard to the narrative contained in the last four books of the Pentateuch, modern criticism has chiefly employed itself in objections turning upon the numbers. The multiplication of the Israelites, as related in Genesis and Exodus, has been declared to be utterly and absolutely incredible. The sudden exodus from Egypt of a body of two millions of persons in the way narrated has been pronounced an impossibility. The subsistence of such a multitude, with their flocks and herds, in the Desert of Tih for forty years, or even a single year, has been said to be inconceivable. Many minor objections, turning on the same point of numerical difficulty, have been urged, and the conclusion has been drawn that the entire narrative of Exodus, Numbers, Leviticus, and Deuteronomy is unhistorical—a romance drawn up at a comparatively late period of the nation's history, having perhaps a certain historic foundation, but in its details wholly and entirely imaginary.*

Now, with respect to these objections, let it be observed, in the first place, that they all turn upon the one point of number; and that the numbers of the sacred texts are (as has been already observed) exactly the part of it which is most liable to corruption and least to be depended upon. So that if the difficulties of the multiplication, as stated, of the exit from Egypt, the march, the passage of the Red Sea, and the sojourn in the wilderness, were all allowed to be as great as represented, it would be enough to reply that there may have been a corruption of the numbers—the addition (say) of a cipher in each case—and that the whole narrative would stand good, and the difficulties disappear, if for "six hundred thousand that were men" in Exodus xii. 37, we were to read 60,000, and so on—the entire exodus being

* Colenso. "The Pentateuch and the Book of Joshua."

thus made one of 200,000 instead of two million souls. But this mode of meeting the difficulty is not, perhaps, here the right one. The numbers may be defended as they stand. In Germany the best critics, including so subtle and little credulous a writer as Ewald, accept them. They seem required by the general tenor of the whole narrative, especially by the great unwillingness of the Egyptians to let the people go, and by their power, within little more than a generation to conquer and occupy Canaan. Assuming therefore the numbers to be sound, to have come to us as they were delivered by Moses, let us inquire what the great difficulties are of which so much has been made, and see if they are really so insuperable.

In the first place, as to the multiplication in Egypt. Now here, before we can form any judgment, two things have to be determined—"What was the number of the Israelites when they entered Egypt," and "What was the duration of their stay there?" What was their number when they entered Egypt? We are commonly told, "seventy souls." Now, no doubt, these words occur in Scripture, "All the souls of the house of Jacob, which came into Egypt, were threescore and ten."* But, when we come to look into details, we find first, that the seventy souls of Jacob's descendants comprise only two women, the married daughters and

* Gen. xlvi. 27; compare Ex. i. 5.

grand-daughters of Jacob not being mentioned, who yet, we are told, followed the migrations of the tribe,* and no account being taken of the wives of his sons and grandsons. Supplying these omissions, we have for the family of Jacob as it entered Egypt, the number 267, instead of the number seventy, or nearly four times the ordinary estimate. But this is far from being all. The children of Israel entered Egypt with their households, or retainers.† What the size of a patriarchal household was we may gather from the history of Abraham, who had 318 trained servants born in his house, capable of active military service. It has been well observed that "we shall scarcely find so many in a clan of three thousand souls."‡ Jacob's retainers are likely to have been more numerous rather than less numerous than those of Abraham; and the conclusion of Kurtz, that they amounted to "several thousands" § is therefore perfectly reasonable. It appears to me quite probable that the tribe which took possession of the Land of Goshen on the invitation of Joseph and Pharaoh was a body of five or six thousand persons.

Next, as to the duration of the sojourn in Egypt, the

* Gen. xlvi. 7.

† Gen. xlvi. 5. The word *taph* (טַף) here, translated "little ones" means "households." The Septuagint translate it by *οἰκία* or *συγγένεια*.

‡ Payne Smith, "Bampton Lectures." p. 89.

§ History of Old Covenant, vol. ii. p. 149. E. T.

Hebrew text lays it down very positively that it was 430 years.* The best MSS. of the Septuagint agree. There was a tradition among the later Jews which brought down the term to 215 years; but this tradition cannot reasonably be set against the plain words of Exodus; and consequently we must take 430 years as the duration of the sojourn.

Is it then, or is it not, conceivable, that under the circumstances of the time and country, a tribe or clan of 5,000 persons may have increased in 430 years to one of two millions? Here it has to be remembered that there were two modes whereby they might increase, one that of ordinary natural increase, the other by augmentation of the number of their retainers. The natural tendency of population has been shown by Mr. Malthus, to be to double itself, if unchecked, every 25 years.† The Israelites, having the land of Goshen, a large fertile territory, capable of supporting a population of several millions, assigned them, would be in a position where the checks on the natural tendency, especially at first, would be very slight. Now, according to the estimate of Mr. Malthus, a body of 5,000 persons increasing without check, would have become more than two millions at the end of 225 years; a body of 267 persons would have exceeded the same amount at the close of 325

* Ex. xii. 40, 41.

† Essay on Population, vol. i. p. 8; Encycl. Brit. vol. xviii. p. 340.

years; and a body even of seventy persons would have done the same at the expiration of 375 years; so that, except for the operation of artificial checks, the family of Jacob, had it really consisted of seventy persons only, would have become one of above two millions fifty-five years before the time of the exodus. But, no doubt, as the increase took place, the artificial checks, which keep down the natural tendency of population, began to operate, and the result was, that if the original immigrants were, as I have supposed, about 5,000, the actual rate of increase had been a doubling, not once each twenty-five years, but once each forty-eight years, or not very much beyond the rate which prevails in our own country at the present time.

If we add to this the consideration that the Israelites, being in a very flourishing condition during the earlier portion of their sojourn in Egypt, would naturally augment, by purchase, the number of their households, and might even receive, by agreement, whole tribes into their body, we shall not be surprised that at the end of the 430 years, the clan had grown to be a nation of two million souls.

With respect to the difficulties of the exit of this large body of persons from Egypt in the sudden way which the narrative in Exodus seems to describe, they depend (I think) mainly on the broad and general manner of description habitual to Oriental writers, who do not trouble themselves with details, or with exceptions, but describe *in the mass*, stating that to be done by all which was done by most, or by those of most account; regarding a nation as concentrated in its heads; and directing attention to the main events, to the neglect of the various details into which they were broken up. A candid reader, making fair allowance for these characteristics of Oriental style, and for the brevity of the sacred narrative, will scarcely be much troubled by the difficulties of the start and the march, as they have been urged by some critics. It is certain migrations of tribes, quite as large as that of Israel is said to have been, have from time to time taken place in the east, and indeed in the west also. Such migrations have frequently been sudden—the emigrants have started off with their women, children, and all their possessions on a certain day*—they have traversed enormous distances, much greater ones than the Israelites traversed, and have finally settled themselves in new abodes. That the Israelites made such a migration there cannot be a doubt. The Egyptians, Greeks, Romans, all accepted the fact as certain. Cavils as to their exact numbers, or as to the particular expressions used in Exodus, do not touch the

* It was on the 5th of January, 1771, the *day* appointed by the high priests, that Oubacha began his march, *with seventy thousand families.* Most of the hordes were then assembled in the steppes, on the left bank of the Volga, and *the whole multitude followed him.*"— Hommaire de Hell, Travels, p. 227, E. T.

main fact, but show (if they show anything) either that our ancient manuscripts are here and there defective, or that an early Oriental historian does not write in the exact and accurate style of a nineteenth-century occidental critic.

The difficulty which attaches to the subsistence of the Israelites for forty years in the wilderness of Tih, concerns almost wholly the sustenance of their flocks and herds, which are said to have been numerous, and have been calculated at two million head of cattle. The answer to this difficulty may be very brief. In the first place, we are not told that the cattle did not very rapidly decrease; for no mention is made of the people possessing any considerable number in the later portion of the sojourn, until an enormous booty is captured from the Midianites;* and in the second place, there is ample reason to believe that the wilderness was anciently very much more fertile than it is at present, and quite capable of furnishing pasturage to flocks and herds of a large size. The recent explorations of Mr. Tristram and Mr. Holland have placed this fact beyond a doubt, and have shown that the Sinaitic peninsula, at any rate, was a "desert" merely in comparison with the richly agricultural countries of Egypt and Palestine.

Historical difficulties are scarcely alleged with respect to the portion of the Biblical narrative which follows upon the

* Num. xxxi. 32, 33.

sojourn in the wilderness. The conquest of Canaan by the immigrant Israelites is a fact too well attested to be denied; and the subsequent chequered history of the race, as delivered to us in Judges and in the First Book of Samuel, is for the most part too modest and unpretending an account to tempt the assaults of sceptics. The exploits of Gideon and Samson are viewed indeed with incredulity; but merely on the ground that they are intrinsically improbable. It is not until we come to the time of David and Solomon that any further difficulties, really of an historical character, present themselves, and that an examination of the difficulties by the light of historical documents becomes possible.

The sudden rise of the Israelites to power and greatness in the reign of David, the grandeur, magnificence, and extent of the kingdom of Solomon, and the entire collapse of the empire at his death appear to some, not merely in themselves strange and improbable, but incompatible with what is known from history of the condition of the neighbouring countries. The little country of Palestine was placed midway between the territories of two great and powerful monarchies, of which it may be said, in a general way, that for a thousand years before the rise of the Persians to power, they contested the sovereignty of the East. Overshadowed by the grand forms of Egypt and Assyria, how could Israel (it may be asked) emerge from obscurity, how especially advance at a bound from a dependent to a dominant position, asserting, and for above fifty years maintaining, her place among the great ones of the earth? We may answer, that, in the first place such a revolution has numerous analogies in the history of the East, where the rapid rise of petty states to greatness, the sudden conversion of an oppressed into a dominant power, is the rule rather than the exception; where Babylon, Media, Persia, Parthia, where the histories of Timur, Yenghis Khan, Nadir Shah, all illustrate it. But further, in this particular case, we can see not only a general analogy, but a fitness in the peculiar circumstances of the time for the production of such a phenomenon as that which Scripture places before us. The monumental evidence of the two countries shows, that exactly at the time when the conquests of David and the Empire of Solomon are placed, both Egypt and Assyria were exceptionally weak. Egypt, after the time of Ramesses III. (ab. B.C. 1,200). ceased to be aggressive on the side of Syria, and continued until the accession of Sheshonk or Shishak, (ab. B.C. 990) to be a quiet and unwarlike power. Assyria, which, about B.C. 1,100, extended her sway into the valley of the Orontes, and threatened Palestine with subjection, passed under a cloud soon afterwards, and did not again become a terror to Syria, till about B.C. 880. For a Jewish Empire to arise it was necessary that Egypt and

Assyria should be simultaneously weak. Such simultaneous weakness is found for the hundred or hundred and twenty years between B.C. 1,100 and B.C. 990. And exactly into this interval fall the rise of the Jews to power under Saul and David, and the establishment of their empire under Solomon.

Doubts were thrown a few years since, by an able writer, on the expeditions of Shishak against Rehoboam, Solomon's son, and of Zerah, the Ethiopian, against Asa, Rehoboam's grandson;* which, it was suggested, might be mere embellishments of a history, otherwise tame and uninteresting. The careful analysis which the inscription of Shishak at Karnac has undergone at the hands of Mr. Stuart Poole,* and Dr. Brugsch,† not to mention other scholars, and the evidence thus furnished of the reality and the importance of his expedition into Palestine, render the continuance of incredulity, as to the former of these attacks, impossible. The analysis has thrown a flood of light on what was previously obscure in the scriptural narrative. It has shown that Shishak went up, not so much with any extensive scheme of conquest, as to settle his *protegé*, Jeroboam, in his kingdom, where he was in great danger from the Levitical

* F. Newman's "Hebrew Monarchy," pp. 160, 161.
† "Dictionary of the Bible," ad voc. SHISHAK.
‡ "Geographische Inschriften," vol. ii., p. 32, *et seq.*

and Canaanite towns not being in his hands. These Shishak reduced and made over to Jeroboam, thus giving him a firm hold on the northern kingdom. Having done this, he was content to receive the mere submission of Rehoboam, and allowed him to retain the southern kingdom, perhaps not wishing to make Jeroboam too strong. It was the constant practice of the great monarchs of Egypt, Assyria, and Babylon, to maintain, on dependent thrones, a large number of petty princes, who were checks upon each other, and could easily be dealt with, if they shewed any inclination to rebellion.

The expedition of Zerah has not yet received any distinct confirmation from monuments. But the recent discovery that there reigned about this time a king called *Azerch*-Amen in Ethiopia, has removed the difficulties which attached to the name and the description of the invader, and has indicated to the dispassionate and candid student, that here, too, the Jewish historian had probably contemporary records to guide him, and related real facts of history, not figments drawn from his imagination.

A real historical difficulty meets us soon after this, in the sacred narrative, in the invasion of the kingdom of Samaria, by Pul, who is called a "king of Assyria," and is said to have put Menahem to a tribute of a thousand talents of silver.* We possess the history of Assyria for this period,

* 2 Kings xv. 19.

apparently in a state of completeness; and this history shows us no monarch at this time (or indeed at any other time), bearing a name in the least resembling that of Pul. The predecessor of Tiglath-pileser on the throne of Assyria, was a certain Asshur-lush (or Asshur-likkis), whose predecessor was Asshur-dayan, who followed on Shalmaneser III. It seems impossible that any one of these kings can be Pul. Moreover, Assyria, in the time immediately preceding the accession of Tiglath-pileser, instead of being a great, aggressive power, capable of marching armies into Palestine, was in a depressed state, troubled by frequent insurrections among her own subjects, and quite incapable of sending out distant military expeditions. Thus "Pul, king of Assyria," constitutes to the modern historical inquirer a real difficulty—a difficulty which it has been proposed to meet in various ways.

The best explanation hitherto suggested is, I think, the following. Pul, who was called by Berosus, the great Babylon historian, "king of the Chaldeans," was probably a monarch who reigned at Babylon, while Assur-lush was reigning at Nineveh. In the troublous decade of years which preceded Tiglath-pileser's accession, he became a powerful prince, perhaps deprived Assyria of her western provinces, and invaded Syria and Palestine from the quarter from which Assyrian invasions had been wont to come. Presenting himself to the Israelites as the representative of the great Mesopotamian power, with which they had been contending for centuries, they termed him loosely "king of Assyria" when he was in reality a king of Babylon, who had possessed himself of a portion of the Assyrian dominions. In the same way, they subsequently termed Nabopolassar, the father of Nebuchadnezzar, and even Darius Hystaspis, "kings of Assyria." *

A difficulty used to be felt with respect to "Sargon, king of Assyria," who is said to have taken Ashdod by the hand of one of his captains.† Sargon's name is not contained in the historical books of Scripture, nor is he mentioned by any of the classical writers, who speak of Shalmaneser, Sennacherib, and Esarhaddon. The occurrence of his name in Isaiah was thought to indicate an irreconcilable difference between the historical data possessed by that prophet and those of the writer of Kings. Even his existence was doubted, and different writers proposed to regard his name as a mere variant for those of each of the three princes just mentioned. The Assyrian inscriptions have completely cleared up all this obscurity. Sargon is found to have been the successor of Shalmaneser; the predecessor and father of Sennacherib. He speaks of having captured Ashdod. All that Isaiah says of him is confirmed; and it appears to have

* 2 Kings xxiii. 29; Ezra vi. 22. † Isaiah xx. 1.

been quite accidental that the writer of Kings, who more than once alludes to him,* does not mention his name.

The strictly historical character of the later portion of the Old Testament narrative, especially of that delivered to us in Kings, Chronicles, Ezra, and Nehemiah, and in the contemporary prophets, Jeremiah, Zechariah, and Haggai, is generally admitted, even by sceptics. The only writings belonging to this period, whereto exception is taken are the Books of Daniel and Esther, which many still regard as full of historical inaccuracies, and as quite unworthy of credence. I shall therefore conclude my observation on the alleged historical difficulties of the *Old* Testament, and the light thrown on them by modern discoveries, by a brief consideration of these two books and of the objections taken to them.

The chief historical inaccuracies alleged against Daniel are the following: He is said to have invented two kings, Belshazzar, and Darius the Mede, whose existence is not merely unknown to history, but precluded by it; to have falsely ascribed a government by satraps to the Babylonians; to have incorrectly represented the condition of their "wise men"; to have made Susa a residence of the Persian monarchs when it was not even built; to have wrongly made the last king of Babylon a son of Nebuchadnezzar, and to have

* 2 Kings xvii. 6; xviii. 7, 11.

misrepresented his fate; to have misconceived the relative position of the Medes and Persians at the time of the capture of Babylon; and to have related an utterly incredible circumstance, viz. that Daniel was admitted among the Babylonian "wise men," and even constituted their head.*

Now of these charges some are quite incapable of being either substantiated or distinctly refuted from our insufficient knowledge of the times to which they refer. Nothing is really known of the classes into which the "wise men" of Babylon were divided in Nebuchadnezzar's time, excepting what we learn from Daniel himself. The authors supposed to contradict Daniel on this point, write of the state of things in their own day, which happens to be eight centuries later! And they do not write about the Babylonian "wise men" at all, but about the divisions of the Persian magi, an entirely different class. We do not even know enough about the "wise men" to say whether there was anything strange and unusual in a foreigner being placed at their head. We may suspect that it was so, but we have really no sufficient evidence on the subject. The little evidence that we have is to the effect that the "wise men" were a learned, not a priestly, body; and that they admitted

* Von Lengerke, "Das Buch Daniel; Einleitung," § 13; p. lxiii. "De Wette, Einleitung in d. Abte Testament," p. 225, a; Davison, "Introduction to the Old Testament," vol. iii. pp. 174-192.

foreigners among them—more we do not know; but there is certainly not the slightest difficulty in supposing that the despotic power of a Babylonian monarch would have been amply sufficient to overcome any repugnance which any class of his subjects might have felt towards one of his appointments.

Similarly, we have no sufficient knowledge of the Babylonian governmental system to say that it was not, at any rate, to some extent, satrapial. A satrapial system is simply one in which governors are appointed over the provinces, instead of their being suffered to remain under the rule of native kings. Our present Indian system is in part satrapial, in part a government by means of kings. The Assyrian government was one of the same kind; and, on the whole, it is most probable that so was the Babylonian. Gedaliah, who succeeded to King Zedekiah in Judea, was a "governor,"* that is, a satrap, appointed by Nebuchadnezzar; and Berosus speaks of a "satrap of Egypt, Cœle-Syria, and Phœnicia," as holding office under Nabopolassar, Nebuchadnezzar's father. Thus there is no "inaccuracy" in Daniel's speaking of Nebuchadnezzar as summoning, among his other great officers, his "satraps."† That the *word*, which is Persian,

* 2 Kings xxv. 23.

† Dan. iii. 2. אחשדרפניא, translated in our version, "princes," but really the Hebrew equivalent of the Persian *khshatrapa*, "satraps."

was not used in Babylonia is probable; but Daniel, writing for Jews under Persian government, who were perfectly familiar with the term, employed it for a corresponding Babylonian expression.

The charge that Daniel misapprehended the relative position of the Medes and Persians at the capture of Babylon, regarding the supremacy of the Medes as still continuing, is unjust, and rests on an omission to look carefully to the original text. It is true that the Medes are placed before the Persians in the words of the handwriting upon the wall, and also in the formula, "according to the law of the Medes and Persians, which altereth not." But this honorary precedence assigned to the Medes is a mere trace of their ancient supremacy—a trace much more strongly marked in Greek writers, who actually call Cyrus and his successors "Medes"—and is not an indication of its continuance. Daniel twice marks very strongly the subordinate position of the Medes, stating in one place* that Darius the Mede "*received* the kingdom"—*i.e.*, was given it by another; and further declaring that he "*was made king* over the nation of the Chaldæans,"† using in this case an expression which distinctly implies that he derived his position from some superior authority, which made him king.‡

* Dan. v. 31. † Dan. ix. 1.
‡ See Pusey's "Lectures on Daniel," pp. 124, 125. 3rd edition.

The notion that Susa, or at any rate, its palace, was not built at the time when Daniel says that he saw himself in vision there, rests wholly upon a statement made by Pliny, six hundred years later, that "Susa, the ancient regal city of the Persians, was built by Darius Hystaspis."* Now this statement, one of very weak authority, had we nothing to set against it, is contrary to the declarations of various other classical authorities, among them notably of Herodotus; and is completely disproved by the Assyrian inscriptions, which show that Susa was one of the most ancient of all the Mesopotamian cities, and that its "palace" was famous for many centuries before the time of Daniel. The truth which underlies Pliny's statement, is the fact that Darius Hystaspis was the first Persian monarch to build a palace at Susa after the Persian fashion; but the ancient residence of the Susian kings, the Memnonium, as the Greeks called it, had existed for considerably more than a thousand years when the son of Hystaspes began his edifice.

Of the two remaining charges, which concern Darius the Mede, and Belshazzar, one—and that the more important of the two—has been completely rebutted by the evidence of the Babylonian monuments. These monuments show that Nabonnedus (or Labynetus), the king of Babylon attacked by Cyrus, had a son named Bel-shar-ezer, or Bel-

* H. N. vi. 27.

shazzar, whom during some years he associated with him in the government. This son may well have been on the mother's side descended from Nebuchadnezzar, as Daniel says that Belshazzar was;* he may have played the part in the siege which Daniel states that he did, while his father (as Berosus mentioned) defended the fortress of Borsippa; and he may have fallen in the general massacre during the night in which Babylon was taken, while his father was subsequently made prisoner, and kindly treated by Cyrus. All the supposed contradictions of profane history by Daniel in connection with this matter, are entirely removed by one little document, exhumed in our own day from the soil of Mesopotamia, by the exertions of an English gentleman.

With respect to Darius the Mede, nothing has been as yet discovered. It is clear from Daniel that he was not a king in his own right, but a viceroy set up by Cyrus. He held his government probably for not more than two years. Perhaps he is to be identified with Astyages, the Median king, whom Cyrus deposed but treated kindly; perhaps he was merely a Median noble, whom Cyrus advanced, as he did other Medes, to a position of trust and importance. The monuments have not at present thrown any light on this matter; but he would be a bold person, who, after the discovery with respect to Belshazzar, would undertake to

* Dan. v. 11.

say that there may not, ere many years are past, be as much light thrown upon the obscure history of this monarch, as has been recently thrown on the history, formerly at least as obscure, of his predecessor.

I cannot leave this matter and turn to another without strongly advising those who have any doubts as to the genuineness and authenticity of the Book of Daniel, which have been of late so fiercely attacked, to study carefully the recent work of Professor Pusey upon the subject. They will find in it a complete answer to all the objections, historical, and critical, which have been urged against this portion of Scripture.

The historical difficulties alleged against the Book of Esther, are chiefly the following. Assuming Ahasuerus to be Xerxes, which is no doubt a highly probable identification, it is said that Esther's position is impossible, since Xerxes had but one wife, Amestris, who cannot be Esther. Nor could any Persian king have married a Jewess, since there was a law that the kings should take all their wives out of seven noble Persian families. Such a feast as that described in the first chapter, where all the princes of the provinces were entertained for 180 days, could not have taken place, since the governors could not without ruin to the empire have been so long absent from their governments. It is incredible that a Persian king should have given the command, said to have been given by Ahasuerus to Vashti. The edicts ascribed to Ahasuerus are all incredible—especially the second and third. No king would have consented to the murder of 2,000,000 of his subjects; nor would any king ever have allowed at a later time those two millions to stand up and slay as many as they pleased of their enemies. Finally, the honours granted to Mordecai are said to be excessive, and such as no monarch would have allowed to a subject.

With respect to the first of these objections, we may reply that though Amestris cannot be Esther, she may well be Vashti; and that though the classical writers tell us of no other wife of Xerxes, yet it is quite possible that he may have had several. Polygamy was the rule with the Persian kings. Amestris was no doubt on the whole the chief wife of Xerxes, and if she at one time fell into disgrace, must have been afterwards restored to favour; but the accounts which we have from the Greeks do not at all preclude the possibility of such a temporary disgrace, and of the elevation of another wife to the first place for a time. As to its being impossible that any Persian king could have married a Jewess, it is sufficient to remark, that though the Persians had laws, the Persian kings were above the law, and could always disregard its restraints. When Cambyses having conceived an affection for his full sister, Atossa, asked the royal judges if they could find a law allowing a Persian to marry such a near relative, their reply was, that they could find no law permitting the marriage of brothers and sisters, but that they found a law, that the king of the Persians might do what he liked.*

The objection to Xerxes feasting *all* his princes for 180 days is an objection, not to anything contained in the Book of Esther, but to something which the critic who makes it has intruded into the book. The writer of the book tells us that Xerxes "made a feast to all his princes and his servants" (ch. i. 3), and subsequently relates that the feast lasted "an hundred and fourscore days" (verse 4); but he nowhere states that the princes were all present during the whole of the time. Indeed, the reader possessed of common sense sees clearly enough that the very duration of the festivity was probably contrived, in order that all the princes might in their turn partake of it. The critic says, "it is not so stated in the text," which is true: but neither is that stated which he has thought that he saw in it.

The command given to Vashti is undoubtedly strange and abnormal. It was an outrage on Oriental custom; and as such the narrative sets it before us. The king does not issue the order until he is "merry with wine"; and the Queen refuses to obey, because she feels the order to be an insult. But can we say that no Oriental king could possibly

* Herod. iii. 31.

have issued such a command? Is it not more reasonable to allow, with a German critic of the sceptical school, that the narrative is here "possible on account of the advancing corruption in Xerxes' time, and through the folly of Xerxes himself"?* Indeed is it not clear that we can set no limit to the caprices of absolute power, or to the orders that may not be issued by a proud and silly despot?

Considerations of this kind go far also to remove the difficulty which has been felt as to the main facts of the narrative of Esther, the intended massacre of the Jews, and the counter-edict allowing them to defend themselves and slay their enemies. Such facts are altogether out of the ordinary experience of Western nations; and it is not surprising that they have been met with incredulity on the part of those whose knowledge of the past is limited to an acquaintance with the course of European, and especially of modern European, history. But can it be said that they are altogether out of nature? that they have no counterpart in the history of the East? that they transcend altogether what authentic history relates of the doings of Oriental tyrants? Here again the German sceptic is more cautious than some of those who have sought to popularise him, and allows that from what we know of the base character and despotism of Xerxes it may perhaps be believed that Haman obtained from

* De Wette, "Einleitung," p. 267.

him a decree for the extirpation of the Jews, and Mordecai in return a corresponding counter-decree*. All that he objects to is, the fierceness with which the Jews set to work, and the consequent massacre by them of above 75,000 persons. This fact he thinks "incredible." It may be allowed that had the persons slain been, as the objectors suppose, "Persians," the circumstances related would have been extremely hard of belief; but it is on the whole most probable that there were few or no "Persians" among them. A religious sympathy united the Persians with the Jews; and it is scarcely likely that any of them would have taken part in the proposed destruction of the Jewish nation. The adversaries of the Jews were to be found in the ranks of the conquered nations, not of the conquering one. They were Persian subjects, not Persians. There is no reason to think that the loss even of 75,000 of such persons would have been felt by Xerxes as a matter of much importance. We must remember, however, that the number 75,000 is doubtful. The Septuagint version has 15,000; and this number is more in harmony than the other with the 800 slain in the capital.

Finally, to the objection that the honours granted to Mordecai are excessive, it may be replied, in the first place, that they are analogous to those granted to Joseph,† and

* Ibid. loc. cit. † Gen. xli. 42, 43.

Daniel,* and therefore such as were occasionally allowed to subjects by Oriental sovereigns; and secondly, that if there were anything abnormal in them, it would be sufficiently accounted for by the wild and extravagant temper of Xerxes, which delighted in strange acts and exhibitions of an unusual character. Haman, who knew his master's weakness, might well speculate upon it, and suggest extraordinary honours, since he imagined that it was himself for whom they were intended.

I have now noticed *all* the historical difficulties of any force or weight, which have come before me in the course of my studies on the history of the Old Testament. I have dwelt particularly on those connected with the Pentateuch and with the two Books of Daniel and Esther, because of late years the attacks of sceptics have been especially directed against those portions of the Sacred volume. I have left myself but scant time for noticing historical difficulties connected with the narrative of the New Testament; but this is of the less consequence, since there are no more than one or two such difficulties on which any stress has recently been laid by our opponents.

It has been said that St. Luke, in connecting the name of Cyrenius with the "taxing" which caused Joseph and Mary to go from Nazareth to Bethlehem, "undeniably contradicts

* Dan. v. 29.

history."* Cyrenius (or Quirinus) was appointed governor of Syria about ten years after the death of Herod the Great, and made a census of his province shortly afterwards. This census St. Luke is accused of placing ten years too early. The answer to this charge is, that the words of St. Luke (chap. ii. 2) cannot possibly mean that Cyrenius was governor at the time of the taxing; had it been St. Luke's intention to express this, the verse would have run thus: "This taxing was made when Cyrenius was governor of Syria," and not "this taxing was first made," etc. "First," that is, which is manifestly the emphatic word of the sentence, would then have been absent from it. Evidently, therefore, St. Luke's words must bear some other meaning. They may signify, "*this* taxing was made *before* Cyrenius was governor," and so before that better known taxing which he ordered. This is an allowable translation of the passage. Or they may mean, and I think they do mean, "this taxing was first completed —first took full effect—when Cyrenius was governor;" that is to say, the taxing ordered by Augustus, and commenced under Herod the Great, was interrupted (as it may easily have been, since the Jews were very bitter against it), and the business was first accomplished under Cyrenius. This is a sense which the Greek verb translated in our version "was made" sometimes has.

* Strauss, "Leben Jesu," § 32.

Again, it has been said that St. Luke erred in stating that Lysanias was tetrarch of Abilene (iii. 1) in the fifteenth year of the reign of Tiberius Cæsar.* Lysanias, it is said, died sixty years previously; and St. Luke has ignorantly made him alive, being deceived by the fact that Abilene continued to be called "the Abilene of Lysanias," after its former ruler, for sixty or seventy years subsequently. Now here it is in the first place assumed, without any word of proof, that the Lysanias who died B.C. 34 once ruled over Abilene. Secondly, it is assumed, also without any word of proof, that Abilene came to be known as "the Abilene of Lysanias," from him. I venture to assert that there is absolutely no ground for believing that the old Lysanias was ever ruler of Abilene; and I venture to maintain that Abilene came to be called "the Abilene of Lysanias" from a second or later Lysanias, a son of the former one, who is the person intended by St. Luke. Till recently, Christian apologists were defied to show historically that there was ever more than one Lysanias, and were accused of inventing a second to escape a difficulty. But a few years since, a discovery was made which must be regarded by all reasonable persons as having set the whole matter at rest. This was an inscription found near Baalbek,† containing a dedication of a

* Strauss, "Leben Jesu," § 44.

† See Krafft, "Topografie Jerusalems," Inscr. 29.

memorial tablet or statue to "Zenodorus, son of the tetrarch Lysanias, and to Lysanias, her children," by (apparently) the widow of the first, and the mother of the second Lysanias. Zenodorus was already known as having succeeded the first Lysanias in his government. It is thus clear, that there were, as previously suspected, two persons of the name, a father, and a son, and there is not the slightest reason for doubting St. Luke's statement that the latter was tetrarch of Abilene in the fifteenth of Tiberius.

I know of no other cavil against the historical accuracy of the New Testament, that I can regard as worthy of being dignified with the name of difficulty. It has been denied that any decree ever went out from Cæsar Augustus, that all the world should be taxed,* but as Savigny, the best authority on Roman antiquities, holds the contrary to be certain, this denial need not detain us. It has been asserted that if the massacre of the Innocents had taken place, it *must* have been noticed by Josephus;† but this argument from omission is too weak to deserve more than a passing notice. Nothing is more familiar to historical students than the unaccountable omissions which occur in the works of almost all historians. Scepticism has searched in the most minute and unsparing way every detail of the Gospel and the Acts, and has endeavoured earnestly to find

* Strauss, L. J. § 32. † Ibid. § 34.

"differences" and "divergences" between these facts and those of profane history; but again and again has it been compelled to own that the divergences are slight, and the differences such as may be reconciled by natural and probable suppositions. The entire result of the searching criticism, whereto the historical character of the New Testament has been exposed, has been to show that not only the general narrative, but all its minutiæ, are trustworthy. No evangelist has been convicted of error in respect of any historical statements. Where a shallow learning and a defective knowledge of the records of the past have led men to think that they had found a slip or a mistake, and a shout of triumph has been raised, profounder research has always demonstrated the veracity and accuracy of the sacred writer, and has exposed the ignorance of his assailant. The historical character of the New Testament is, I think I may say, in the eyes of all sober historical critics established.

MYTHICAL THEORIES OF CHRISTIANITY.

BY THE

REV. CHARLES ROW, M.A.,

OF PEMBROKE COLLEGE, OXFORD.

MYTHICAL THEORIES OF CHRISTIANITY.

It is hardly possible to over-estimate the importance of the issues to which it will be my duty to address myself in this lecture. They involve the central position of Christianity; viz., the all-important question whether Jesus Christ was an historical person, or a creation of the imagination. Is the Church which is erected on Him founded on an historic fact, which had an objective existence; or is the Jesus of the Evangelists a subjective creation which existed only in the minds of its originators?

Many of the attacks which have been made on Revelation are directed against its outworks merely; this is one directed against the very key of the Christian position. If it can be carried by our opponents, the whole line of our defences becomes untenable. Let us not deceive ourselves. If the Gospels are not *in their main outlines* historically true, Christianity is no more divine than Shakespeare. It may be the highest development of man; but it can have no pretence to be esteemed a revelation from God.

The objections of this school have done more to undermine the belief of the educated classes in Christianity as a divine revelation than any one single cause. They have largely created the so-called rationalism of the Continent. They are widely diffused in America. In our own country, a numerous class of writers who obtain ready access to our periodical literature are not only imbued with similar views, but write with the quiet assumption that the historical foundation of Christianity cannot be defended.

As my subject is a wide one, I must address myself to it without any preliminary observations. The question before us is simply this, Are the Gospels credible histories, in the sense that other writings of the same description are? or are the larger portion of their contents fictitious?

It should be observed that although these schools support their views by an immense critical apparatus, the real σκάνδαλον of the Gospels is the supernatural element which they contain. Apart from this, their historical character would never have been questioned. The theory that miracles are impossible underlies the entire mass of these objections. But the question of the miraculous has been already handled by another lecturer. I shall therefore only observe on it that it forms no portion of a strictly historical inquiry. It appertains to the abstract regions of thought. History has to deal with evidence, not with abstract dogmas or philosophical questions. To begin an historical inquiry with the assumption that miracles are impossible, and that any event which involves the supernatural must be a fiction, is quietly to assume the point at issue.

But as the Christian Church is an institution which actually exists, and as its origin can be traced up to the times of Jesus Christ, and as it is erected on the Gospels as its foundation, these schools are fully aware that the question cannot be settled by the quiet assumption that miracles are impossible. The case stands thus. The Christian Church exists. It has had its origin in the events of past history. The Church itself asserts now, and has asserted in all ages, that it is founded on the historical truth of the divine person of Christ our Lord, as He is depicted in the Gospels. If the Gospels are true, they give a rational account of its origin, But those with whom I am reasoning deny that they are a statement of historic facts, and consequently that they are not the true account of it. But as the Church is an historic fact, they are quite aware that any mere general assumption that miracles are impossible is not sufficient. They find themselves, therefore, compelled to do two things, —first, to invent a critical apparatus to destroy the credibility of the Gospels; and, secondly, to propound a theory which shall account for the origin of the Church on principles purely human. The solution propounded is the mythical and Tübingen theories.

This critical apparatus keeps two aims in view,—first, to prove the existence of statements in the Gospels at variance with those of contemporaneous history; secondly, to show that these narratives abound with a multitude of contradictions. To effect this latter purpose, every variation of statement is made to assume the character of a contradiction. The extent to which this has been carried is scarcely credible.

This process having as they hope destroyed the substance of the Gospels, the next procedure is to invent a theory out of the imagination as the account of the origin of Christianity, and to propound it as true history.

At first sight it would appear to have been the easiest course to assert that they are simple forgeries, in the same sense in which the Donation of Constantine or the False Decretals are forgeries. But this is what no unbeliever of the present day who regards his literary reputation ventures to propound as the alternative to their historical credibility, Why is the simple course abandoned, and an infinitely complicated theory substituted in its place? The answer is that their entire phenomena negative the supposition that they could have originated in directly conscious fraud.

A more elaborate theory, therefore, has to be substituted for the simple one. It must be observed that I can only speak of it in its general aspect, for its modifications are extremely numerous, and hardly any two writers can be found who take precisely the same view. But the following may be stated as the principles which underlie these systems of modern unbelief, throwing aside their minor details.

First. That miracles being impossible, no supernatural element whatever enters into the character of the historical Jesus.

Second. That He was probably a very great man, though, whenever the exigencies of the system require it, it is necessary to assume that He was deeply implicated in the prejudices and superstitions of the age in which He lived.

Third. That He probably believed Himself to be the Messiah expected by His countrymen, though as to the precise nature of His Messianic claims my opponents are not agreed.

Fourth. That He succeeded in inspiring a crowd of followers with an enthusiastic attachment to Him.

Fifth. That they were honest people after their fashion; but were impelled by an enthusiasm only equalled by their credulity.

Sixth. That they invented a multitude of fabulous

stories, ascribed them to Jesus, and in time mistook them for facts.

Seventh. That out of these and kindred elements, aided by a succession of developments, the human Jesus was gradually metamorphosed, in the course of the seventy years which followed the crucifixion, into the Christ of the Synoptic Gospels, and in a hundred and thirty into that of the Gospel of St. John.

Now, as these schools deny the existence of the supernatural, this whole development must have been due to causes which are purely human; in one word, to the laws which regulate the developments of the moral and spiritual worlds. As those of the natural world have been effected through the agency of natural laws, so the creation of the Jesus of the Evangelists is due to laws which regulate with equal potency the action of the mind. Both sets of laws are equally constant and invariable.

To examine the critical apparatus which has been applied to the Gospels for the purpose of proving their unhistorical character, could only be accomplished in a work of considerable length. I shall therefore only make two observations on the principles adopted.

First. These schools assault the Gospels by charging them with containing a multitude of inaccuracies, discrepancies, and contradictions. While they do this they carefully keep in the background the minute accuracies, agreements with contemporaneous history, and plain indications of autoptic testimony with which they abound. Such a line of conduct is the same thing as to place before the Court which is to try the cause everything which an acute counsel can adduce in opposition, and to suppress the whole evidence for the defence.

Secondly. A great majority of these objections are founded on a view of the Gospels which their writers expressly repudiate. It is taken for granted that the Gospels are histories in the strictest sense of that word. By a strict history I mean a narrative in which the events are connected together in accordance with the sequences of time and place. This is the arrangement which is generally adopted in modern histories and biographies. But the Gospels expressly assert that they belong to a different class of writings. They are not *histories*, but *memoirs*. In a memoir, the arrangement of events in the strict sequence of time and place is not the predominant idea. The Gospels are not only memoirs, but memoirs of a peculiar character. They are details of the actions and teachings of Jesus Christ written for the express purpose of teaching the Christian religion. In works of this kind the arrangement and grouping of events are formed on very different principles from those adopted in the composition of pure histories.

As this is a most important point, I must adduce proof of it which is beyond all contradiction. St. John's Gospel asserts, in as many words, that it was the purpose of its author to write such a memoir, and not a strict history. At chap. xx., ver. 30, 31, he says, "And many other signs truly did Jesus in the presence of His disciples, which are not written in this book: but these are written, that ye may believe that Jesus is the Christ, the Son of God; and that believing ye may have life through His name." Again, in the last verse of the Gospel it is expressly stated that Jesus did many things which the writer has not recorded.

The author therefore clearly asserts that he has made a selection of certain events in the life of Jesus Christ, from a very much larger number, with which he was acquainted, and that the principle which guided him, both in the selection and arrangement, was a religious one. "These are written that ye may believe that Jesus is the Christ," etc. It is impossible more distinctly to assert that the Gospel is a religious memoir.

No less clear is the statement of St. Luke. He says "that he wrote in order to the most excellent Theophilus, that he might know the certainty of the things in which he had been instructed." The original shows that the instruction was given with a definite religious purpose. The Gospel is "a declaration of those things most surely believed among Christians." In one word, the work is a memoir, and not a history.

If it be replied that Luke says that he wrote "in order," (εν ταξει), I answer that there are other orderly arrangements besides those of time and place; and that if a work is a religious memoir, the arrangement would be regulated, though not exclusively, by the reference of the facts to the religious end in view.

The assertions of the other two Gospels are not so express, but viewed in connection with their contents they prove that they belong to the same class of writings. Mark writes, "The beginning of the good news of Jesus Christ, the Son of God." Here a religious purpose is asserted to be the guiding principle of the work. Matthew, in accordance with Hebrew phraseology, entitles his work "The book of the generation of Jesus Christ, the Son of David, the son of Abraham." The whole contents of the Gospel answer to this description. It was written to prove that Jesus was the Messiah of prophecy according to the conceptions of Jewish Christianity.

Such being the distinct assertions of the writers of the Gospels as to the character of their works, it is absurd to criticize them as one might be justly entitled to do if four Boswells had set forth four lives of Dr. Johnson, the arrangement of which was professedly regulated by the historical sequence. The writer of a religious memoir is entitled to adopt a very different order of events in his narrative from that which ought to be adopted by the writer of a history.

An illustration will make this matter plain. If I were to compose a biography of Wesley, I should be bound to narrate the events in the order of time, with a distinct specification of the order of place; but if I were to compose a memoir for the purpose of teaching the doctrines of Wesleyanism, I should follow a very different arrangement. Still more remarkable would be the variation in the arrangement if I wrote his memoir for the purpose of proving that Wesley never designed that the Church which he founded should dissent from the Church of England.

Such being the character of the Gospels, objections which would be serious as against regular histories are harmless against compositions of this description. A large portion of their alleged discrepancies arise from the different arrangement of the events narrated in them, owing to the predominance in them of the religious idea.

Now observe that in compositions of this description it frequently happens that the connecting links which would make events perfectly harmonize together, are wanting, simply because the purpose of the writer has not led him to record them. I adduce a single instance where the connecting link has been accidentally preserved, and which at once converts a narrative against which most serious objections might have been alleged, into one of the strongest proofs of the historical truthfulness of the Evangelists.

We all remember the account of the murder of John the Baptist. It is told with all those minute and delicate touches which are the peculiar indication of autoptic testimony. It places before our eyes the great feast—the young lady dancing her lascivious dance—the words of Herod's vow—the girl's going out with excitement to her mother—the demand of the Baptist's head in a large dish—the sorrow and reluctant consent of Herod—the mission of the executioner—the presentation of the head to the girl, and by her to her mother. Everything betokens the presence of an eye-witness.

The narrative is open to this obvious objection: How could the disciples of Christ, mean and low as they were, procure so accurate a description of an event which happened in the palace at the great feast? There were neither newspapers nor reporters in those days. But this is only the beginning of the difficulty. The authors of the Gospels profess to give us the *ipsissima verba* which were uttered by Herod, in the retirement of his palace, when the reports brought him of the fame of Jesus rendered him conscience-stricken. The words are most remarkable, and leave no alternative between their being the words of Herod or a forgery. "It is John," says he, "whom I beheaded: he is risen from the dead, and therefore mighty works do show forth themselves in him." Our version spoils the force of the last words—*αἱ δυνάμεις ἐνεργοῦσιν ἐν αὐτῷ*—which, rendered literally, are, "The powers energize in him." This is certainly a most singular expression, and one open to a strong suspicion of forgery; for how could the followers of Jesus have got hold of the very words of an utterance of Herod spoken in the retirement of the palace?

But besides all this, the words *αἱ δυνάμεις ἐνεργοῦσιν ἐν αὐτῷ* plainly imply that it was the general idea that a large number of miracles had been wrought by our Lord. My opponents suppose that the historic Jesus only attempted to work miracles in a very few questionable cases, and that the multitude of miracles which have been subsequently ascribed to Him are the inventions of His deluded followers. Such are the difficulties. Now for their solution.

It has been observed that the author of the Acts of the Apostles tells us that among the teachers of the Church at Antioch during Paul's sojourn there, was Manaen, who was a foster-brother of Herod the Tetrarch. This is told us in a manner which is purely incidental, and supplies us with a possible source from whence the information might have been derived. Still it by no means follows that a man who had the same wet-nurse as Herod was an inmate of his palace, or witnessed the great feast.

But a passage of the most incidental character in St. Luke's Gospel supplies us with the source of information which we want. In narrating our Lord's last journey to Jerusalem, Luke tells us that He was accompanied by the twelve apostles, and several women who ministered to Him. Of these he designates three by name. One of these is described as Joanna, the wife of Chuza, Herod's steward.

Here then we have the very person we are in want of. Chuza's office of ἐπίτροπος, or steward, imposed on him the duty of superintending the great feast. He therefore witnessed the whole procedure, and his wife was in constant communication with the disciples. His office must have brought him into daily communication with his master. What more likely than when he waited on Herod for his orders, he would ask him the news; and that he should report to him the fame of the great teacher with whom his wife was in attendance? He was therefore in the exact situation to have heard Herod's conscience-stricken exclamation. The source of information is before us. The incidental mention of Joanna and her husband affords to this narrative an attestation such as few events in past history possess. If this incident had been lost, the difficulty would have been insuperable. The manner in which little circumstances dovetail into one another in the Gospels is only consistent with their historical character. It would be impossible if they were bundles of myths or legends.

I adduce one instance of the manner in which the Gospels fulfil the conditions of history, even where the absence of the connecting link has occasioned serious difficulty. You all know that the want of any reference in the Synoptics to the miracle of the resurrection of Lazarus is the stronghold of those who deny its historical credibility. In the absence of any direct information, we are driven for the solution of the difficulty to the regions of conjecture.

Let us suppose, then, that the story is a myth. If so, it is obvious that it is a very grand and perfect one. The inventor must have been a man of the highest genius in his way. If a person wished to invent a description of a resurrection, he would find it impossible, in the same number of words, to surpass its perfection. If the author of St. John's Gospel has failed to depict another resurrection in an equally graphic manner, it was not for want of sufficient genius. Yet the Gospel asserts the fact of another resurrection—that of Jesus Christ; but it utters not one word descriptive of it. All that it says is that Mary Magdalene came in the morning, and found the tomb empty.

I put it to your common sense to determine, on the supposition that this Gospel was written by a partisan for the purpose of throwing a halo of glory around the person of his Master, whether the author of the resurrection of Lazarus would not have forged a still more magnificent description of the resurrection of Jesus Christ. His failure to do so is clearly not owing to lack of ability.

But how stands the case on the supposition that the Gospel is historical? Everything is exactly as it should be. The Evangelist has given his pictorial description of the resurrection of Lazarus, because he witnessed it. He has not done so with respect to the resurrection of Jesus Christ, because no human eye beheld it. The narrative therefore fulfils the conditions of history, and breaks down under the tests which belong to fiction.

The limits of a single lecture necessarily preclude me from entering on any minor consideration.* I therefore proceed at once to address myself to the demolition of the central position of my opponents, that while the Gospels contain a few grains of historic truth, buried beneath a multitude of fables, the greater portion of their contents is a spontaneous growth which sprung up in the bosom of the Christian society in the last seventy years of the first century; and that by means of a number of mythical and legendary inventions,

* Those who wish to see the cumulative force of the entire argument will find it in "the Jesus of the Evangelists." It is impossible to compress its reasonings.

and a succession of developments, a good and holy Jew, named Jesus, was metamorphosed into the divine Christ of the Evangelists. In reasoning on this point, I shall assume nothing but what is conceded by the Schools in question.

What are the concessions which I ask as the foundations of my reasoning? Very simple ones indeed, and such that no man can deny me. First, that the Gospels exist; secondly, that the three first Gospels were in existence about A.D. 100, and the fourth about 160; thirdly, that in addition to the facts or fictions which make up our Gospels, they contain the delineation of a great character—Jesus Christ.

On the existence of this character my argument is founded. I now concentrate your attention on it, which I shall call for the future the portraiture of Jesus Christ our Lord. I need not prove that it exists in the Gospels, for the most ordinary reader perceives that it is there. The question is, How did it get there? It is very easy to say that the Gospels consist of a mass of fictions. But this is no account of the origin of the portraiture. St. Paul's Cathedral undoubtedly consists of an immense multitude of stones. But to say that a multitude of quarrymen dug them, and that a multitude of masons arranged them according to their spontaneous impulses, is no account of the origin of that magnificent structure.

Let us carefully observe what this great portraiture of Jesus Christ, as it is exhibited in the Gospels, consists of. It is the delineation of a great moral and spiritual character dramatized over a wide sphere of action. This portraiture is not the result of the artificial delineation of a character such as we see very commonly presented to us by historians, and of which we see very numerous examples in Lord Macaulay's History of England. Such characters are the artificial creations of the historian, and exhibit his view of what his heroes actually were. But neither of the authors of the Gospels have once attempted thus to delineate the character of his Master. But the portraiture of Jesus Christ is delineated in the Gospels most clearly and most distinctly. Of what materials then does it consist? Only one answer can be returned. It is the combined result of all the facts, or, as my opponents say, fictions, which compose the Gospels.

Now as the existence of this portraiture is not a theory, but a fact, it is plain that it must be accounted for. The assumption that the Gospels are historically true, and that their authors have truly delineated the actions and sayings of one who had an historical existence, is a rational account of its origin. But as these Schools deny their historical character, they are bound to tell us how the portraiture got there. The only answers which they propound are the mythic and Tübingen theories.

According to these theories, a good and holy Jew, who had attracted a crowd of enthusiastic and credulous followers, was gradually metamorphosed by them into the divine Christ of the Evangelists. The inventors of the character were impelled by purely spontaneous instincts. They had no intention of conscious deception. They mistook their Master for the Messiah. In the depths of their enthusiastic credulity, they invented multitudes of fictions, and in time mistook them for realities, and innocently ascribed them to Jesus. Development succeeded development. The fruitful mind of the infant Church created myth after myth. Party spirit raged. Compromise followed compromise. Spontaneous impulse by the end of the century had created the materials of our present Gospels. At last three unknown men appeared who arranged these materials into their present form, and produced the Synoptics. Sixty years later, another great unknown arose, whose character must have been a compound of mysticism, enthusiasm, and imposture, and produced the fourth Gospel, which he successfully palmed off on the Church as the work of the Apostle John, some seventy or eighty years after he was silent in the grave. Such is the alternative which modern unbelief presents as a substitute for the historical reality of the portraiture of Jesus Christ as we behold it in the Gospels.

One cannot help pausing to observe the kind of analogy

which exists between these theories and those of a certain class of philosophers who attempt to prove that the moral and religious being whom we designate man has been slowly developed out of the lower forms of life by causes purely physical. Like as in the one case each development became an improvement on its predecessor, so in the other the lower fabulous creations must have died out, and the nobler ones prevailed, until at last there emerged from them Christianity and the glorious Christ of the Gospels. Physical philosophers, however, work at a great advantage in developing an ape into a moral being, compared with the mythologists who developed a Jew of the year 30 into a Christ. The one can draw cheques to any extent on the bank of eternity. If a million of years is not sufficient, a million of millions may be easily had. But in the other case my opponents are limited by the stern conditions of history; and the respective periods of seventy and one hundred and thirty years are all that they venture even to demand.

Now, observe; the portraiture of the Jesus of the Evangelists consists of a multitude of parts which harmoniously blend into a complicated whole. It is composed, in fact, of as many distinct portions as there are incidents recorded in the Gospels, which all concur in imparting to it a common effect. Those with whom I am contending admit that the character is a very great one. Many of them allow that it is greater and more perfect than any which has ever existed as a fact or been conceived as a fiction. Yet the character, taken as a whole, presents us with an essential unity. This is obviously the case in the three first Gospels, and will hardly be disputed except on a very few subordinate points. But it is equally remarkable that of the various traits which compose the character, and which are very numerous, each presents us with a similar unity, although they are dramatized over a very wide sphere of action. To this fact I earnestly invite your attention. In the portraiture of Jesus at least twenty distinct aspects of moral character are blended together, and a number of subordinate ones not easy to be counted; and each of these constitutes a separate unity, which harmoniously blends with the others, and together compose the great unity of the portraiture. Numerous as they are, and dramatized over a wide sphere of action, they are yet depicted with a faultless propriety, even in the most minute details. Nor does it to any serious extent differ with the fourth Gospel. This is certainly the case as far as the actions attributed to Jesus are concerned, though it is not so obvious in the case of the discourses. Still even in these an underlying unity of conception can be found.* The four Gospels contain, in

* See Appendix to "St. John's Testimony to Christ," in Professor Leathes' Boyle Lectures. No one who has not read this can form an

fact, four portraitures of one and the same Christ, only differing from each other in the point of view from which they are taken.

Now the obvious course would have been to have assumed that the conception of the original character was the creation of some great poet, and that the fourfold modification of it which our present Gospels exhibit has been the work of four subsequent poets. But this supposition the facts and phenomena of the case consign to the region of hopeless impossibilities. It is therefore necessary to assume that the character itself, and the Christianity of the New Testament, have been gradually elaborated bit by bit, not by a succession of great poets, but of credulous, enthusiastic mythologists; and that the Synoptic Gospels originated in piecing together a multitude of tales which in the latter end of the first century were floating on the surface of the Christian Church.

It is impossible to deny that the Jesus of the Evangelists is an immeasurably finer conception than either the Prometheus of Æschylus, which exhibits the divine in suffering, or the Macbeth or Hamlet of Shakspeare. Each of these characters is distinguished by a unity of conception which proves that as characters they are the creation of a single mind. But supposing we were to be told that these, and the

idea of the extent of similarity of thought and expression to the fourth Gospel which underlies the Synoptics.

dramas which contain them, were not the creations of single poets, nor even of a succession of poets, but had been slowly elaborated, step by step, during a considerable interval of time by a number of credulous enthusiasts. My opponents would be the first to receive such a suggestion with shouts of derision.

It is plain that if the portraiture of our Lord be an ideal creation, those who framed it must have been gifted with a high order of genius.

Let me illustrate the position by the art of painting. High genius in painting is analogous to high genius in poetry. Let us suppose that we are contemplating a great ideal picture,—*e. g.*, the Marriage Feast in Cana of Galilee, at the Louvre,—and that we are told that it is not the work of a single artist, nor even of four, but of a succession who gradually developed it.

Nor, to make the case a parallel one, is this all which we should be asked to believe. As I have already observed, the portraiture of the Jesus of the Evangelists is made up of a multitude of parts, each of which has a separate unity, from the union of which the unity of the whole results. These are said to have been elaborated out of a number of myths and developments which have been the creations of many minds. In a similar manner the picture of the Marriage Feast at Cana consists of a number of separate figures which harmoniously blend into a whole, and to which the magnificent colouring has been adapted. Now suppose that we were told that each of these figures had been gradually developed into its present form by a set of improvements effected unconsciously by a succession of painters; and that all that the artist who formed the picture did was skilfully to combine these separate figures, and place them in juxtaposition. Surely one would not be uncharitable in assuming that the author of such a suggestion had escaped from a lunatic asylum.

Similar is the theory of these Schools as to the origin of the Gospels, and of the great character contained in them. Such a theory of their origin demands our acquiescence in a greater miracle than all the miracles of the New Testament united together.

Viewed in its great outlines, this theory is self-condemned by its inherent absurdity. But when we apply a sound logic to its details, it vanishes like one of the palaces of the Arabian Nights. Professing to be based on rational principles, it violates all the laws of reason. For historic truth it substitutes wild dreams of the imagination.

You will please to keep steadily in mind that the means by which my opponents undertake to metamorphose a Jew of the year 30 into a divine Christ, stated generally, are a succession of mythical and legendary creations and developments, contests and compromises, between hostile sects evolved in conformity with the laws of the intellectual and moral world. Let us now assume the truth of their position, and see how it will work.

If the Jesus of the Evangelists be a development, it is evident that it must have had a starting-point. This could have been none other than the atmosphere of thought and feeling which existed in Judæa during the first thirty years of the first century.*

But none more firmly profess their belief in the reign of law in the world of mind and matter than those whose theories I am controverting. In consequence of this belief they pronounce all supernatural interventions in human affairs impossible. I thankfully concede to them the fact that all developments affecting the mind of man which are of purely human origin must be brought about in conformity with law. Let it be clearly understood, therefore, that my reasoning is based on this assumption.

This point being clear, the question immediately presents itself, what is the nature of the laws which regulate the mental developments of man, especially in his character of a moral and religious being? Are they rapid, or do they require

* To give precision to the argument, it is necessary to determiné its definite character. But it is impossible to do so within the limits of a single lecture.

long intervals of time for their elaboration? Are great changes in our moral or religious ideas of aquick or a slow growth? The answer to these questions is of vital importance to the argument, because on the showing of my opponents they have only seventy years at their command during which they can develop the Christ of the Synoptics, and the Christianity of nearly all the Epistles, from the religious and moral ideas of the Judaism of the year 30.

Fortunately for us, the universal testimony of history answers these questions with no ambiguous voice. The developments of man, whether moral, social, or religious, are slow. The whole course of civilization, including within that term everything which relates to the growth of the mind of man, and which tends to his refinement and higher culture, is a very gradual one; and its successive stages require long intervals of time for their development. Whenever unbelievers attempt to account for the growth of human civilization from a savage state, or to develop a man out of an ape, in the one case they demand tens of thousands and in the other millions of years for its accomplishment. As this point is of great importance to the argument, I must adduce distinctive proof of it.

No truth is more certain than that it is impossible for men, either individually or collectively, to raise themselves except by very gradual stages above that moral and spiritual atmosphere in which they were born. We are united by the closest ties of habit and education with the past. We breathe from the dawn of our consciousness the very atmosphere of its thought and feeling. Every succeeding state of society is most closely bound to that which preceded it. Every great change in thought or feeling has been produced by a succession of changes leaving no deep gulf between. Individual progress, unless external influences are brought to bear on the mind, follows the same law of gradual growth.

Even genius, and what are called the creative powers of the mind, are fettered by these conditions. All greatness is relative to and bears the impress of the age which produced it. Great men differ from others only in being able to advance a few stages beyond ordinary humanity. But the greatest genius is unable to elevate itself into a very high region of thought or feeling at a single bound, or to sever the links which unite it with the past. The utmost effect which the greatest of men have been able to produce on those by whom they have been surrounded is to cause their actual developments to advance at a somewhat accelerated ratio.

To the truth of these general principles all history testifies. When we measure each stage of human growth, we find that it has occupied long intervals of time. So gradual is the process, that considerable changes can only be discovered after the lapse of lengthened periods. The whole history of philosophy, art, morality, and religion testifies to this. All philosophic schools of thought have been of gradual growth. The daub of a savage has never suddenly developed itself into the creations of a Michael Angelo or a Rubens, nor have his rough imitations of the human form passed but by a succession of gradual stages into the perfection of a Phidias. Poetry, the most creative of arts, is subject to similar conditions. The ideas with which the poet works are those of the age in which he lives. He paints the phenomena and reflects the line of thought, the morality, the religion, the intellectual and social conditions of the times which gave him birth. What he accomplishes is to exhibit them under new combinations. A bushman never at a single bound became a Homer or a Shakspeare.

The history of philosophy bears witness that the universal law of our nature is a gradual growth. Each of its developments was closely allied to that which preceded it, and directly grew out of it. Each School has occupied a considerable time in its development, has grown out of that which preceded it, and prepared the way for its successor. The interval which separates the respective stages is small. Each great race of mankind has also created a philosophy stamped with its own impress, and directly related to its peculiar character. A native of Australia has never suddenly elevated himself into a Socrates.

The same law is no less applicable to religions. We know no instance of the direct creation of one. It is true that the origin of many is buried in the obscurity of the past. Yet as soon as they emerge into the light of history, it is clear that they are subject to a law of gradual growth; and after they have attained their full development, to a no less remarkable law of gradual decay. All the religions on earth, with the exception of Christianity, bear witness to this rule. What have been called new religions, have been evolved out of previously existing materials, modified and adapted to the growth and decay of civilization. No Fetish worshipper, however lofty his genius, could have evolved the systems of Brahmanism or Buddhism by a single bound of his imagination.

If the law of the growth of religions is a very gradual one, that of our moral ideas is far more so. Improvements in the great moral principles which regulate the life of man are most painfully slow. All the great races of mankind have presented the same general outlines of character, with only slight improvements, from age to age. I quote only two examples, the modern French and Germans. How strikingly like are certain portions of the character of the former, to the picture of the Gauls given in the pages of

Cæsar; or to the descriptions of the same race inhabiting a distant region which the great apostle has drawn in the Epistle to the Galatians. We may still read the general outline of the character of the German race in the pages of Tacitus. Developments there have been, and the slowness is sadly disappointing to the philanthropist. To be able even to recognize progress, we must survey long intervals of time. The optimist has indeed need of patience; and the most enthusiastic may be certain that long ages before any considerable advance is made, according to the mere laws of natural development, he will be slumbering in the grave.

But it must not be forgotten that the developments which our opponents postulate are always in the way of progressive improvements. Stern historical fact compels us to assert that developments are frequently retrogressive.

No less gradual is the moral progress of the individual. It is also a painful but undeniable fact that retrogressive ones are much more rapid than progressive ones. The moral ideas in the midst of which we are educated cling to us with the firmest grasp. The best men exhibit only a slight advance above the general morality of their age.

I now draw your attention to the fact that the inventive powers of the composer of fiction are limited by the same laws. He too, in the strict sense of that term, is unable to create the new. The materials with which he can work are the idealization of the times in which he lives. Whether he be poet or novel writer, he can neither invent a new religion or a new morality. Mythical inventions of every kind embody the state of thought, feeling, and general idealization of the times which produced them. The entire mass of existing mythology testifies to this fact.

Such, then, are the instruments and materials with which my opponents have to work in the elaboration of Christianity out of Judaism, and in metamorphosing a human Jesus into a divine Christ. Let us examine the possibility of the attempt.

We must place ourselves in the position of the followers of Jesus on the evening of the crucifixion. His individual influence had gathered around Him a number of enthusiastic and credulous followers who mistook Him for the Messiah of popular expectation. The crucifixion certainly dashed their hopes. But according to the theory of my opponents, in the height of their enthusiasm they determined to believe in Him as the Messiah still. To carry out this resolution, it is obvious that new ground had to be taken. A development of some kind was absolutely necessary. No amount of credulity could mistake a dead body mouldering in the grave for the Messiah of Jewish expectation.

It was absolutely necessary, therefore, if His Messiahship

could become a possibility, that the crucified Jesus should be rescued from the tomb. If a resurrection could not be effected in reality, it was indispensable that one should be in imagination. Until His followers could be brought in considerable numbers to believe that this had happened, no developments in the direction of the Gospels were possible.

The most obvious expedient to have accomplished this would have been for some of the disciples to have done that which, according to one of the Evangelists, the Jews accused them of, viz., to have stolen the body, and report that Jesus was risen from the dead. But those against whom I am reasoning do not venture to accuse them of conscious fraud. This assumption all educated unbelievers have long abandoned as hopelessly untenable. Such a basis will certainly not bear the weight of the Christianity of the New Testament. In place of this, they assume that the credulity, idealism, and enthusiasm of the followers of Jesus was bottomless. With this machinery they think that He can be rescued from the grave.

Two theories have been propounded for this purpose. One is that some enthusiastic woman—Mary Magdalene, for example—thought that she saw Jesus with the mind's eye, or mistook the gardener for Him, and converted this appearance into a bodily reality. She communicated her enthusiasm to the rest. Others may have imagined that they saw Him in a similar manner, and committed a similar mistake. The other theory is that He was buried in a swoon, that He managed to creep out of His grave, that He partially recovered, and died shortly after in retirement. On such a foundation my opponents propose to erect the whole weight of the historic Church, and from such a chimera to develop the portraiture of the divine Christ.

The second theory I should not have mentioned if it had not been dignified by the name of Bunsen. It is obvious that it will not support the weight of the Christian Church. What! a man who died from weakness shortly after creeping out of his grave, metamorphised by his followers into a divine Messiah, and seated on the right hand of God! If He lived in retirement, and died in Phœnicia shortly afterwards,—according to an assumption for which there is not even the ghost of historical testimony,—His followers had access to Him or they had not. If we adopt the former part of the alternative, no amount of credulity could have mistaken Him for a glorious Messiah rescued from the tomb. The very sight of Him must have acted as a complete extinguisher on the powers of the imagination. If we adopt the latter, it falls under the general head that the belief in the resurrection was merely due to an excited imagination. All the assistance which it renders is to dispose of the dead body.

Now, in theory, nothing is easier than to say that an excited woman saw Jesus with her mental eye, mistook it for a bodily reality, and communicated her enthusiasm to the rest of His followers. But in practice, such things are not quite so easy. Although it is no hard matter to persuade the credulous to believe in the appearance of ghosts and phantoms, yet I do not know that the whole history of man presents us with a single example of a great institution which owes its origin to such a belief. But even the credulous believers in such apparitions are very difficult to persuade that they have actually seen a man who once had died again restored to life. I doubt whether the entire mass of fictitious literature presents us with anything at all analogous to the supposed belief of the credulous followers of Jesus in the resurrection of their Master. Even persons who have a most imperfect knowledge that nature is governed by law, are quite aware that dead men do not revive. The followers of Jesus could have been hardly more credulous than modern spiritualists, yet these latter have not yet succeeded in erecting a great institution on the basis of an actual resurrection from the dead, or even on the presence of a spirit in a table. Supposing, therefore, that some fanatic follower of our Lord made the mistake in question, it could really have been no easy matter to have communicated this enthusiasm to the rest, damped as their spirits were by the crucifixion. Still more difficult would it have been for any considerable number to have made the mistake of converting a flight of the imagination into an objective fact. At any rate my opponents must concede that to have persuaded any number of men under such circumstances that the crucified Jesus was actually risen from the dead must have required a considerable interval of time.

It would be much more easy to create a belief in a resurrection after the lapse of a century, than within a few years of the event. When we survey a past event through the haze of time, it helps to confuse our ideas as to what is possible. But long intervals of time so convenient for the physical speculator are precisely the things which my opponents have not at their disposal. Seventy years is all which they themselves think it possible to ask for; and as all developments are slow, one or two entirely exhaust it, and they require a multitude to effect their purpose. But not only was it necessary to get some of the enthusiastic followers of our Lord to believe in His resurrection, but also to constitute a society founded on its basis. Until this was done, all development was impossible. But each step requires a considerable interval of time. But how could the Church be held together while the belief in the resurrection was forming?

But even supposing that Jesus by the power of the imagination had been rescued from the grave, it became a very serious question what to do with Him. No amount of credulity could have brought Him into daily communication with His followers. If He continued on earth, His not doing so was a very serious affair. The obvious expedient was that He should be taken up into heaven, from which at some future day he should come back again and take possession of his Messianic throne. Such is the idea adopted by these schools of thought, and they are never wearied with telling us that the chief if not the only article in the primitive belief of the followers of Jesus was His speedy return to realize their expectations of His Messianic glory.

Be it so; for the consequences are very serious to the position of those whose views I am combating. His followers then expected Him to return as the Jewish Messiah. Now nothing is more certain than as long as this expectation lasted there could have been no development in the direction of the Christ of the Gospels. How long, then, did this state of stagnation last in the bosom of the Church? When did it occur to the followers of Jesus that the expectation of the speedy return of their Master was a baseless one, and that they must set themselves to work to develop a different conception of a Christ? It is a fact that such beliefs do not speedily die out, and that they can survive many a disappointment. The modern prophetic School affords a striking proof of the tenacity of such hopes. They have repeatedly prophesied that the Advent will happen in our times; and notwithstanding the falsification of their predictions, I believe that they still cling to this belief. At any rate it has required a long interval of time to undeceive them; and as credulity was, according to the views which I am combating, the leading trait of the followers of Jesus, it must have been a considerable interval of time before they could have been persuaded to part company with their darling expectation. But as long as a Jewish Messiah satisfied their aspirations, the Church could have developed no new Messianic conceptions.

But to afford something like a basis for reasoning, I will suppose these obstacles to have been surmounted; that the work of development has commenced, and that the womb of the Church is at last become pregnant with its future Christ. Fresh and ever-increasing difficulties present themselves for solution.

Let it be observed that, after they have effected the resurrection, all which has been accomplished was to repair the damage inflicted on the Church by the crucifixion, and to restore to it, as a necessity of its existence, a living instead of a dead Messiah. That Messiah was still the

Messiah of Judaism. They have scarcely advanced a stage in the creation of the Gospels, and of the Christ therein delineated,—not to say of the entire moral and spiritual teaching of the New Testament.

Let us observe the steps of the process by which the metamorphose must have been effected. It is, say my opponents, very uncertain whether the historic Jesus ever attempted to perform a miracle. But according to the conceptions of the times, His followers thought that the Messiah ought to have performed them. To supply the defect, they invented a mass of miraculous stories, and in their fond credulity thought that Jesus had actually performed them, and thus the delusion of His miraculous wonder-working was propagated in the Church. But all experience proves that mythic and legendary miracles are grotesque. Yet those in the Gospels are all sober ones, and stamped with a high moral tone. They must therefore have undergone a succession of developments before they could have assumed their present form. Still a Jewish Messiah has yet to be transformed into the Jesus of the Evangelists. After a while a happy thought occurs to these uninstructed Jews. They determine to invest the Teacher with whom they had habitually conversed with a character at once divine and human. The mythic faculty is again invoked, and the human Jesus, by the aid of development after development, gradually assumes the aspect of the divine Christ. In a similar manner they feel that the moral aspect of the Messiah of their fondest expectations must undergo a change, and in due time the triumphant King becomes the meek and the lowly Jesus, and the morality of Pharisaism becomes that of the New Testament.

Few persons are at all aware of the enormous difficulties which would have beset any persons who, whether consciously or unconsciously, set themselves to metamorphise a Jew of the year 30 into the Christ of the Gospels. Familiarity with the character induces numbers to think that poets or fabulists, inventors of myths and legends, might easily have created it. To form a correct estimate of the difficulty, it is necessary to transport ourselves out of the nineteenth century into the Jewish atmosphere of thought and feeling of the century which preceded the Advent. A starting-point it must have had. There could have been no other than it.

Let it be observed that before the elaboration of the Jesus of the Gospels, those who fabricated the conception were wholly without a model to guide them. All ancient fact or fable fails to furnish anything at all analogous to this great character. Such models as they had would have guided its inventors wrong. The only ones which they possessed were the popular Messianic conceptions of the period, and the prevailing Jewish ideas of religion and morality. Besides these, they might have fallen back on the general ideas contained in the Old Testament Scriptures and the apocryphal books. The ideal of a Jewish hero would certainly not have helped them in forming the conception of the Evangelical Jesus. One apocryphal book has been frequently referred to as affording considerable aid —the Book of Enoch. I have fully discussed this subject elsewhere,* and the conclusion to which I have arrived is, I think, incontrovertible, that even if we grant that its Messianic portions were composed prior to the Christian era (a concession which I am by no means prepared to make), the aid which it would have afforded the mythologists who invented the Christ of the Gospels would have been inconsiderable. To avoid a lengthened controversy as to its date, I am quite willing that these schools of thought should make all the use they can of them.

Let me point out a few of the difficulties which must have beset the path of the inventors of the great portraiture of the Gospels.

Every reader at once recognizes that the character who is there depicted is a superhuman one; or rather, to speak more accurately, it is exhibited as uniting the human and the divine. This is a plain matter of fact, and is quite

* "Jesus of the Evangelists," chap. x.

independent of the question whether the Evangelists were right in so representing it. Nor is my argument at all affected by any supposed difficulty in defining, in the terms of an abstract creed, the precise measure of the divine which they have ascribed to it. All that I contend for is that the Jesus of the Evangelists is dramatized as uniting a divine and human consciousness, and that it is exhibited with a faultless propriety.

Now the moment the mythologists made a movement in this direction, a hundred problems of a most difficult character must have demanded their solution before they could advance a single step. I can only adduce one or two examples. How was the human to be represented as acting in union with the divine, and the divine with the human? In what proportions were they to be combined? How was the one to be prevented from swallowing up the other? Let it be observed that there was no model to guide them. The attempt to exhibit the divine and human in a single personality had never been attempted before.

The difficulty will be at once seen from a reference to the Old Testament. The nearest approach which it exhibits to uniting the human and the divine is in the act of prophetic inspiration. But in this the two factors are invariably distinct. The Old Testament prophet, when under the influence of the prophetical illapse, invariably prefaces his utterances with "Thus saith the Lord." These words are never once placed in the mouth of Jesus throughout the entire Gospels. Instead of them, His most solemn utterances are introduced with the words, "I say unto you." The prophet is generally vehemently excited. The Jesus of the Evangelists is invariably calm.

You must never forget that the position of those against whose theories I am reasoning compels them to assume that the contents of the Gospels have been elaborated by the action of a multitude of minds. Be it so. It follows that these problems must have received as many different solutions as there were minds engaged in the attempt. Instead of the character which resulted therefrom presenting a unity of aspect, it would have been a mass of hopeless confusion.

My limits will only allow me to draw your attention to one or two of these difficulties out of the vast multitude. The historical Jesus was unquestionably crucified. How was a crucified man to be represented as divine? He died in agony. How was an artist to dramatize the divine in suffering? If my hearers are not aware of the difficulties which would have attended the solution of these and kindred questions, I advise them to study the creation of the great Grecian dramatist, the Prometheus Vinctus of Æschylus, and compare it with the Jesus of the Gospels. I am sure that correct taste will pronounce that the creation of the fishermen of Galilee utterly transcends that of the genius of the great tragedian.

Nothing is more difficult, even in works of fiction, than to combine the attributes of holiness and benevolence as harmoniously acting in the same person. In living men they almost invariably jar. They possess them imperfectly, and one generally counteracts the action of the other. The difficulty of combining them is greatly increased if the being uniting them is to be represented as both human and divine. Holiness and benevolence are in fact opposite sides of character, and no more difficult problem can be presented to the imagination than to exhibit them as acting harmoniously in the same character. No question in theology is more embarrassing than the mode in which they coexist in God.

It follows that if the contents of the Gospels were due to a multitude of minds, they must have exhibited as many aspects of the character of a Christ as there were fabulists engaged in its creation. But the character of the Jesus of the Gospels, in its combination of holiness with benevolence, presents us with a complete unity. Not only is the unity complete, but the perfection of the picture is inimitable. Where can we find, either in fact or fiction, anything like the perfection of the holiness and benevolence of the Jesus of the Evangelists? Yet we are asked to believe that it has been a gradual growth created by successions of credulous mythologists.

The moral and religious teaching of the Gospels forms a subject by itself of large dimensions, and it is impossible for me within the limits of a lecture to do more than glance at it.* It consists of two perfectly distinct portions: first, the subject of morality and religion as it is exhibited in the person of Jesus Christ; secondly, as He taught them for the use of ordinary men. Most unbelievers will admit that the portraiture of Jesus Christ, as it is exhibited in the Gospels, is one of the most spotless moral beauty, and the greatest elevation. I am quite aware that a few exceptions have been made to it; but some of them are obviously founded on misapprehension, and others are evidently incorrect. At any rate it cannot be denied that the entire moral aspect of the person of Christ is unique in human literature.

No less remarkable is His moral teaching for the use of ordinary men. It is pure, elevated, beneficent, grand. It bears the unquestionable marks of having been the elaboration of a single mind. The parts are adapted to each other and to the whole.

But our Lord's moral character, and His moral teaching as they are exhibited in the Gospels, consist of a number of

* See "Jesus of the Evangelists," chap. v.

detached portions, which together make up a complicated whole. Their solution involves such a multiplicity of questions, as to render it difficult to count them. They are questions which the profoundest thinkers have solved in the most varied manner. Yet in the Gospels the mode of their solution is a complete unity. They coalesce with an inimitable beauty. Let unbelievers cavil as they may, an overwhelming majority of the holiest and the best of men have bowed before the character of the Jesus of the Evangelists in humble adoration, and felt that it was immeasurably above them. Numbers of these subjects were inquired into by ancient philosophers with the keenest interest, but they found no adequate solution. My opponents assert that this great character, around which the entire morality of Christianity centres, is not an historical one. How did it then originate? The answer is, that it is founded on the traditional reminiscences of the teaching of a Jewish peasant who died in early manhood; and that the numerous parts of which the character and His teaching consist were unconsciously elaborated in the course of many years by a multitude of credulous, enthusiastic mythologists.

I must now advance to another stage of my argument. As my opponents assert that the development of the Gospels, and of the portraiture of the Christ which they contain, were entirely due to natural causes, it is evident that they must have been effected in conformity with the laws which regulate the developments of the human mind. Let us test this principle.

Taking the atmosphere of Jewish thought and feeling as it existed in the year 30 as the starting-point, it is evident to every one at all acquainted with the subject, that the interval which separates its conceptions from those of the Gospels is far greater than that which separates any two types of human thought. To take a single example. The interval between the free spirit of morality as it is exhibited in the New Testament, and the casuistic and ritualistic tendencies of moral thought which ultimately developed themselves into Rabbinism, is profound. If, therefore, Christianity grew out of Judaism by a succession of natural causes, the interval between them must have been bridged over by a succession of developments. So, again, with respect to Messianic conceptions. A profound interval separates that of Christ from that of Barchocebas, to which Jewish Messianism was then tending. That of Barchocebas was a natural growth out of the popular Messianic conceptions of the year 30, and separated from them by no great interval. But their development occupied no less than a century. But if the Jesus of the Evangelists grew out of the popular idea of the year 30, it is evident that the succession of developments must have been very numerous, and have required long intervals of time, before it was possible to create the portraiture of Christ.

Let me take another example, which those against whom I am reasoning cannot refuse to accept. The interval which separates the state of religious and moral thought involved in the primitive Mosaic institutions from that of the year 30 is considerable, though far less than that which separates the latter from that contained in the Gospels. In adducing this example, I use one most favourable to my opponents. Christians maintain that this development was accelerated by supernatural causes. The proper subject of comparison would have been one which both sides are agreed to have been effected by causes purely natural. I need not however fear making the concession, for it will more than bear the weight of my argument. We will suppose that the entire history of Judaism, as those with whom I am reasoning say, contained in it nothing supernatural. I ask you therefore to observe that the development in question was completed only after an interval of more than a thousand years from its commencement. Yet we are invited to believe that the Christianity of the Synoptics, and of the larger portion of the Epistles, was evolved in a period of seventy years, and the Christian Church erected on them, as its foundation, and that of the fourth Gospel in 130 years.

Let us take another mode of measurement of my opponents' own choosing. The Synoptic Gospels, as they say, are separated from that of St. John by an interval of sixty years. Is it possible to bridge over the interval which separates the Synoptics from the Jewish atmosphere of thought and feeling of the year 30, in seventy years, if it required sixty years to effect the development in question?

Against one convenient assumption I must present a most respectful protest. Whenever it suits their purpose, the human Jesus is represented as a very great man, who towered high above the ordinary conditions of humanity. Again, when it is convenient He is represented to have been a very little man, the prey of all the superstitions of His age. I am prepared to reason on either side of this alternative, but not on both. These Schools postulate greatness whenever they want to make a prodigious leap in religion and morality; littleness when they want to account for the miraculous element in Christianity. But while I am ready to assume as the basis of the argument that the human Jesus was a great man, let it be understood that He could have been great only in the sense in which all other great men have been great. Those who deny the possibility of physical miracles must not, when it suits their purpose, assume the existence of moral ones. His greatness must have been limited by the conditions imposed on it by the environment of a Jew of the year 30 who was born a peasant, and perished at thirty-five years of age.

Observe again, the miracles of the Gospels have to be invented somehow. I am ready to concede that miraculous stories of a certain type have been invented in rich abundance. But the whole class of fictitious miracles invented in credulous ages are stamped with a peculiar trait from which those of the Gospels are free. The one are monstrous, undignified, and grotesque. The others are sober, dignified, and I think that my opponents will allow, if miracles are possible, worthy of God. The preservation of the apocryphal Gospels enables us to know what sort of miracles the mythic spirit commencing with the next century attributed to Jesus Christ. I have examined the subject elsewhere. The following passage sums up the result :—

"The case stands thus: our Gospels present us with the picture of a glorious Christ; the mythic Gospels with that of a contemptible one. Our Gospels have invested Him with the highest conceivable form of moral greatness; the mythic ones have not ascribed to Him one action which is elevated. In our Gospels He exhibits a superhuman wisdom; in the mythic ones a nearly equal superhuman absurdity. In our Gospels He is arrayed in all the beauty of holiness; in the mythic ones, this aspect is entirely wanting. In our Gospels, not one stain of selfishness defiles His character;

in the mythic ones, the Lord Jesus is both pettish and malicious. Our Gospels exhibit to us a sublime morality; not a ray of it shines in those of the mythologists. The miracles of the one and the other are contrasted in every point. A similar opposition of character runs through the whole current of thought, feeling, morality, and religion." *

I ask my opponents to account for this difference, and specially to say why in the second century the mythic spirit began to create a ridiculous Christ, and in the first it produced a glorious one; and through how many stages of development the creation passed until it culminated in what we read in the Gospels, and the interval of time to be assigned to each.

But according to the theories I am combating, the Messianic aspects of the character of the Jesus of the Evangelists must have passed through a succession of developments before they could have attained their present form. Different parties had to invent different aspects of it. Next, these had to procure acceptance in the various Churches. Each party would cling to its own views. The formation of hostile sects in the Church was a certain con-

* "Jesus of the Evangelists," p. 381. The entire collection of apocryphal Gospels has been translated by Mr. Cowper. I am sure that their perusal will greatly confirm our faith in the historical character of the true. The order of mind which invented the one could not have invented the other.

sequence. If they gradually wore themselves out, all experience of sectarian warfare proves that the interval must have been long. We know as fact that nothing is more difficult than to effect compromises between contending religious factions; and that they are only, if at all, possible after long and bitter experience. I ask you to compute for yourselves how many developments and compromises must have been required, and the interval of time each must have occupied?

Far more difficult and more numerous must have been the developments by which the moral aspects of the Gospels and of their divine Christ must have been elaborated out of the Judaism of the year 30, and the popular conceptions of its Messiah. I shall select for illustration only two examples out of a vast multitude. One of the most marked distinctions between Gospel and ancient moral teaching is this: the whole aspect of ancient moral teaching assigned the highest place to the heroic and political virtues, and a subordinate one to the mild, meek, benevolent, and humbler ones. This is precisely reversed in the morality of the New Testament. Again: the aspect of a Jewish saint and hero, as it is depicted in the Old Testament, forms a singular contrast to that which the New Testament has assigned to Jesus Christ. I have proved that moral developments in the direction of improvement are very slow. I propose, therefore, the following problem for my opponents to solve. Through how many stages must these have passed before the creation of the Gospels became a possibility, and how many years must they have occupied?

But all the while that the Christian Church was creating a mythology, and struggling with developments and contentions and external opposition, it is an historical fact that it succeeded in extending itself over a wide geographical area. This greatly aggravates the difficulty of developing an improved Christ out of her pregnant womb. The wider the geographical area over which she gradually extended herself, the more difficult would have become the interchange of ideas necessary for developments and compromises. It by no means follows that one little society would immediately swallow the mythic creation of another.

I must observe that this portion of the argument is cumulative, and admits of being pressed to an indefinite extent.

It now remains for those against whose theories I have been reasoning to count the number of these developments, and to assign a reasonable interval for each. If they will do so, they will then find that these theories are hopelessly untenable.

I have hitherto argued, on the chosen position of my opponents, that the Synoptic Gospels were written about the year 100, and the fourth about 160. Such dates are entirely fallacious, and against all evidence. But as far as my reasoning is concerned, it matters little when the Gospels were composed. If I can prove that the portraiture of Christ and the general aspect of the Gospels were familiarly known in the Church at a much earlier period, it is not the smallest difference for my argument whether they existed in an oral or a written form. The concession of seventy years for the creation of the Synoptic Gospels, and one hundred and thirty for that of St. John, has now to be entirely revoked.

The most extreme of the School that I am opposing concede that the four most important epistles of St. Paul are unquestionably genuine, and written by him within less than thirty years after the resurrection. The genuineness of at least four others is conceded by the most eminent unbelievers. We have, then, before us genuine historical documents of Christianity, composed by its most active missionary at about the same distance of time from the resurrection as that which separates us from the repeal of the Corn Law Act.

Now by the aid of these epistles it is possible to prove by a multitude of incidental allusions that all the great features of the portraiture of Jesus Christ were fully developed when St. Paul wrote them. Nay, what is more, the manner in which the allusions are made prove that this portraiture was not a new one, but that it had been long known in the Christian Society. To exhibit this proof would require a lecture of equal length to the present. As I have given it already elsewhere,* and it has not been assailed, I shall assume that my position is incontestable.

The period of time during which the human Jesus must have been developed into the divine Christ of the Gospels, if the portraiture be a fictitious creation, must be reduced to one of less than ten years. But whether it be ten, seventy, or one hundred and thirty, it contradicts the laws by which all human developments are regulated. Its creation involves a moral miracle of the most stupendous character.

My opponents postulate a number of conditions which history and philosophy refuse to concede. They require a long interval of time; history will only grant them a short one. They require that developments should be rapid; they are always slow, especially moral ones. They require the creation of elevated moral sentiment; their only instruments with which to work are credulous mythologists. They require that developments should be always progressive towards higher perfection; history declares that they are frequently retrogade ones. They postulate party spirit, but it produces endless division. They require compromises, but they must be made by credulous enthusiasts. They

* "Jesus of the Evangelists," chap. xvii.

require unity of result; they postulate a multitude of agents. They ask for credulity, and are confronted by sobriety. They ask for seventy years; historical fact will concede them less than ten. They deny physical miracles, and ask us to believe in moral ones.

Such is the position of the school of thought against whom I have been reasoning. They are called by a sad misnomer rationalistic. I ask, are these theories rational, probable, or possible? Defenders of revelation have no grounds for dreading an appeal to reason. If the Gospels, and the glorious Christ therein delineated, have been evolved in accordance with the various theories against which I have been contending, it involves a greater miracle than all the miracles of the New Testament united together.[1]

THE EVIDENTIAL VALUE OF ST. PAUL'S EPISTLES.

BY THE

REV. STANLEY LEATHES, M.A.,

PROFESSOR OF HEBREW, KING'S COLLEGE.

THE EVIDENTIAL VALUE OF ST. PAUL'S EPISTLES.

THE attacks upon that body of traditional belief and received thought which is conveniently expressed and commonly understood by the term Christianity have turned very much of late years upon the authenticity of the several books composing the New Testament. Inquiries of this nature have commended themselves to an age which we need not shrink from characterising as critical and discriminating. There is a manifest and a very intelligible pleasure to be derived from reopening questions which many have been accustomed to regard as settled, from proving former conclusions erroneous, or showing that considerable doubt still remains where certainty was believed to exist; and in the natural enthusiasm attending investigations of this kind, it is by no means a matter of surprise if the actual importance of the results has been somewhat overrated. The inferences following from the conclusions arrived at, have been estimated in proportion to the supposed certainty of the conclusions. If a particular Gospel can be shown to be falsely, or at any rate with doubtful truth, ascribed to its traditional author, the inference drawn, or at least suggested, is the comparative depreciation, if not worthlessness, of that Gospel. We know not why, but it is frequently assumed that if everything is not in exact accordance with the popular belief in any matter, nothing which is popularly associated with that belief can reasonably be maintained. The whole edifice will fall, or must even be destroyed, because a stone here or there is faulty, or out of place. Because investigation shows that the foundation does not lie as it was thought to lie, therefore there is no foundation at all. The rashness and precipitancy of any such inference will be at once apparent to every thoughtful mind. Because the reasons usually assigned are inconclusive, it by no means follows that no reasons can be given. The central questions really involved, may be altogether unaffected by the technical and subordinate question, who was actually the writer of some particular book. The critical investigation of authorship may have positively no bearing at all on the opinions expressed, or the facts recorded in the book. Whether or not this be so in any given instance, it is at any rate conceivably possible in the abstract.

In the case now before us, however, we have to deal with a converse position. There are four Epistles in the New Testament which have been admitted on all hands to be the veritable productions of the Apostle Paul. These are the two Epistles to Corinth, the Epistle to the Church at Rome, and the Epistle to the Galatians. The writers, if any, who have ventured to call in question the authenticity of these Epistles are so few, and so insignificant, as to be unworthy of mention. We may safely pass them by without fear of challenge or dispute. There is absolutely no room for any reasonable doubt that we have in our hands in these four letters the true and genuine compositions of Saul of Tarsus, after he had become a Christian.

It will be my business, then, on the present occasion, to examine and weigh the precise value of this admission of authenticity, which can only be spoken of as universally made. What is the evidence in support of Christianity which can be fairly adduced from it? In endeavouring to estimate the nature and amount of this evidence, I shall not assume these Epistles to be what we commonly understand by inspired. I shall regard them only as the natural human productions of a certain man whose personal history, to a considerable extent, can be discovered from them. If, on internal or other grounds, there is cause to believe they have any higher authority, that will be another matter. But we shall not assume it in dealing with them. Our aim in the first place must simply be to inquire what the acceptance of these four Epistles as the work of St. Paul legitimately demands of us; what are the inferences fairly deducible from their statements; what insight they give us into the character and motives of the writer, and what information they convey as to the nature and constitution of the early Christian society to which they were addressed.

And first, as to their date. We cannot place the death of the Apostle Paul later than the year of our Lord 68. It may have been the year before; but as he is said by Jerome and Eusebius to have suffered under Nero, and Galba succeeded Nero in A.D. 68, it cannot have been afterwards. Again, we are safe in saying that, on the supposition of the latter date, these four Epistles had been written ten years before the Apostle Paul died; that is to say, they were all written before the end of A.D. 58. Festus probably succeeded Felix in the year of our Lord 60. But Paul had been two years a prisoner at Cæsarea, when Festus came into the province;* and these letters were written while he was still at liberty. We have, then, in St. Paul's Epistles, by which we mean always and exclusively these particular Epistles, undoubted genuine productions of about five-and-twenty years, or not much more, after the death of Jesus Christ. Making all due allowance for possible variation in the requisite dates, we are warranted in saying that the

* Acts xxiv. 27.

interval between the Crucifixion and the sending of these letters to their several destinations, did not exceed by more than two or three years the quarter of a century. It was certainly less than thirty years.

The best way of appreciating such an interval as this is to take a corresponding period in our own lives. We have most of us a very clear recollection, probably, of events which happened in the year 1844 or 1845. The war in the Punjaub, and the Irish famine, which happened shortly afterwards, in 1846, and the great European events of 1848, some two years later, are fresh and vivid in the memory of every person who has arrived at middle age. To others yet more advanced, an interval of five-and-twenty or thirty years can effect but little in effacing events or circumstances which at the time produced a deep and powerful impression. They remember them as yesterday. So it must have been with many who were living at Corinth when the first Epistle to the Church there was written, and who read it on its arrival. But from this Epistle we know* that more than 250 persons who had seen the risen Jesus at one time were still alive and able to give their testimony to that effect. These persons, therefore, must have had as vivid a recollection of the circumstance referred to, as we ourselves have of the battles on the Sutlej. The Queen's coronation is to us an

* 1 Cor. xv. 6.

event farther in the background of the past than the vision of the crucified Jesus was to the 250 brethren who still survived.

And the way in which their experience is mentioned is one which is the more striking because it is so casual. St. Paul alludes to it incidentally as a thing of which he had often spoken to the Corinthians. He could not have done so had this not been the case. They knew perfectly well that he had mentioned it to them. They had not forgotten that it formed a part of his oral communications. He could not have referred to it in this way had it not been so. But so neither is it possible that he could have spoken of the fact had the 250 witnesses been the mere invention of his own brain. Were there no shrewd men of common sense in the Church of Corinth who could have detected an imposition so gross as this, if it had been one? Had there been even a small minority of such men, we should have had no second Epistle to the Corinthians, or the second Epistle would surely have been very different from what it is. We are obliged, in accepting the first Epistle to Corinth as the veritable work of St. Paul, to conclude that during his stay in that city he had habitually spoken of the fact, which none could call in question or deny, that there were living at that time more than 250 persons who had a distinct recollection of having seen Jesus Christ at some period less than six weeks after He had been crucified, *but who never saw Him again.* St. Paul not only said this, but the whole Corinthian Church knew that what he said was true, for otherwise he would not in this way have dared to say it.

There is no occasion now to discuss the question what it was these people saw, because that would carry us far astray. All we need for the present insist upon is the fact that we have contemporary evidence of the very best kind, in the form, namely, of a genuine letter, that a large number of persons were still alive, say in the year of our Lord 58, who believed that they had seen a person, not merely as a spectre or vision, but as a living and substantial man, whom they knew to have been crucified and buried but a short time before, and who likewise knew that there were many more who could have corroborated their evidence on this point if they had not been dead.

We fully admit, then, that this is a circumstance which is open to explanation in various ways, the true explanation being determinable upon other and additional considerations; but what we do maintain is that upon the premises conceded to us by the most rigid criticism, it is not possible to set aside the evidence on which it rests, be its explanation what it may.

And here it is worth while asking, before we pass on, how we should feel ourselves justified in regarding the testimony of 500 persons now, not more credulous or weak-minded than ourselves, to an event which had passed under the cognisance of their own senses, even though that event were the posthumous appearance of a man who had been put to death as a malefactor? Is it not certain that any such supposed appearance would be calculated to make an impression on the beholders which might well last for five-and-twenty or thirty years, and should we not regard their uniform agreement in the matter as a very remarkable circumstance imperatively demanding some solution?

The first point, then, which the existence of this Epistle establishes, is the fact that at the time it was written there were living many competent eye-witnesses of what was believed by them to have been the reanimation of a body which had been dead and buried, and that their testimony was accepted by a very large number of persons who implicitly believed it. Here, then, we have written evidence to the effect that a particular event was amply testified and very generally believed upon the testimony.

But, again, the same Epistle shows that this belief was by no means unquestioning. The very same chapter proves that there were those at Corinth who said there was no resurrection of the dead.* They did not believe, that is, in the doctrine that the dead will ultimately rise. They held no doubt in common with others that the resurrection

* 1 Cor. xv. 12.

was "past already;" that the change which had passed upon the Christian upon belief in Christ was so radical and so complete, that he might literally, without any violent figure of speech, be said to have risen again from the dead. They acquiesced so fully in the truth expressed by St. Paul in the second Epistle, "If any man be in Christ, he is a new creature,"* that the felt newness of that spiritual creation seemed to satisfy all their longings after life, and they relegated to the insignificance of a non-essential and a dreamy unreality the thought of a resurrection of the body yet to come. The way, then, in which the Apostle meets this form of unbelief is in the highest degree noteworthy. He argues from the known to the unknown, from what was believed to what was not believed, from what these early doubters implicitly accepted to that which they sceptically rejected. "Now, if Christ be preached that He rose from the dead, *and ye believe it*, how say some among you that there is no *future* resurrection of the dead? For if there be no *future* resurrection of the dead, then is Christ not risen? *but ye know and believe Him to be risen, otherwise ye would not be what ye are.*"

This, and nothing else than this, is the drift of the Apostle's argument. It shows us plainly, therefore, that there was a discriminating exercise of reason at work in men's

* 2 Cor. v. 17.

minds at Corinth. The struggle between reason and faith had landed them in a logical inconsistency. They rejected the future resurrection on what seemed to be rational grounds, because it appeared to them contrary to reason and experience, but they forgot that they had already submitted their reason to a belief no less absolute and imperious, which, if logically held, would stultify their scepticism.

And there is no setting aside the inference from this argument, that the tendency of the mind which rejected the future resurrection was to reject likewise the personal resurrection of the Lord Jesus, and the testimony of the greater part of the 500 brethren yet surviving who had seen Him after He was risen. That is to say, the character of the faith in the one case is enhanced by the scepticism in the other. Just as the belief of Thomas after his doubt, accepting for the sake of illustration the narrative in St. John,* was the stronger and more convincing because he had only adopted it upon conclusive evidence, so is the belief of the Corinthians in the resurrection of Jesus of the greater value evidentially, because we know it to have been their habit of mind not unquestioningly to believe.

We arrive, then, at this further position that we may not lightly regard the belief of the Corinthian Church in the

* For evidence as to the authenticity of this Gospel see the Boyle Lectures for 1870, "The witness of St. John to Christ."

validity of the evidence for Christ's resurrection as the belief of persons who were credulous enough to believe anything. Upon fairly estimating all the circumstances, there is abundant and conclusive proof, which we may call contemporary, that the resurrection of the Lord Jesus was believed in as a fact by a vast number of persons who were convinced they had received that fact upon ample or sufficient testimony.

We must not forget, also, the nature of the fact that was believed. The resurrection of a dead body is so contrary to all reason and experience, that the difficulties in the way of believing it may be estimated as practically equal in all cases. No one can profess to believe it without being fully conscious of the absurdity of that which he professes to believe. It is a point in which the imagination can scarcely hope to take the reason at a disadvantage, or at unawares. In only two ways is deception possible. First, on the supposition of the unreality of the previous death; and secondly, that the subsequent appearance was unreal. Now in the first case the notion of unreality is precluded, because it was firmly and universally believed, and not by Christians only, that Christ had died; and there is no vestige of any evidence to show that He died in any other way than on the cross. This death was as needful an element in the creed of the Corinthian Church as His resurrection, not to say that any true belief in His resurrection involved the belief in His death. It will not do to explain His supposed resurrection on the ground that His death was unreal. Where would have been the foolishness of the cross, if Christ had not died? To secure the resurrection of Christ at the expense of His death would have been simply absurd, for two reasons: first, because that would have made the resurrection after all no resurrection—an unreality; and secondly, because the death of Christ alone and by itself was a fact that was implicitly believed, and without which the faith of the Church cannot be conceived or comprehended. We are reduced, therefore, to the necessity of explaining the resurrection of Christ on the alternative supposition that the subsequent appearance was unreal. And here we are met by the transcendent difficulty, that it is antecedently in the highest degree improbable that any sane man should be found to believe that the appearance of a person after death, who had been crucified and buried, could be other than imaginary and delusive. And we become, in fact, bound to determine whether in the abstract it is more improbable that multitudes of competent persons should believe in what was contradicted by universal experience, and especially by their own, or that something may have occurred which, in spite of themselves and their experience, had compelled them to this belief.

For we must not fail to remember that the two suppositions are mutually destructive. If Christ died, then the belief in His resurrection can only be explained on the theory that His subsequent appearance was unreal. If His subsequent appearance was unreal, then, to say the least, it is entirely gratuitous to deny the fact of His having died, because if He did not truly die, there is no discoverable reason why His supposed appearance after death should not have been real. We may choose which explanation we deem preferable. We cannot alternately or simultaneously adopt both.

I am not now called upon to prove more than what is clearly proved, that the existence of this one Epistle as the genuine work of St. Paul affords abundant evidence that the resurrection of Jesus Christ from the dead was accepted as a fact by large numbers of men, some of whom, at least, can only have accepted it on evidence which seemed to them sufficient to counteract the adverse testimony of their experience, their reason, and their senses. And it is almost needless to observe that the belief in the resurrection as here depicted, involved also a belief in the burial* of Jesus Christ, in the main and essential features of His death,† that it was on the third day that He arose,‡ that His appearances after His resurrection were distinct and manifold,§ and that the Apostle who depicted it had himself been among the

* 1 Cor. xv. 4.
† 1 Cor. xi. 27.
‡ 1 Cor. xv. 4.
§ 1 Cor. xv. 5—8

most vehement opponents of this very belief in the person of the Lord, whose resurrection he proclaimed.* All this is established by the admission of this letter as genuine, and by the admission which cannot be denied, that the writer was giving a natural and plain statement of the truth, and not a fabricated or ideal narrative of fictitious occurrences.

That is to say, so far the testimony of this Epistle is in conformity with the framework of the Gospel history. If the four Gospels were lost to us, the life, and death, and resurrection of Jesus Christ would still remain firmly and distinctly imbedded in the original faith of the Corinthian Church. We know from this letter that less than thirty years after the death of Christ, there was a very large body of men at Corinth who believed implicitly that He had risen from the dead, and that they knew that many persons were still alive who were eye-witnesses of the fact.

I ask you, then, very carefully to observe that this does not prove the fact. It only shows us conclusively that less than thirty years after the fact there were many persons who believed in it as such.

And let us put a parallel case. Suppose a person coming to London in the present day, and declaring that less than thirty years ago a certain man in a distant country who had been put to death as a malefactor, had risen from the dead

* 1 Cor. xv. 9.

the third day, and was still alive. What success think you would he meet with? Most assuredly there would not be half-a-dozen people who would believe him. But if, on the contrary, a new society should be formed, consisting exclusively of persons professing to believe all this, would not the circumstance be so remarkable as to lead us to infer that there must be some adequate cause for it? If the persons professing this belief were of all stations and classes, and many of them, as is proved by this Epistle, men of intelligence and discernment, should we not be constrained to confess that the only reasonable supposition was that there was something in the evidence which could not be lightly set aside? However strange and mysterious the tale might be, it could not be altogether a cunningly devised fable. There must be something at the bottom of it. No effect can exist without an adequate cause. Here is clear evidence of a very considerable effect existing. What was the cause of it? The cause alleged would doubtless be a sufficient cause, for truth is not only stranger, but mightier than fiction. And it may be fairly questioned whether, under all the circumstances, any other cause can be discovered which would be sufficient. There is so far, therefore, an antecedent probability that the cause alleged was the true cause.

Again, it is to be observed throughout all these Epistles of St. Paul that the resurrection of Christ was to him not a past influence, but a present power. If the evidence of the first Epistle to Corinth is less than thirty years after the death of Christ, the evidence of the second carries us back to nearly half that time. The writer speaks of himself as being in Christ more than fourteen years before.* This brings us virtually to not more than a dozen or fifteen years from the actual occurrence of the resurrection; and in all probability the Epistle to the Galatians carries us back even further still. Critics are divided as to the computation of the time mentioned in it. But if the "fourteen years after" of chap. ii. are to be added to the "three years" after which Paul "went up to Jerusalem to see Peter," then the whole period can be little less than twenty, and the extreme limit referred to scarcely more than ten years after the resurrection.† At that time, then, St. Paul himself fully and implicitly believed in it. At that time he had made great sacrifices for his belief in it. At that time, or shortly after, he had not improbably suffered privation and persecution because of it. But the faith which he held then he is found holding as tenaciously as ever fourteen or twenty years afterwards, holding it, in fact, so tenaciously that he is able to bring many others to share it with him. A man must be something more than an enthusiast who for fourteen years could retain a conviction so monstrous as this, if false, and

* 2 Cor. xii. 2. † 1 Gal. ii. 1, and i. 18.

at the end of that time could make more converts than before. Surely this is not the ordinary experience of mankind, that it is so easy to get men to believe as a fact, contradicting their own experience, what after all is no fact at all. It is one thing to win converts to our *opinions* or our *principles*, and quite another to gain credence for a *fact* that it is every one's interest to disprove.

For at that time what secondary advantage could there be in the profession of a faith which was universally despised, and which exposed its more prominent votaries to imminent peril, as the eleventh chapter of the second letter to Corinth abundantly shows. It is obvious that at fifteen years after the death of Christ many of the 500 brethren who were afterwards dead were still alive, and it is not too much to infer that St. Paul, from the position he held in the Church, was personally acquainted with many or most of them. He therefore personally must have had numerous opportunities of amply satisfying himself as to the truth of the fact which he proclaimed so persistently. But still it is evident that it possessed for him a power and an influence totally different from that of any ordinary occurrence or event. It was not the Christ who once rose, but the Christ who was risen that he proclaimed. His first rising from the grave was the work of a distinct moment of time. The influence of which He thereby revealed Himself as the centre and source was continuous and inexhaustible. It was this influence which the Apostle felt in his life. He could tell the Galatians in language it would be impossible to counterfeit, "I am crucified with Christ, nevertheless I live; yet not I, but Christ liveth in me, and the life which I now live in the flesh I live by the faith of the Son of God, who loved me, and gave Himself for me."* A declaration such as this is worth volumes of evidence; it is its own evidence; it bubbles up clear and sparkling from the very fountain and well-head of truth. No man could have said it who did not feel it, and no man could have felt it, and not known that what he felt was an intense reality, defying all explanation except on the hypothesis that the central core of it was truth, and not falsehood. If an influence thus operating on the life was derived from the death and resurrection of Jesus Christ, there must have been something very unusual in that death, and something more than a mistake or an illusion in that rising again to set such a force in operation. No other man's death would produce the same effect, (who cares for the death of Socrates?) and no other man's resurrection, whether alleged or proved, could do so; but if this man's death and resurrection did produce it, as it plainly did, then the result speaks for itself. The Epistle to the Galatians, though written more than eighteen centuries ago,

* Gal. ii. 20.

is a standing witness to it. There is no wonder that such an influence was felt then in every part of the known world, and especially in the centres of its life, such as Rome and Corinth, because we cannot but feel it now; and a principle so instinct with life cannot but be superior to and independent of the power of death. Here is the present power of the resurrection acting concurrently with the mass of cumulative evidence converging in the point when it was an event of actual history, and combining therewith to show the truth of it. Nothing can prove more conspicuously the strength of this influence in the personal life of St. Paul than his great Epistle to the Romans. Everywhere Christ is present with him as an energising power, which is vastly more than a mere memory of the past, and is a vital and potent agency still in operation. He did indeed die unto sin once, but evermore He liveth unto God.* The gift of God is eternal life, through Jesus Christ our Lord, who was declared to be the Son of God with power according to the spirit of holiness by the resurrection from the dead.†

But what is not the least remarkable feature about the Epistle to the Romans is the fact that it was written to a Church of which St. Paul was personally ignorant. He had never been at Rome. It is evident, however, that there were many Christians there. These Christians were not his

* Rom. vi. 10. † Rom. vi. 23; i. 3, 4.

converts. He says he had had a great desire for many years to come unto them.* Then there had been Christians at Rome for many years. The many can be scarcely less than ten or a dozen; but if so, this brings us again to little more than fifteen years after the death of Christ. We find, however, these Christians professing identically the same belief in the same person and the same facts as St. Paul himself. They also believed in a Jesus Christ who had been crucified, and who had been raised from the dead. How they came to believe in Him we cannot tell. It is plain they did believe in Him. It is also probable in the highest degree, nay, it is impossible but that many of them from whom they received their faith, had either been eye-witnesses, or companions of eye-witnesses of the life of Jesus Christ. At any rate, it is obvious that the substantial framework of belief was identical with that which was current among the Churches of Galatia, and in the Church at Corinth. A man who had been crucified and risen again, was the centre of their hope, their affection, their joy, their confidence. In Him they all felt they were supernaturally united in a supernatural life; and as their knowledge of Christ was altogether independent of St. Paul's preaching, it possesses the value of independent testimony, and presents an additional amount of difficulty in the face of any attempt

* Rom. xv. 23.

to account for the belief in Christ's resurrection on the hypothesis of some error or deception. However unreasonable it was to attempt to account for it in that way at Corinth, the difficulty becomes greater when the case of Rome is added to that of Corinth. Here the personal influence of the enthusiastic Paul is removed, and yet the results produced are manifestly undistinguishable. Their faith had been spoken of throughout the whole world,* and it was faith in a crucified and risen Jesus; a faith which they as Gentiles were not ashamed to profess in the Jew Christ Jesus, and to be confirmed in by the Jew Saul of Tarsus. There is something very remarkable in these results. How many national and personal prejudices must have been overcome; how many rooted and inherent animosities must have been eradicated; how much stubborn pride must have been bent and mortified; and how many acute sensibilities deadened, before results such as these could have been obtained. And what was it all for? No earthly advantage had been or was likely to be secured. No hope of visible reward was offered. Simply the loss of self-respect, in having believed what was only a gross absurdity if it was not the truth, was incurred. The knowledge that under any circumstances their temporal condition would have been far better if they had never heard of Christ

* Rom. i. 8.

Jesus; that the belief in His name could give them neither lands nor houses, but only lay upon them additional hindrances in the way of gratifying their natural inclinations, only expose them more and more to the hatred and contempt of men. If in this life only they had hope in Christ, they were of all men most miserable; there was no one redeeming point, no one compensating advantage. They had believed a lie, and they were all the worse for it. These two points at least are clear: that they thought it no lie, and that under the circumstances they must have been strangely constituted, if, being a lie, it had the power to sustain them as it did.

For observe, connected with the faith of Christ there was not even the gratification of flattered vanity in the case of these first believers. There is an intelligible pleasure that a man can find nowadays in constituting himself the apostle of unbelief. There is the promise of a certain intellectual glory in the effort to overthrow an ancient faith like that of Christianity. The hope of possible triumph is dazzling. There is a pleasure in seeming to be so much wiser than so many others, in having outstripped the accumulated wisdom of ages, in being the pioneer of intellectual emancipation, the harbinger of light that has emerged from every trace of religious darkness, the forerunner of the downfall of superstitious prejudices, the demolition of the last and oldest of the creeds. There is something to attract the imagination in all this, something to foster a self-complacent estimate of self, together with a kind of malevolent joy in indulging the passion of destructiveness. But what was there to flatter the vanity in the belief of a proclamation which was foolishness to the Greeks? What was there to exalt the intellect, or to magnify the self, in the doctrine of Christ crucified? We do not deny that it was possible for the self to enter in and mix even with the doctrine of the cross; but it could only do so as a principle that was fatally antagonistic to it. The two could not co-exist; one must destroy the other. The belief that a crucified malefactor had risen in triumph from the grave, was subversive of everything calculated to honour the intellect, or to please the natural desire of man to worship and admire himself. There was no harvest to be reaped from belief in the Crucified on this score. We are at a loss to discover in any one point what secondary motive can, with any show of probability, be attributed to the first believers, as predisposing them to their belief, if the motive was not a simple and sincere conviction of its truth. And yet if so, the difficulty becomes still greater in *assuming* that what they believed was not the truth, but a flagrant lie. For it must ever be remembered that it *is* an assumption after all. It is certainly not less difficult to *prove* in the face of all the evidence that Christ did not rise, than it is to *prove* upon that evidence that He did. If the result of the whole argument in the one case is a *presumption*, it most assuredly is not less so in the other.

Once more, it cannot for one moment be asserted that the Epistle to the Romans originated in any way the faith which it assumes. It is absurd to suppose that an unknown man merely on the credit of his reputation could have substantially modified the belief of a particular Church by simply inditing a letter to it. The state of things assumed at Rome, and the faith depicted in the Epistle to the Romans, are only intelligible on the supposition that they are true. It is obvious that the body of the writer's faith was substantially identical with that of those to whom he was writing. Both were attached to a particular person whom they believed to be the Son of God, who had been crucified, dead, and buried, had risen again, and was then sitting at the right hand of God as an intercessor.* And more than that, both believed that this person was the giver of a new Spirit which influenced both, and animated all believers, and made them all one, and was not only the evidence to them of the actual truth and resurrection of Christ, but was also the pledge that they themselves were accepted in a new relation to God by Christ.† This gift of the new Spirit was the invisible bond between

* Rom. i. 4; vi. 6—9; viii. 34. † Rom. viii. 14, 16, 17.

them and Christ, between them and one another, between them and the Macedonian Christians, between them and the brethren of Corinth, between them and St. Paul himself.

Nothing the least like this Spirit had been known before in their own experience or in that of the ages past. It was a new phenomenon which they felt, and saw, and acknowledged, and could not deny. Now the eighth chapter of the Epistle to the Romans contains incontrovertible proof of the operation of this Spirit. No letters from Paul could have made the Christians at Rome imagine they were influenced by it. We can see for ourselves that it was not less familiar to them than it was to him. No message of his had made it familiar to them. Years before they had known it, although from whom they had received it none can tell, but it is perfectly certain that a condition of belief like that at Rome could not have been the work of a day. It must have taken time to grow. And yet at the same time it is no less clear that it was a product of the existing generation. There was not one of those to whom the Apostle wrote who had not in his own being the consciousness of a prior condition of unbelief. Many of them had probably been defiled with some of the dark catalogue of crimes enumerated in the first chapter, but they had been justified by faith, and had found peace with God through our Lord Jesus Christ.* They

* Rom. v. 1.

knew this; they were conscious of the double experience; they could compare the one with the other. The Apostle's letter had not originated these experiences of their consciousness: it had reflected and expressed them. The notion of the Epistle to the Romans being an imaginary letter written under imaginary circumstances to imaginary persons, describing imaginary incidents and imaginary feelings, is too monstrously preposterous to be for one moment entertained. It has preserved the real and irresistible evidence of a vast spiritual influence at work among a large body of men which was precisely contemporaneous with one event—their belief, namely, in the resurrection of a man who had been crucified in Palestine.

Now it must be admitted that in this alone and by itself, if it was not true, there is nothing that can be discovered which is adequate to the production of results so remarkable. When it is asserted that the death of Jesus Christ is surpassed in excellence and sublimity by any other death, the one question that suggests itself is, If this be so, how is it that the results which followed that death were not more remarkable than or so remarkable as those which followed the death of Jesus? This is a simple fact that no criticism or scepticism can destroy, that the preaching of the death and resurrection of Jesus Christ in the first thirty years afterwards did produce results, as testified by these Epistles, which are simply unparalleled in the history of the world. If the death was not a real death, or the resurrection not a true resurrection, then the responsibility must rest upon us of discovering some other explanation sufficient to account for effects which are too palpable to be ignored, and can assuredly be accounted for on this supposition, but have not yet been adequately accounted for on any other.

It is no part of my present design, and time would fail me, to enlarge upon all the points in which the history of the Gospels is confirmed by these Epistles. I am not now concerned to establish the credibility of the Gospels, but only the general credibility of the Gospel history; and therefore it may suffice to say that we find St. Paul and the Romans believing that Jesus Christ "was made of the seed of David according to the flesh," * an admission which, coming from the pupil of Gamaliel, who must have had the requisite technical information, is very remarkable; but "separated as the Son of God with power," which is at least consistent with our Gospel narrative, that makes Him the Son of God, but born of a virgin, and especially characterised during His ministry by miraculous powers; that in each of these Epistles the custom of baptism is expressly mentioned or implied; † that if the

* Rom. i. 3, 4.

† Rom. vi. 3; 1 Cor. i. 13; Gal. iii. 27; cf. 2 Cor. i. 22.

origin of this rite is not directly to be referred to the institution of Christ, as recorded in the Gospels, we are altogether ignorant of its origin; that the practice of it was clearly universal, which is so far consistent with the belief that it was derived from the express command of Christ; that in the first Epistle to the Corinthians* the writer speaks of Jesus Christ taking bread the same night that He was *betrayed*, and blessing it, and speaks of it in terms almost identical with those of the Gospels, thus showing not only that the death of Christ, but that the main circumstances of His death were commonly known, and the record of them so far unvarying, and that consequently the supposition of any great or substantial divergence is precluded; that the portrait of Jesus which all recognised was, in all its principal and important features, identical with that which we recognise now; and that, therefore, as the existence of some Gospels is, under the circumstances, a matter of necessity, the question is not so much whether *our* Gospels are true, as whether there are any others which can be regarded as truer and more trustworthy.

And when we bear in mind that at this time the interval of thirty years had not yet elapsed since the death of Christ, we can partly estimate the possibility of dim or uncertain recollection in the case of events so clearly defined, and so

* 1 Cor. xi. 23.

simple, and so important, by the freshness with which we ourselves remember other events more complicated that have happened within a similar period of time. There is, moreover, clear evidence that at the date of these Epistles two practices were universal in the Church—those, namely, of baptising converts, and of commemorating what was called the Lord's Supper. These practices must have had a commencement, and have had an origin. The period of thirty years, before which there is no trace of the second, even if the first existed in other forms, is too short a time for their origin to have been forgotten, or for the practice of them to have become materially modified. But the commemoration of the Lord's Supper is unmeaning, except in connection with the death of Christ, and St. Paul declared, "As often as ye eat this bread and drink this cup, ye do show the Lord's death till He come;"* and whatever relation there may have been between baptism as practised by the Jews or by John the Baptist, and Christian baptism, it is certain that baptism in the name of Jesus is unintelligible, except on the supposition of His having risen from the dead, or having in some way established His claim to be the Son of God, or the founder of a new society. St. Paul, however, distinctly says that Christ sent him "not to baptise, but to preach the Gospel,"† as though He had sent others to do

* 1 Cor. xi. 26. † 1 Cor. i. 17.

both; or at any rate, had sent others to baptise. The prevalence, therefore, of these significant practices, which is clearly traceable less than thirty years after the death of Christ, is well-nigh equivalent to contemporary evidence, both as to their origin and to the reality of the events they signified. If Christ had been a shadow, or a myth, or a mere crystallised idea, it is absolutely impossible that we should have the kind of evidence we have as to the universality of these practices. We can account for them on no theory but the express command of Christ, which must have been substantially identical with that recorded in the Gospels.

It is perfectly clear, therefore, that the known writings of St. Paul contain incontrovertible evidence of the whole framework of the life of Christ, which was the basis of the Christian faith less than thirty years after His death. They show us the existence of a large and organised society, which was held together solely by the attachment of its members to His person; and which, but for faith in Him, would have had no existence at all. This society was notorious for the profession and the practice of a very high morality, such as had never before been seen, and can never be surpassed,—at least, it is such a morality these Epistles inculcate. The occurrence of one or two flagrant breaches of this morality in the Church at Corinth, only serves as a foil to what was, beyond all question, its general standard;

but, in addition to this, there were other features in it of a wholly exceptional and unprecedented character. One of these was what we may call, for want of a better name, its unworldliness. Every one must feel that there is that in the writings of St. Paul which is distasteful to the common humanity of the world. It is as if a new sense had been suddenly created, and the writer was bent upon satisfying it. The whole range of sympathies and requirements and tastes is new. It is not a natural thing for men to care about communion with Jesus, or prayer to God, or participation in the Holy Spirit, to have hearts overflowing with gratitude to the Divine Being for having redeemed them, for adopting them into His family, and making them partakers of the holiness of His own nature. However this is to be accounted for—if it can be accounted for—it was not then, and is not now, a condition of mind natural to man. Now, take away the expression of these feelings, and the letters of St. Paul come to an end, and the occasion for writing them comes to an end, and the existence of the society for which they were written comes to an end. But as the letters exist, the occasion for writing them must have existed, and the society for which they were written must have existed; and none of these things can have existed without a sufficient and analogous cause. They are inseparably connected with the preaching of Jesus and the belief in His name. Take away these two things, and they would not have existed at all. But their very existence is a proof at the same time that they can only have made their way in opposition to the prevailing tendencies of human nature, because they cherished and exhibited a condition of mind which is foreign to the natural tastes and inclinations of mankind. There is internal evidence, therefore, in the writings of St. Paul that the faith which he preached had only succeeded, wherever it was successful, by triumphing over much that was naturally and fatally opposed to it; thus showing that we cannot refer to any natural causes the success of a scheme of religious belief which was itself contrary to nature, and is still felt to be contrary to nature.

But there is another feature, wholly exceptional and unprecedented, which characterised the new society; the evidence for which is too distinct to be set aside or explained away—the first Epistle to Corinth affords conclusive proof of the existence of miraculous gifts in the Church there. These gifts were of various kinds; the most mysterious of them being the gift of tongues. Whatever this was, it is sufficiently clear that it was over-estimated, and that it was abused. The possessors of it were puffed up on account of it. They were disposed to prefer it before charity, and the less obtrusive gifts of the Spirit. We can only conclude, therefore, that this gift was a reality which was acknowledged and envied by others, but a reality likewise which was peculiar to the Church, and which was limited to the area of belief in Christ. Now we must not assume that the possession of this gift was miraculous; all we may insist upon is the validity of the evidence that it was real, and of this the fourteenth chapter of the first Epistle to the Corinthians presents incontestable proof, and consequently the existence of this gift is a distinguishing characteristic of the effects which followed the original profession of the faith of Jesus. Not only was the standard of morality raised by it, not only were new dispositions awakened by it, and new capacities and tastes created, and new desires and hopes implanted, not only were the original propensities, inclinations, and antipathies of nature resisted, thwarted, and overcome; but in addition to this, there is a plain evidence of new powers and endowments being conferred upon the first believers concurrently with their belief in Christ. Now it is obviously impossible that delusion can have operated in all these cases; but unless it did, the multiplicity and combination of them supply no inconsiderable confirmation of the reality of that event, the belief in which was the very basis of their existence. Multitudes believed in the fact that Christ had risen from the dead, and the profession of that belief was followed by one or other of these results. A great change was wrought in numerous instances which was unprecedented in the experience of the individual, and which could find no counterpart in the experience of the heathen world; and if the results which followed the proclamation of a fact were conspicuously so real, is it possible that the fact itself was less so? For there is only one alternative—if the cause producing these results was not a fact—namely, that *belief* in a particular event which was not a fact, produced them. In other words, not only was the faith of the early Church self-originated, but moreover, all the phenomena of its existence were the product of that which itself had no existence.

We need not fear to admit that a very strong conviction may suffice to produce considerable results, even though the conviction may be based upon a falsehood; but we may well question whether all the results here manifested, combined, could have been produced by mere belief in the resurrection of a man whose resurrection was not a fact. What was there in this belief, supposing it to have been based upon a lie, which could have wrought so powerfully and so generally on the minds of men as it did? Could such a belief have made them morally new, have made them willing to encounter shame and contempt, and endowed them with powers which rendered them the objects of envy to their fellow-believers? If we think it could, we must still confess that a combination of circumstances like these, taken all together, is so exceptional as to be virtually without a parallel in the history of the world.

There is, however, another point in the Epistles of St. Paul which deserves our notice when estimating their value as evidence, and that is the witness they afford us of his own altered feelings with regard to Christ. He speaks, in his letter to the Galatians, of having been formerly a devoted Jew, and having persecuted the Church of God and laid it waste.* If we had no other evidence than this, it would be sufficient. There is no reason to doubt what the Apostle says. He had been a bitter enemy of Christ. But there is no evidence whatever that while he was thus hostile to Christ he had ever believed His death and His resurrection to have been an unreality. Had he disbelieved in these events as facts, it is more than probable that some trace of such disbelief would have escaped him in his writings. But it is not so. The death of Christ was manifestly a notorious fact which neither he nor any one cared to deny. The resurrection of Christ, though perhaps received more questioningly, was nevertheless put by or explained away rather than actually denied. The tradition mentioned at the end of St. Matthew's Gospel, as commonly reported among the Jews,† is probably a fair sample of the indolent spirit in which the story of Christ's resurrection was met by them, and, perhaps, regarded by Saul of Tarsus. In

* Gal. i. 13.

† St. Matt. xxviii. 15.

his own case it was not so much that he disbelieved these things as facts, as that he was ignorant of their power. The death of Christ was no more to him than the death of any one else. The resurrection of Christ was to him nothing more than an idle Christian tale. He disregarded both rather because of the principles associated with them than because of their intrinsic falsehood. But the time came when it was otherwise. "It pleased God, who separated him from his mother's womb, and called him by His grace to reveal His Son in him."* He then found that the man whose death he had known as a fact, though not as a power, was intimately connected with himself, that he had a share in His death, and had been crucified with Him, and the resurrection, which had been to him before but as an idle tale, he now found to be the unfailing source of a new spiritual life to him. This was probably more than twenty years before he wrote any one of these Epistles. If we place his escape from Damascus under Aretas in the year of our Lord 39, this will bring his conversion to the year of our Lord 36. Now, I ask you notice this date very carefully. It is as late as we can well fix the conversion of Saul; some have fixed it much earlier. But supposing it to have happened as late as A.D. 36, this was but five or at the most six years after the death of Jesus Christ, which happened in A.D. 30, or, as I believe, in

* Gal. i. 15, 16.

A.D. 31. Now, if the death of Christ was an unreality, He would in all probability at that time have been still alive, as He would not yet have been forty years old, and His death by natural means was not likely to have occurred. But conceive for one moment the impossible absurdity of the conversion of Saul taking place and the active life of the Christian Church going on for many years while Christ, who was supposed to have died upon the cross, was actually living in obscurity in some unknown corner of the world. The idea is simply preposterous. The supposition of Christ not having died as He was believed to have died is too impossible to be maintained.

If we have got Christ's death then as a positive historical fact which is unquestionable, we have a platform of reality on which to rear our superstructure of evidence for the reality of His resurrection. If Christ did not truly rise, there is one very important question to be answered which has not been, and which never will be answered, namely—What became of His dead body? The production of that dead body by the enemies of Christ would have been absolutely fatal to all the preaching and the faith of the Christians; the Christian Church would have been effectually stifled in its very birth. I should not now, after an interval of almost nineteen centuries, be lecturing in St. George's Hall on the evidences of Christianity if the dead body of Christ had been produced, and yet nothing, surely, would have been easier for His enemies to do. If, then, the disciples stole Him away from the sepulchre while the soldiers slept, and so made away with the body, we must admit that these Epistles of St. Paul, which at least are unrivailed in the literature of the world, and which cannot again be produced at will, owe their origin to a deliberate lie; and that after an interval of five-and-twenty years, which might have sufficed for it to have been successfully exposed. And we must confess that one of the most distinguished and highly educated of the Jews of that time, who himself had been a violent persecutor of the Christians, was induced against his will, and apparently not by Christian influence, to connive at this collusion or become the victim of it, and that in such a way as to ruin all his worldly prospects, to entail upon him years of hardship, and to inspire him, or at least to leave him, after almost a quarter of a century, with all the tact, wisdom, and discretion which are so conspicuous in his letters to the Churches at Rome and Corinth. Verily this supposition is absolutely precluded by the very nature of the case.

There remains then but one other to be advanced, and that is this. The primitive Christians and St. Paul himself were alike the victims of delusion. The testimony of the first disciples was based upon an error. The vision which had arrested Saul on his journey to Damascus, and changed the whole current of his life, was nothing more than the hallucination of a sunstroke. The preaching in which he passed so many years of his life, and breasted so much resistance, was only an infatuation; the hope, and peace, and joy of which his letters are so full, and which had taken permanent possession of him upon belief in Christ, were all a lie. He had sacrificed himself for nothing, he had toiled and suffered for nought. He had thrown away his life for a dream. We do not deny that such a position is conceivable; but we do deny that the letters of St. Paul give evidence of it. Had the resurrection of Christ been merely a delusion, the Epistles to Rome, Corinth, and Galatia are not the kind of fruits we should have expected it to produce after so long an interval; nay, there is room for the gravest possible doubt whether, being a delusion, it could have produced them.

This, then, is our standing ground. We do not assume that St. Paul was inspired. We do not say that his writings are authoritative or binding upon our faith. We take up no such position. We take only what we find—the genuine letters of an early convert to Christ, which were certainly written less than thirty years after the death of Christ, which contain internal evidence on the part of their writer to his belief in the central facts they proclaim, at an interval of little more than five years after those facts occurred. We treat these letters as the natural productions of any ordinary man.

We deduce from them only such evidence as we should deduce from the letters of Cicero, or any one else. We do not affirm that they are in any way supernatural, but we say that they supply conclusive evidence to the very wide-spread belief in centres of life so far removed as Rome, Corinth, and Galatia, in a supernatural fact less than thirty years after it occurred. We do not say that this wide-spread belief proves the fact to have occurred; but we do say that if the fact really did occur, it would account for the belief, and we do say that taking all the circumstances into consideration there is at least room for the very gravest possible doubt whether had it not occurred, the phenomena we witness would have been presented. Given the resurrection, and St. Paul's Epistles are explained; deny the resurrection, and you cannot account for them. Given the resurrection, and St. Paul's own character is the natural consequence of it, St. Paul's conversion its natural product; deny the resurrection, and he is the greatest of all inconsistencies, and his conversion, *with its effects*, the most inexplicable of all enigmas.

And here we might be content to leave the case, confident that we have not overstrained it, and confident in its own intrinsic soundness and inherent strength, for the more the character, the history, and the writings of St. Paul are fairly studied, the more disciples they will win to Christ;

but it may, perhaps, be expedient to notice briefly one or two points in their bearing on this position. It will, of course, be said that no amount of belief in a fact will prove it to have been a fact, which is obviously true. The resurrection, if a fact, is a miraculous fact, so far removed from the limits of ordinary experience and natural law as to be well-nigh sufficient to cover almost any contradiction of the one, or any violation of the other. It is no part of my present business to discuss the question to what extent a belief in miracles is defensible; that has already been done in a previous lecture of this course; but I may make this observation, that, granting the actual occurrence of a miracle like the resurrection, there are those to whom it would be impossible to prove it by any testimony whatever. Nay, there are those who would not believe it on the evidence of their own senses, or, at least, who say so. Any demonstration, therefore, of a miracle, even if it could be demonstrated, would be clearly useless for them. It would, of course, on this hypothesis, fail to reach them. Now, we may concede at once that Christianity is wholly unable to offer any such demonstration; nay, we may go further, and say that if it could, it would be no nearer to the overcoming of such opposition. But let it be observed that the existence of such opposition by no means proves the evidences of Christianity to be unsatisfactory or unsound. The person who declares that he would not believe a miracle like the resurrection even though he were himself the witness of it, is not likely to believe it on the testimony of a second person, be he never so trustworthy, even if it had actually occurred. And this is a fact that deserves to be borne in mind, because so far from showing that the evidences of the great Christian miracle are inadequate, it rather shows the absolute impossibility of their being adequate to meet successfully the case in point. It rather concedes the strength of those evidences, from mere eagerness to affirm that nothing could make them strong enough.

But, besides this, it must be remembered that, granting the reality of a miracle like the resurrection, it is obvious that, having been witnessed by a limited number of witnesses, it must necessarily be dependent afterwards for its acceptance upon testimony. On the supposition of its actual occurrence, a few only could receive it upon ocular demonstration, and the vast majority of mankind, if they received it, could only do so upon the testimony of others. It is therefore clearly conceivable on the hypothesis that many who rejected it might do so in direct contravention of the truth. Indeed, all who rejected it must do so.

Because, then, there are found those who reject the evidence of the resurrection of Christ, it by no means follows they have not done so in contravention of the fact. The question really is not whether there is still left any possible room for doubt—for that we have seen there always must be—but whether the existing testimony is sufficiently unbroken, and sufficiently uniform, and sufficiently valid, to be reasonably conclusive. And on this point the known Epistles of St. Paul are singularly clear. They witness to the fact of five hundred persons having seen the risen Jesus at one time, of the universal acceptance of belief in the resursection, so that neither in the Churches of Rome, Corinth, or Galatia, does there seem to have been a single Christian who doubted it. They witness to the fact that St. Paul himself had lived in familiar intercourse with Peter, James, and others, who had known the Lord, and that he had originally joined the Christian body at the most six or seven years after the resurrection, when he must have had abundant opportunities of testing the validity of its evidence, and when it would have been impossible for him to have given in his allegiance to an event so contrary to his experience, except upon conclusive proof.

Bearing in mind that under any circumstances some must content themselves with belief on testimony, it is difficult to conceive of any testimony which could be more convincing or more satisfactory than that of this Apostle; especially seeing that he was at the first a violent persecutor of the faith he preached; that he must have had ample means of sifting the evidence on which it rested; and, because, living at the time he did, so near to the death of Christ, that which his testimony loses in the matter of personal eye-witness it more than gains, all things considered, in the matter of deliberate conviction and devoted lifelong service.

That is to say, the conversion of the persecutor Saul of Tarsus is itself a wondrous evidence of the resurrection of Jesus Christ. The letters of the Apostle are the expression of his mature belief; but at the time when that belief was formed he must have had ample means of knowing how far he had followed a cunningly devised fable, and how far that which he believed was truth and was no lie.

Lastly, it may be said, If the evidence for Christ's resurrection was so satisfactory when it was first proclaimed, why was it not universally believed? To this we may answer, Why was Paul the Apostle at any period of his history Saul the persecutor? or Why were there any that believed if there were some who doubted? It is gratuitous to affirm that the want of universality on the one side is more remarkable than on the other. We can only say that faith is the great touchstone of man's moral nature. To the end of time it will be true that some will believe the things that are spoken, and some believe them not.* Why are there now any intelligent and able men who believe in Christ's resurrection if it is absolute folly

* Acts xxviii. 24.

to believe in it? That it is not folly to believe in it we can show to demonstration, while if, as a matter of fact, it did occur, as for the moment we may assume it did, it is obvious that the actual effects are what we see them now to be. There are those who believe, but there are those also who disbelieve. It is from the nature of the case impossible that a fact like the resurrection should appeal to man's acceptance like any ordinary fact of history, a battle or an earthquake. It cannot do so. If it did, there were no place for the question, "Why should it be thought a thing incredible with you that God should raise the dead?"* In accepting the resurrection of Christ, we accept also the inference that it was God who raised Him from the dead, and that He did so for a special purpose—the purpose, namely, of testifying to His life, His character, His mission, His teaching, and His claims, which are inseparable from His teaching. In accepting the resurrection, we accept not only a bare fact, but a fact that influences our relation to God and our thoughts of God—a fact involving antecedently many important principles, and resulting in momentous consequences.

But be it remembered that if the resurrection is established as a fact at all, it is established as a fact for all time; no progress of mind, no advancement of science, no change of

* Acts xxvi. 8.

circumstances, no distance of time, no lapse of ages can affect its truth. That which has happened once has happened for ever. The undisputed Epistles of St. Paul furnish what may be regarded virtually as evidence of a contemporary character to the truth of Christ's resurrection. Had it not truly happened, they could not have been written; for the pulse of resurrection life beats strong in every page. Had it not truly happened, those exigencies of the early Church would never have occurred which were the occasion of their being written, for without the death and resurrection of the Redeemer the Church of the redeemed is an impossibility. Had it not truly happened, the Christian Church would have had no existence now, and the commentary of eighteen centuries on the advice and judgment of Gamaliel, when confronted with the first preaching of the resurrection, would have been quite other than it is: "And now I say unto you, Refrain from these men and let them alone; for if this counsel or this work be of men, it will come to nought; but if it be of God, ye cannot overthrow it, lest haply ye be found even to fight against God."

For further treatment of this subject the reader is referred to the Boyle Lectures for 1869—"*The Witness of St. Paul to Christ.*"

CHRIST'S TEACHING AND INFLUENCE ON THE WORLD.

BY THE RIGHT REVEREND

THE LORD BISHOP OF ELY.

CHRIST'S TEACHING AND INFLUENCE ON THE WORLD.

My subject is a large one, and my time is short; therefore, I will say but very few words of preface. I propose to assume nothing but the patent facts of history, admitted even by the most advanced sceptics of the day. Heartily as I myself believe in all the canonical scriptures, and in all that they teach us, I do not ask you to admit the truth of miracles, or the inspiration of the Apostles, or the genuineness of the fourth Gospel, or anything which any moderately reasonable man can doubt of. All I would assume is this, that we have in history a general outline of the life and teaching of Jesus Christ, that that outline corresponds with what we read in the three Synoptical Gospels. There is really no discordant account or contradictory tradition either among the early Christians or the early heretics, or the contemporary

heathens. It is everywhere one and the same. It may b
more filled up, more coloured, more draped in one pictur
than another; but the features and the lineaments belon
unmistakably to one Man. In all the biographies, all th
letters, all the traditions, and they are many and mos
unusually numerous and diversified though not diverse,
there is in reality nothing like the discrepancy which w
observe in the character of Socrates as portrayed by hi
disciple Xenophon, and the character of the same Socrate
as drawn by his other and more famous disciple Plato. The account in the first three Gospels is uncontradicted by that in the fourth, by what we read in the Acts, by the letters of the early disciples, by the traditions carefully gathered up by men like Papias, some seventy years after the events, by the general belief of after ages, or by the few notices to be found in the writings of enemies and unbelievers.

I shall ask, then, that you admit the general truth of the history of Jesus as handed down to us by St. Matthew, St. Mark, and St. Luke, just as you would generally admit the evidence of common men, even if some choose to think that they were credulous men.

I. Let us first look at the character of Christ as so depicted. I venture to say, in the first place, that it exhibits the most perfect picture of sublime simplicity ever drawn. The Gospels seem very much like notes taken from memory by men who were anxious not to lose some record of One whom they had known and loved. It is impossible to imagine anything more simple or more simply graphic than their style—it is still more impossible to imagine anything more removed from the vulgarity of rhetoric or display or effort at effect, than the character of Jesus Christ. People have spoken as though He had been merely a first-rate political reformer, a demagogue belonging to a type of unusual disinterestedness. Surely His retired, unseen youth, His gentle, quiet manhood, His calm, dignified, unimpassioned words are the very opposite in tone and character to those of the noblest demagogue or the purest political leader that was ever heard of. "He went about doing good," seems almost to record His history. "He was meek and lowly of heart," seems almost to sum up His character. The most untiring energy, the most patient endurance, the most tender and affectionate benevolence strike us in every act and every word of Christ. And yet there was nothing feeble, nothing effeminate, nothing sentimental about Him. Simple as the gentlest child, He was brave as the hardest warrior. Weeping with the tenderness of a woman for the sad and the suffering, He rebuked with inflexible sternness the base, the cruel, and the hypocritical. With the most unsullied purity of thought and life, He had yet a heart of such large and gentle sympathy that the very outcasts of mankind could come to Him for help and counsel, and He never rejected them. He did no shrink from touching the leper, and the leprous sinner wen away from Him a new man, with a new heart and a new life But the covetous, the proud, the treacherous, the actor in religion, were rebuked by Him in words which have made a new language in Christendom; Scribes, Pharisees, hypocrites, sounding to us no longer as writers of the law, members of a religious body in Palestine, and actors in dramatic per formances, but as synonyms for all that is untrue in religion and in life. And there is one thing which signally separates Him as a teacher from all other teachers of religion and morality, viz., that the great lesson was Himself. I must speak further of this presently. What I mean here is, that the biographies, though they give many of His discourses, set before us most of all, not what He said, but what He did; and His actions are to us, and have been in all time, the most impressive lessons ever given to man. Probably all men—even those who do not believe in Him—would confess, that if they could see anyone living just the life which is related to have been the life of Jesus, the man so living would be perfect in all parts, the very ideal of humble-hearted, active-spirited, pure-minded, high-souled humanity. He taught Himself, by simply living Himself; and His life is the great lesson to every age of man.

And the originality of His character is almost as observable as its excellence. He was not simply the Great Teacher, like the philosophers of old, to whom crowds of disciples were gathered to listen. He was not the contemplative thinker, living retired from human society. He was no ascetic, frowning coldly on the innocent happiness of man. On the other hand, with all His marvellous activity, there is not the smallest appearance of restlessness, excitement, impetuosity. He was, if He be rightly described by His biographers, what no other man ever was—perfectly unselfish, living, acting, thinking, speaking, always with reference either to the service of God or the good of man.

Of course, as I do not assume the truth of miracles, I am unable to ask you to give unlimited credence to all that His followers have recorded concerning Him. But this is evidently the impression that He left upon their minds, viz., that He possessed amazing power, but that it was united with infinite condescension, and that it was constantly engaged in doing good, and never exerting itself to do mischief. They believed that He had power to do all things, but that he restrained it from doing evil even to His greatest enemies; that He never used it to gratify Himself, nor to save Himself from trouble, or even from suffering; that it was always exercised for the benefit of others; that in fact the *Self* which was unspeakably grand was incessantly restrained and denied.

II. Now let us turn for a few moments to His teaching. It was as remarkable as Himself. Other moral philosophers, or teachers of the art of living, argued with their followers, setting forth moral systems or propounding theological theories. He used no arguments, propounded no theories, weaved no elaborate systems. All He said was with an authority which astonished His hearers, and all the more, because of the humility of His life and the self-denial of His character. His whole system of casuistry would be contained in four or five pages of common printing; and though much of it was new, and all of it of the severest stringency, it yet commended itself at once to the consciences of them that heard Him; it has commended itself in the main to the consciences of all subsequent ages, and in principle at least it yet rules the morality of all Christendom, and in great measure even the morality of the followers of Mohammed.*

It is easy to sketch out a few of the great principles which He thus set forth. At the root of all lay truth. The Easterns, among whom He taught, have always been accounted as too ready to practise deceit. There was nothing

* It must always be remembered that Mohammed learned the best of his morals and his theology from Jews or Christians.

Jesus Christ condemned so much as dishonesty or hypocrisy—the very word hypocrisy, as I have said already, and all our instinctive hatred and contempt of it, being due to His denunciations of it to His disciples. Closely connected with this was the stress which He laid on purity of thought. To impose a weight and put a strain on outward conduct was all too little: it would very likely lead to superficial character, to the dreaded and denounced hypocrisy. From the heart come evil thoughts, and evil words, and evil actions. And the axe must be laid to the root of the tree. Make the tree good, and its fruit will be good. To give way to the desire of evil is to do evil.

Again: there was plenty of partial goodness. The heathens and even the Jews had learned an ardent patriotism, but it was linked, as to its *alter ego*, with a burning hatred of their country's enemies, never stronger in Palestine than when Jesus taught there. And this principle of love to country and hostility to aliens came home, too, into private life. It was an axiom that men should "love their neighbours and hate their enemies." Never before were those words clearly uttered upon earth, "I say unto you, love your enemies." Imperfectly, miserably ill indeed, as they have been acted on, they have revolutionized human thought. It was not only "Spare your enemies," not only "Forgive your enemies," but "Love your enemies." Like everything that He taught, it was to have its seat deep down in the heart. It was essential to every Christian that he should from his *heart* forgive everyone his brother their trespasses. It has been objected to His teaching that it undermined the principle of heroic virtue, absorbing active patriotism in a dreamy philanthropy. But the objection is false. His teaching was at the farthest possible distance from dreaminess or sickliness. The benevolence He taught was, like His own, active and energetic, busying itself, as everything practical must, first on those most easily and most naturally within its reach, but then extending to every created being, made by the same God, and loved by the common Father. There did, indeed, arise a new kind of patriotism, to which I may, perhaps, allude hereafter; but can anyone read our Lord's lamentations over Jerusalem, or St. Paul's utterances of his heart's desire for Israel, his almost wish that he himself might be lost if he could save them, and yet maintain that patriotism in its truest essence was quenched either in the heart of Jesus or in the feelings of His most devoted followers?

But whatever else may have been peculiar and exceptional in the teaching of Christ, that which chiefly distinguishes Him from all other teachers is this. Moral philosophers like Socrates, ever kept themselves in the background. It was philosophy that was everything, Socrates was but the humble tyro, feebly feeling after truth. Prophets of every religion,—

Moses, Zoroaster, Mohammed, all spoke the word which God put into their mouths. He was all; and they were at the best His honoured subjects and servants. But Jesus Christ, the meek, the gentle, the humble, the unselfish, the self-denied, the self-devoted, not only showed Himself as the Pattern of life, but even propounded Himself as the Object of faith, hope, love, obedience, loyalty, devotion, adoration, worship. It is impossible to deny this without rending to pieces every Christian record. It is argued, I know, that this was no part of Christ's original teaching, that it grew up after His death among His devoted followers, who looked back upon Him as a loved and lost friend and teacher, and who by degrees invested Him with Divine attributes and paid Him Divine honours; and especially it is thought that the writings of St. John, or rather writings in the second century falsely ascribed to St. John, and the later epistles attributed to St. Paul, fostered this exaggerated belief. I may well leave the genuineness of these later writings to those who have so ably and so amply dealt with them before me. All I wish to say now is, that if St. John's Gospel and St. Paul's Epistles had never come down to us, we should still be just where we are. This special teaching of Christ by Himself is fully developed in every portion of the three synoptical Gospels. They are interpenetrated by it from end to end. If it never came from Christ, the writers of those Gospels have misconceived Him altogether, and their record is mere fiction and falsehood. And so it is of every document which we possess—history, letters, traditions, anecdotes, apocalypses—they all turn the same way, they all speak the same tongue. Nay; I have often thought that if we had only the three synoptical Gospels left, though we should suffer terribly indeed by losing the deep theology of St. John the Divine, we should still have the clearest possible statements—though of the character sometimes called undesigned, or more properly indirect and incidental—as to the Godhead, Kingship, Priesthood of Christ; and that we should have none, or at most but one or two of those passages which have been thought by many to be inconsistent with the highest belief in our Lord's supreme, co-equal, co-eternal Deity. It is in fact in St. John and in St. Paul that we find the most developed form of the New Testament theology, but on that very account the appearance, for appearance it is only, of inconsistency and difficulty.*

Let us briefly recall our Lord's words in the first

* In answer to this theory of development or afterthought it may be said that all the early records, the writings of the Apostles and Evangelists, the writings of the Apostolic fathers, are clear about the Godhead of Christ. It was comparatively late that doubters arose, heretics like Cerinthus and Theodotus, and philosophic Christians like Justin Martyr, Clement of Alexandria, and Origen, accepting the gospel indeed, but diluting it by their reasonings upon it.

three Gospels. Constantly He calls Himself *the Son of Man*, meaning—(can we doubt?)—one who had no ordinary interest in mankind, in manhood, in all humanity; constantly He confesses Himself, and is confessed to be, the Son of God; constantly He claims to be King: He demands absolute obedience, boundless love ("he that loveth father or mother more than Him is not worthy of Him"); He forgives sins; He has authority over the Sabbath; He baptizes with the Holy Ghost; He promulgates His own law even where it seems to contradict Moses' law; He is at least *represented* (as I do not assume miracles I must say no more) as with creative power, multiplying bread, restoring sight, calling the dead to life, saying to the tempest, "Peace, be still;" He proclaims Himself the Judge of all the earth, about to sit upon His throne, with all nations, the dead, small and great, gathered before Him, and the angels of God waiting to do His pleasure; He pronounces the sentence, and it runs in words which indicate that the great act of obedience was waiting on Himself in prison, in sickness, in need, and in suffering, that the great sin was neglecting Him, Him as represented by His servants. There is one other scene which seems to me even more telling than all these. Each of the three Evangelists relate, St. John alone omits to relate, the institution of the Last Supper. There distinctly—whatever may be held by differing sects as to its meaning and its blessing—there distinctly Jesus Christ presents Himself to our faith as the Power which sustains all spiritual life; pointing to Himself as the great Sacrifice, the anti-typical Paschal Lamb, and then professing that His Body and Blood can feed and sustain the souls of all disciples in all coming time. What is this but, first to proclaim Himself the Lamb of God which taketh away the sin of the world; and then to attribute that sustaining, strengthening, life-giving power to Himself which can be predicated of nothing short of God?

I therefore fearlessly assert that, if our Christian records be in any way better than waste paper, if they be any records of Christ at all, we cannot but learn from them that He presented Himself to His followers, not as Prophet merely, not as Teacher only, but as their Priest, their King, their God.

Now, observe, first, the perfect originality of this. No one ever professed anything like it before. All the heathen fables about gods coming down among men, all their belief or half belief that some men were the offspring of deity, meant nothing like this. Their gods were themselves but deified men or personified powers of nature. It was easy to make mythic stories about their bodily appearance, or about their earthly loves and their earthly progeny.

Or, to speak of something grander, though perhaps less

poetical, the great pantheistic religions gave ready room for the fancy that there was a spark of deity in every sentient being, and that it might be more and more developed into God. In them, indeed, God is but the general principle of life and intelligence which runs throughout all the universe; it is duller in one spot and brighter in another; here it may almost go out in darkness, and there it may burst forth into the light of heaven and of glory. But it is not a person; at the highest it is an impersonal power. It may dwell therefore in the Bull Apis, it may reside in the Lama of Thibet, it may grow to be the highest intelligence in Buddha. In none of them is it really God. It is but the embodiment and the kindling up of a spark of Divine Being, but not a living, thinking, willing maker of the universe and ruler of all things. But Jesus Christ, when He was upon earth, lived among the only people on the earth who had a clear conception of one great and personal God, so one and so personal as each separate man is one and personal, man having been made in the express likeness of God. Jesus Christ lived among a people who esteemed that one personal God so great and so awful that they dared not even speak His name, the name by which He had specially revealed Himself, for they thought that that name, if human lips should utter it, would shake heaven and earth. Yet it was this great, only, incommunicable, unutterable Being, whose Son He called Himself, whose very essence He claimed for His own.

Let it not be said, that He came at a moment when Jewish hopes were all centred on some heavenly Messenger to redeem and restore them, that He only fell into their notions, took advantage of their expectations and flattered their prejudices. They expected a Messiah, no doubt, with much in him that was heavenly (if you will, Divine); they expected Him to redeem their nation, to overthrow their enemies, to advance their kingdom. But they never thought that their Messiah would claim to be the Supreme JEHOVAH, they never thought that He was to redeem, not their bodies, but their souls, by dying as a lamb sacrificed upon the altar; they never thought that, instead of satisfying their patriotism and elevating their nation, He would teach them to subordinate patriotism to universal love of man, and that instead of extending the earthly kingdom of Israel through the world, He would found a kingdom which should be wholly moral and spiritual, and which would place the Greek, the Roman and the Samaritan on the same footing with the long-favoured children of Abraham. So far were they from any thoughts like these, that it was because of all this that they crucified their Christ.

And if all this were original in Jesus, it was as bold as it was original. The humble, unostentatious, unselfish, Jewish peasant declares Himself the One Eternal God. If it was assumption only, it deserved the death which was its consequence.

But just let us consider it for a moment. Was it fanaticism? I have already pointed to the calmness, self-possession, soberness of Christ. No character in history exhibits these qualities so markedly. There is not a symptom of restlessness, excitement, intemperance, of any kind in one of His discourses. His eloquence—and no one can doubt His eloquence who has read, "Consider the lilies of the field," who has heard "Come unto Me, all ye that travail and are heavy laden"—but His eloquence, though more heart-thrilling than any human eloquence, was never rhetorical, never emotional. It carried conviction because it sounded like *truth uttered by love.* In fact, fanaticism or insanity are charges that cannot be made against Him on any ground whatever, except on the ground that He believed what He taught, and that no reasonable man could believe it. And if so, I think the charge must be abandoned, for Bacon, Locke, Leibnitz, Newton have believed it, and it is still believed by the most reasoning minds in Christendom.

Imposture is another charge. I have reminded you that the great principle of Christ's teaching was truth. If there was one point on which it could with some colour of probability be said that He was an enthusiast, it would be in His love of truth, and His scorn for all that was false and hypocritical. It would be strange indeed that such a teacher should lay the foundation of His teaching in falsehood. And be it remembered, that the supposed falsehood was not to please popular tastes, or to take advantage of popular prejudices, but to run counter to and offend them all, having apparently no purpose, but the purely disinterested purpose of mending men's manners against their wills, and having evidently no earthly end but persecution, suffering, and death. The fanaticism is the most inexplicable, the imposture the most improbable ever heard or thought of.

III. And now let us see what the teaching of this so-called fanatic or impostor has done.

I suppose it will be acknowledged that He lived at a time when the world was singularly *in want.* Heathenism had failed to satisfy it. The world had outgrown its infancy, and had tossed away its dolls. The philosophers derided, even the poets could hardly play with, their old heathen deities. Society was corrupt to its core. The old monarchies had sunk one by one,—Egypt, Assyria, Babylon, Persia, Macedonia—oppressed with their own vices. Rome had indeed reached the height of power, but it was power to be vile and so to be miserable. And there was a groan uttered from universal humanity for something to save it from the utter exhaustion of sensuality hard by suffering, of moral, social, and political degradation. Judea itself, where still God was worshipped, was no exception to the general rule, though it had yet hardly fallen to the depth of imperial Rome. And what of philosophy? Certainly it could never have had a better trial. The greatest moral philosophers the world ever knew, Socrates, Plato, Aristotle, had taught at Athens. The sound of their voices reached Rome, and echoed through all the civilized world. Without doubt, their teaching was valued, without doubt it was valuable to the thinking few; but the effect produced upon the many is too truly described by Ovid, "Video meliora proboque, Deteriora sequor." The salt of society had not been discovered; for society stank, and was corrupt throughout.

And then Jesus Christ set forth a remedy, and it was HIMSELF. It cannot be too emphatically said, or too steadily borne in memory, that CHRISTIANITY IS CHRIST. So He taught; so His disciples after Him—not a law—not a theory—not a code of morals—not a system of casuistry—not even an elaborate theology—but "they ceased not to teach and to preach Jesus Christ."

And this did satisfy human wants.

(1) Moral philosophy never moved more than a few

thoughtful minds. A strong law, like the law of Moses or the laws of Rome, may put a curb on men's passions and keep them in by bit and bridle, lest they fall upon you. But there was something vastly more powerful in the teaching of Christ. He propounded Himself to His followers, as the one great object of their loyalty and love. Now love and loyalty are the very groundsprings of noble and disinterested life. The servant of law lives in obedience to law, because to break law is to incur its penalties. The moralist trains himself with special reference to himself. The very necessity of his training turns the moral eye inward, creates self-consciousness, and produces, perhaps despondency from failure, perhaps self-confidence from success. The effect of loyalty is altogether otherwise. The eye, the heart, the hope, are all turned outwards—and in the case of the Christian—not outwards only but upwards. The result is, not the calculating morality, which may easily make a man selfish, but the absorbing love of a master, which makes him self-devoted. And coincident with the love and loyalty to the Master, came the brotherhood of all who loved and obeyed that Master; a close tie of brotherhood towards them, and earnest desire to bring others into that brotherhood, and so an universal charity to mankind. Thus did the Great Teacher provide for the wants of man, considered as a *moral being*.

(2) Let us see how He provided for His wants as *a spiritual being*. It is the witness of all religious antiquity, that, whilst the soul longed to look up to, and rest in something above it, it was ever striving to bring that which was above it down to a level with itself. It could not grasp infinity, and it was ever trying to make it finite. So it devised man-gods and idol-gods. So it degraded God to be no higher than man, nay, "likened its Maker to the grazed ox." What Jesus Christ did was to bring God down to man, but not to degrade and lower Him by doing so. He professed not to be a Man-God,—like the Saturn and Jupiter of Latium, like the Lama of Thibet, or like the Buddha of Ceylon and China; but the God-Man, God dwelling in human flesh, and manifesting all the character of infinity in the person of the finite. So He satisfied the yearnings of the human soul, without lowering the dignity of the Divine Spirit. It is impossible to remember the fables of heathenism without feeling that Deity is not only lowered, but utterly lost in them. But I appeal to your experience and to your hearts, whether the conception of God conveyed to us through Christ is not raised, rather than depressed—raised even above the conception of the High and Lofty One which inhabiteth eternity, as discovered by our reasonings, or as revealed to our faith, in the theism of the philosopher or the writings of the Jewish prophets.

(3) Once more, He provided for man's wants *as a social and political being.* Social polity has ever oscillated between an absolute despotism and a pure democracy. There are many who say that the only ideal of good government is either a paternal despotism, or "liberty, equality, and fraternity." It is most true that our Lord declined persistently to mingle Himself with earthly politics, or to meddle in the affairs of earthly kingdoms. But He declared that His mission was to set up in this world a kingdom not of this world. And the principles, the polity of that kingdom combined in a marvellous manner the unopposed will of the Father-King with the fraternal equality of all the people. As King of the kingdom of God He exacted the most devoted loyalty and the most unswerving obedience; but to the members of the kingdom He said, "All ye are brethren." He forbade any to aspire to pre-eminence, or authority, like the kings of the Gentiles; to those who desired to sit on His right hand and on His left He only promised that they should drink of His cup of suffering, and be baptized with His baptism of blood.

(4) Lastly, He provided for man's natural wants *as a sinful being.* Every religion witnesses to the anxiety of the religious mind to throw off a weight from the conscience by austerities, or by sacrifices, or by gifts. I am aware that I am treading on ground which may lead me into controversy,

and from this I must guard myself. Still I think every one who reads the Gospels must confess that the Christian history and the Christian faith culminate in sacrifice. I do not wish to reason on it; I readily admit its deep mystery, and the great difficulty of explaining it; I only assert, and I assert without fear of contradiction, that Christ set forth Himself, and that His disciples set Him forth to the world as One who suffered for the sins of that race which He had made His own; that He first bound them closely to Himself, and then drained off to the dregs that cup which their sins had prepared for *them*. He came into mankind that He might carry off the curse which sin had cast into the midst of it. And I know, indeed, that there are some, and some for whose scruples and difficulties I feel deep respect, who, acknowledging all the debts due to Christianity, for raising, ennobling, and purifying human life and human thought, yet say that they could accept every portion of it save only its doctrine of atonement and sacrifice. They think it derogatory to the mercy and to the love of God, and they doubt if the sins of feeble beings like ourselves can ever be so offensive to His majesty as to need such an intervention, or to cost so tremendous a price. I say I respect their scruples, for in some cases I believe they have been the scruples of men very pure in life and very loving in heart. But of this I am most certain, that there is nothing in Christianity which has so commended it to the acceptance of mankind at large. And certainly its effect, if fully exhibited, is very remarkable. Its effect is first to enhance our sense of sin, and secondly to enhance our sense of the love of God. Wellnigh every other system of forgiveness tends to make light of sin. If repentance be easy, sin cannot be so very hard. Wellnigh every other system of religion has created a dread of the Sovereign Ruler of the Universe, and has seldom, if ever, led to devoted love of Him. Strangely enough, too, all past religions had treated sin, when great, as inexpiable, and gave no room for repentance, even though sought carefully and with tears. But the Christian faith in the atoning love of Christ has deepened, beyond all comparison with aught besides, our conviction of the darkness and the danger of sin; has yet assured us that repentance for sin is not impossible, but to be attained and then certain to be accepted; and, lastly, has been the one only convincing evidence that, for all the clouds and darkness in which nature and natural religion have enveloped the Deity, there is yet a loving Heart in heaven, and that we may, with undoubting, filial confidence cast our orphan souls upon the Fatherhood of God. And so it is a fact, which nothing can take away, that, with all its admitted mystery and deep obscurity, the cross of Christ has been, even more than all else in His marvellous history, that which has won human hearts, and which has satisfied human yearnings.

IV. Let us pass to the reception of Christ's teaching in the world. There is not much that is new to be said about this. First, as to the mode of its propagation: it was not propagated by force, like the religion of Mohammed; nor was it a political revolution, as Buddhism was a great rising against the caste system of the Brahmins, joined with a modification or so-called reformation of their theological and philosophical theories. Christ forbade His followers to mix themselves up in the politics either of the Jews or of the heathens; and, as to force, He told them, in words which all Christian history since has verified, that "they who take the sword shall perish with the sword." In fact, the mode of the propagation of the faith of Christ was the simplest conceivable: it was merely a proclaiming of Christ as the Prince and the Saviour of the world. Apostles preached the kingdom of God, invited men to come into it, declared that Christ was its King, claimed from His subjects obedience to His sovereignty, and promised them peace in their hearts here and happiness in His home hereafter. It is a matter of perfect indifference to my present argument whether you acknowledge that this preaching was accompanied with miracles or not. If it was, then *cadit quæstio.* Probably no one in this company will say, as the Jews said and as some of the heathens said, that those miracles were due to Satanic agency. If there were miracles therefore, they were of God. But, if you refuse your assent to miracles, then I only say the result was all the more miraculous. If there was nothing but a simple teaching of Christ—if only men narrated the life of the Jewish carpenter, told of His death, declared him to be their King, set up His cross as their hope, and claimed submission to Him as their God; and if thereupon, in the midst of Jerusalem and Rome, and Athens and Corinth, and Ephesus and Philippi, and Smyrna, and Antioch, and Alexandria, at a time when art and science, and civilization and philosophy were at the greatest height ever known; if then and there, in the space of a single generation, thousands and hundreds of thousands, of all ages and all classes, bowed their heads and gave up their hearts to Christ, I ask what was it that gave such magic power to the so-called "foolishness of preaching?" I answer, It was the force of truth; and I ask again, Has any other answer ever been given?

The progress of Christianity in every stronghold of heathenism soon roused the jealousy of the governors of the world. We need not dwell upon the cruelties with which its votaries were persecuted. Men clothed in garments smeared with pitch, and then lighted up as living torches, to add a horrid lustre to the festivities of the

Emperor. Men crucified with their heads downwards. Men thrown to wild beasts. The heart sickens at the recital of their sufferings, and still more at the ferocity of their torturers. But nothing stopped them. Every human power was exerted. Every device was tried. But neither skill nor force availed. The stream flowed onwards till it became a river; the river spread out till it became a flood. In the short space of three centuries from the death of Jesus, Europe, Asia, and Africa, as far as civilization had reached, owned Him as their sovereign, and marched under His banner. Not a blow had been struck in His favour, though thousands and hundreds of thousands had died rather than disown Him. And then the heathen oracles were silent, the heathen altars were deserted, the heathen philosophers were changed to Christians; Christian presbyters ministered where heathen priests had sacrificed; Christian orators spoke where heathen advocates had pleaded; Christian judges decreed justice in the seats of the prætors and the proconsuls; a Christian Emperor sat upon the throne of the Cæsars. It is so still; the great bulk of the civilized world still retains, and professes to be guided by, laws, customs, and morals, which are really drawn from the teaching of Jesus Christ.

(1) It is said that the spread of Christianity is at least

partly due to mere human and common-place causes. * It is said for instance, that the civilization of the heathen empire was effete, that society was corrupt, that the very world was wearied with its own wickedness. Very true: yet it was in the Augustan age that Christ lived and taught, the very climax of ancient art and letters, and refinement, and philosophy. Very true; but still, that which will be our only refuge if we are driven out of our faith, had offered everything that it can ever have to offer. Moral philosophy had done its best. Socrates, Plato, Aristotle, Epictetus, Seneca, had done all that could be done by reasoning and moral teaching, to win men from vice, and to train them to virtue. And earth, for all that, was wearing the very semblance of hell. Men, no doubt, were weary of it, and they listened the more readily to Him who promised to the weary rest. Is it no mark of design and wisdom, that the remedy was offered at that very time when it was the most needed, and when the need was the most keenly felt?

(2) It is said, that the world then, in its deep dissatisfied restlessness and inquietude, was turning right and left for satisfaction, and that thus it readily lent an ear to the superstitious and the supernatural. It may have been so. It had apparently given up all faith; and the unbeliever passes

* The arguments here considered are those propounded in Lecky's "History of European Morals."

readily into the credulous. But I cannot think it reasonable to conclude, that an age of philosophical scepticism, of unbridled licentiousness, even though it might combine with these some disposition in favour of the marvellous, would be likely to admit the pretensions of Christianity without careful investigation; when Christianity bore with it requirements of the most rigid morality, offered in exchange for its philosophy simple faith, in exchange for its licentiousness the sternest self-denial, and gave it no promise in this life, but of contempt and suffering, and very likely martyrdom.

(3) It is said once more, that the unequalled organization of the Primitive Church made it a firm phalanx sure to win its way through the ranks of the fiercest foes. Very true. The economy of the Primitive Church, with its bishops, priests, deacons, and deaconesses in every city and suburb, with its strict and unbroken unity throughout the world which it had won and was winning, was, no doubt, an organization, a freemasonry, a secret society if you will, which constituted the best possible machinery for preserving and propagating its faith. Is it no sign of the superhuman wisdom of its Founder, that He not only taught the great secret of life; but that He devised means whereby that secret should be guarded and handed on to men?

I must here consider for a moment one of the gravest questions which arises in many minds about the progress of Christianity. Granted that its speed was rapid at the first, why has it ever stagnated since? If it be the great remedy for human woes, and the great prompter of human virtue and morality, why did not its Divine Author, if Divine He be, ordain that it should at once find its way everywhere, and should never fail anywhere? I am ready to admit the gravity of the question. I doubt if there be any greater mystery connected with the faith of Christ. It was objected to that faith by Lord Herbert of Cherbury, perhaps the most eminent of the deists of the last century, and it has tried many a believing, as well as many a doubting spirit, since. We naturally feel, that a religion meant to save all men ought to be made known to all men. In the few words I can say on it now, I do not pretend to clear up all the mystery. I cannot clear up all the mystery of God's actions or of God's will. I would only remind you first, that this is at all events but one specimen of the working of that general law, which seems to rule in creation, in Providence, and in grace. The analogy between the development of nature and the development of revelation was ably traced in the lecture of one who preceded me some fortnight or three weeks back. It certainly seems the principle of the Divine action, that all things should rise up into maturity by steady gradual progress and growth. So the infancy of mankind was left in the glimmer of twilight; then there was a dawning light in the ages of the patriarchs and the prophets, till the day broke full upon the world in the coming into it of Jesus Christ. By the same kind of gradual working, that day-spring from on high has extended its brightness first to one land and then to another. It is no more marvellous that China and India and Central Africa should not yet have seen it all, than that for thousands of years of man's past history, the whole human race, except at most a very small portion of it, should have known nothing of Christ or even of God. There has been an infancy of man, as there has been an infancy of the Universe; and we may well believe, that there may have been a preparation for Christ's coming, and elsewhere a preparation for the knowledge of His coming, corresponding with the preparation through countless ages past for the habitation of man upon the earth.

And as to the imperfect reception of Christianity in some places and times, and its actual retrogression, as from the Mohammedan conquest, in others; is it not plain that we have to expect Christianity to advance by moral means and not by mechanical? Christ left a leaven in the world, that it might work and leaven mankind. We are apt to expect that it should work by magic, and not by its own moral influence. Now, our Lord never so worked on earth. If He worked in His miracles by a mechanical force on nature, He never applied such a force to human wills, nor does His

Gospel work so now in the world. He called His church the salt of the earth; but He warned it that the salt might lose its savour. He said it was a grain of mustard seed, which should grow into a tree and fill the earth; but He never said that there should be no blights, no frosts, no tempests which might check its growth, or nip its leaves or rend off its branches. The apostles themselves knew that they had the Gospel treasure in earthen vessels, and when the vessel was injured the treasure could not be safely conveyed by it. It is very natural to expect that a potent remedy should produce an instantaneous cure. But we are constantly taught by experience that maladies are too deep-seated, or constitutions too sickly, for rapid or perfect restoration. We naturally expect every man under the true influence of Christianity to become perfect: we expect Christianized society to exhibit no defects. But, in reality, we only find that both the man and the people have a new principle, which gradually raises them, that they become instinct with a new life, which shows itself sometimes indeed by vigorous action, but which sometimes, too, becomes languid and feeble. If we make these allowances, there will be nothing to stagger our faith in the slow progress of the Gospel through the world. In the beginning, Christianity was thrown into mortal conflict with heathenism. That heathenism it steadily extirpated, whilst the sounder philosophy which had lived in the midst of heathenism it adopted for its own. In the midst of this there came too often an attempt at compromise. There sprang up a fusion between Christian verity and philosophy, and philosophy, too, of the corrupter heathen type, not of the purest or most divine type. Hence the strange forms of heresy which meet us in the earlier centuries. After the barbarian conquests, Christendom indeed took its fierce captors captive. They who had trod down imperial Rome, bowed lowly before Him whom Roman governors had crucified and Roman emperors had persecuted. Then came a struggle between barbarism and faith, the faith gradually subduing the barbarism, but the barbarism still clouding the faith. And I think we do not enough remember how through the Middle Ages, on which we often look so contemptuously back, there was ever going on a great mission work of the church and of the Gospel, the fierce barons and the rude churls being as hard to win to the obedience of faith as the heathens with whom the apostles pleaded in the early ages of the faith.

On the whole there has been a constant progress, greatest certainly at first, but never seriously slackened, till Mohammed devised a great Christian heresy (for a Christian heresy it was, as much as that of the Gnostics, or that of the Manichees before him,) thereby blighting the growth of the Eastern Church for centuries; still, however, there was progress again in the west, among Germans, and Slaves and Scandinavians; stagnation for a time from the twelfth to the eighteenth century, as far at least as visible increase was concerned; and now, again, progress, through the over-spreading of new continents by Christian colonists, and the bringing in of newly-known heathen tribes to the faith of the Church. Unless we insist that the world should be won by miracle, I do not see that we can ask more evidence to the winning power of the teaching of Christ.

V. And now for its effect on those taught by it, and on the world at large through them. I have argued that philosophy failed; has Christianity succeeded? With the allowances which must be made for the matter on which it has to work, and with the premised condition that it was not intended so to act as a spell that man's will would simply be enslaved by it, his moral responsibility lost, and his state of probation done away with; then I assert that it has succeeded incomparably beyond anything else that has ever been devised, or ever attempted by man.

Let us take great and acknowledged facts. It is confessed that under the influence of Christianity gladiatorial shows, and the throwing of prisoners to wild beasts, were given up and done away with. It is impossible to deny that the worst forms of licentiousness, which were not only tolerated in Greece and Rome, but indulged in openly by their heroes, attributed to their deities, and celebrated in verse by their poets, have been universally reprobated in Christendom, and dare not now show their heads abroad even in the most corrupted centres of modern society. The respect paid to woman is due before any other cause to the honour with which the Great Founder of our faith treated those women who waited on Him, and to His filial reverence for the mother that bare Him. The laws of marriage which now rule in Europe are not heathen, not even Jewish, but pre-eminently Christian. What Christ spoke concerning marriage and divorce regulated the principles of the Church, and the first Christian rulers incorporated those principles into the laws of the empire. Our domestic morals have thus been governed by a few sentences from the lips of one Man. The existence of hospitals for the sick and wounded is entirely due to the charity of the early Christian Church. The softening of the horrors of war, and the better treatment of prisoners, are equally the result of Christian influence. Contrast, for instance, the conduct of the most humane of heathen conquerors with the conduct of any great Christian general. No one among the ancients is more celebrated for his humanity than Titus; yet when Titus had taken Jerusalem, he crucified by thousands its undoubtedly brave defenders, and the historian tells us that "there lacked crosses for the bodies and room for erecting the crosses." When Gustavus Adolphus took a city, he so guarded the lives of its inhabitants, that it is said that no injury passed upon the head of one of them. In the war we have just witnessed, the German army marched into Paris, after fierce fights and long sieges, yet the first care of the invaders was not to slay or torture, but to feed the famished inhabitants of the city they had taken, the conquering army even giving up its rations to supply food to their enemies, who might else have perished for hunger. And as for the prisoners in modern warfare, the wounded and the sick are tended by the surgeons, and nursed in the hospitals of those against whom they have been fighting, and against whom it is possible they may yet live to fight.* This regard for human life is justly regarded by philanthropists as the truest test of a high

* The terrible scenes just enacted, and even now enacting, in Paris, almost seem to contradict my words concerning mercy in war, words written and even printed before Paris was burned and wasted. But let us remember that eighty years ago France threw away its Christianity, and took Atheism for its creed ; that in the last fifty years it has been slowly and painfully recovering its faith ; that Paris has been the centre of the unbelief of Europe ; that so, a large portion of its inhabitants have grown up utterly without religion ; that, according to a friendly witness, "the people of Paris believe not in any God, nor in any man ;"* or, according to another statement, "the Communists acknowledge no God, no man, no faith, no hope, nothing but better wages and more pleasure ;"† that the chief perpetrators of the horrors of the past week not only

* *Fortnightly Review*, quoted in *Times*, May 31, 1871.
† *Times*, May 31, 1871.

civilization; and I confidently ask whether it has ever come but from the influence of Christian teaching and the effect of Christian sympathy.

Let us turn to the question of slavery. It is objected by some that there is no direct denunciation of slavery in the Scriptures. I am not now concerned with the Old Testament; but I may yet, in passing, say, that whilst Moses could hardly refuse to recognise slavery as a prevailing institution, he still gave laws concerning it which mitigated its horrors to the utmost, and placed the Jewish slave in a condition, moral, social, and spiritual, utterly unlike to his condition in any heathen state. As regards the Gospel, we must remember, once more, that Christ was not a political reformer, not professedly a social reformer, not even primarily a moral reformer. His mission was to elevate men's whole spiritual nature; and this He did by the infusion into society of a new religious or spiritual principle. It did not fall in with the purposes of that mission to descend to every detail of social life, still less to regulate political institutions. So, He never denounces war, nor imperial

abhorred Christianity, but murdered priests, only because they were ministers of Christ, and proclaimed Atheism and Materialism to be the very basis of their theory, both in politics and in life. There is nothing to surprise us when we find that those who deliberately cast off religion and humanity, faith in God, and faith in man, fall lower than those who are simply ignorant of the true principles of either. Atheists in the midst of faith are very likely to be much worse than heathens.

tyranny, nor even the political factions of the Jews. It is scarcely a question that sudden emancipation of a great slave population is never desirable. And if the first Christians had preached against a deeply-rooted social institution, they might easily have produced great political convulsions, and have ultimately rendered less tolerable than ever the conditions of those whom they desired to befriend. But the principles of Christ's teaching are directly adverse to slavery, and their progress has invariably tended to mitigate, and at length to eradicate it. The principle of the brotherhood of all men, of their common interest in God, of their common humanity with Christ; the principle that there was neither Jew nor Greek, neither male nor female, neither bond nor free, in the great Christian commonwealth, but that all were one in Christ—this principle cannot be worked out without destroying the abject servitude of one man to another. And, as a matter of fact, this is what it has done. "The change brought about was gradual, but it was sure. At first monks, especially eastern monks, refused to be waited on by slaves. Then missionaries never lost an opportunity of redeeming slaves . . . . Ecclesiastical legislation declared the slave to be a *man*, and not a *thing*, or *chattel*; laid it down as a rule that his life was his own, and could not be taken without public trial; enforced on a master guilty of involuntary murder of his slave penance and exclusion from the communion; opened asylums to those who fled from their master's cruelty; declared the enfranchisement of the serf a work acceptable to God. The abolition of domestic slavery was one of the most important duties incumbent on the missionary energies of the mediæval Church." * It is sad, indeed, to think how the plague of slavery again broke out on the discovery of the West Indies and of America—slavery, too, in one of its most revolting and debasing forms; but it still is true that Christianity and Christian missions have struggled with it from the first, and that now, at length, it seems to be yielding, and there is good hope that it may ere long be utterly subdued.

In every way Christianity has been the pioneer of civilization, and the giver of social comfort and peace. Very truly, many colonists from Christian lands have given to the colonies which they founded not comfort, nor peace, nor civilization; but it has been because they have left Christian lands and not carried their Christianity out along with them. Often, indeed, they have only laid waste heathen lands and oppressed heathen races; and Christianity following after them, has had to undo the evil, which

* Maclear's "History of the Christian Missions in the Middle Ages," p. 417. Macmillan, 1863.

apostate Christians had inflicted. Still we may challenge any one to show a single instance, in which civilization in modern times has spread to any place to which Christianity has not first found its way. We may challenge any one to deny, that, where Christianity has been forsaken or neglected, there have sprung up, instead of it, as in revolutionary France, cruelty, licentiousness, and social degradation.

Christianity, once more, has been favourable at least to the development of mind, the cultivation of letters, the advancement of science. It is easy, of course, to say that there have often been efforts among Christians to check the progress of science, still more frequently panic terrors as to its unexpected discoveries. It is easy to point to Galileo, easy to speak of the fate of geology in the earlier days of the present century, of the reception of Mr. Darwin's theory now. As to Galileo, we may at once disown the Inquisition as representing the Christian faith. But it is unnecessary to deny that an appearance of antagonism between faith and science, or faith and literary criticism, will alarm timid believers, and so may lead to temporary misunderstandings between Christians and men of science or of literature. Yet look at past history and say, first, whether science and philosophy and literature did not for centuries find their only shelter in the Church, even under the deepest shadows of its cathedrals and monasteries. When all the world besides was unlettered and ignorant, learning flourished among the schoolmen, philosophy and even physical science were pursued, as far as they then could be pursued, by ecclesiastics and divines. The name of Roger Bacon stands out conspicuously as one who, in the cell of a convent and under the garb of a friar, carried inquiries into physical truth to a height which, considering his date and his difficulties, may compare even with the great and rapid discoveries of the present day. In short, it may be said truly and fearlessly, that whilst the only other religious systems in the world, which deserve consideration, Mohammedanism, Brahminism, and Buddhism, have either stifled, or at the best stunted science and made stagnant civilization; Christianity has fostered learning of all kinds, and has been in itself the highest civilization ever known.

I have naturally dwelt upon the external development of the religious life of Christians, not upon its inner being. A lecture on evidence, must of necessity appeal to that which can be known and read of all men. Yet I might, if there were time, point to the characters of individual Christians as proof of the elevating, ennobling, purifying, sanctifying power of the teaching of Christ, of the contemplation of Christ, and of the love of Christ. I will content myself with quoting words which many here have read, and read with interest, long ago. The author of "Ecce Homo" writes: "That Christ's method, when rightly applied, is really of mighty force, may be shown by an argument which the severest censor of Christians will hardly refuse to admit. Compare the ancient with the modern world. 'Look on this picture and on that.' One broad distinction in the characters of men forces itself into prominence. Among all men of the ancient heathen world, there were scarcely one or two to whom we may venture to apply the epithet 'holy.' In other words, there were not more than one or two, if any, who, besides being virtuous in their actions, were possessed with an unaffected enthusiasm of goodness, and besides abstaining from vice, regarded even a vicious thought with horror. Probably no one will deny that in Christian countries this higher-toned goodness, which we call holiness, has existed. Few will maintain that it is exceedingly rare. Perhaps the truth is, that there has been scarcely a town in any Christian country since the time of Christ, where a century has passed without exhibiting a character of such elevation that his mere presence has shamed the bad and made the good better, and has been felt at times like the presence of God Himself. And if this be so, has Christ failed? or can Christianity die?"*

Let us apply this test to one or two of the greatest and best of the heathen philosophers. Take Socrates first. Is

* "Ecce Homo," p. 71. Second edition, 1866.

it possible to imagine an apostle of Christ joining, as we know that Socrates joined, in drinking bouts where many were intoxicated, not himself drinking willingly, but when pressed making deeper potations than any one besides, yet never exhibiting symptoms of drunkenness? * It cannot be conceived that the unutterable licentiousness of Alcibiades, manifested during one of those drinking bouts, could have been so manifested, I will not say in the presence of St. Paul or St. John, or in the presence of any Christian clergyman since them, but even in the lowest assembly of English drunkards.

Take Marcus Aurelius: Mr. Lecky, the eloquent and able writer on "European Morals," has held him up as an example of what pure philosophy can do, and has challenged comparison between him and the most exalted and sanctified of the followers of Christ. We may well acknowledge the nobleness, the disinterestedness, the simplicity, and the elevation of his character. No absolute and irresponsible governor of men has ever been more "clear in his high office." Yet the concessions, which his panegyrist has made concerning him, separate him off by a broad line of demarcation from the highest types of Christian holiness. When his wife died, for his children's sake he would not contract a second marriage; but he preferred the society of a mis-

* Platon. Symposium. Steph. iii., 220.

tress. When he persecuted the Christians, an act which we may perhaps attribute to mistaken conscientiousness, he not only persecuted them, but he derided their sufferings. Could we in these days even call a man Christian who could so err? Professed Christians, no doubt, fall into licentiousness, but then they know they are in act repudiating their Christianity. Christians, alas! have persecuted those whom they regarded as heretics. But we must look fairly at the sad history of persecution before we simply say that Roman emperors did no more. In the first place, persecution was not inconsistent with the principles of heathenism, nor is it inconsistent with the principles, if such there be, of atheism or of atheistic philosophy; but it is wholly inconsistent with the principles taught by Christ, and can only have been tolerated when those principles had been perverted or obscured. In the next place, Christian persecutors, believing that their own form of Christianity was the only faith that could save mankind, esteeming therefore those who defiled that faith as more dangerous to mankind than any robbers or murderers, thought consistently, though erroneously, that they were bound to stamp out heresy as they would stamp out pestilence in their cattle sheds, or moral pestilence in their homes and villages. In the third place, though deeds of violence always harden the hearts of those that do them, it is well known that even inquisitors, so far from ridiculing the sufferings of their victims, often decreed those sufferings with trembling hands and broken accents, and eyes filled with tears. Persecutors are no types of Christian excellence; the truest Christianity utterly repudiates them; but even persecutors have generally been so, not from love of persecution, but from a deep and painful conviction that persecution was a duty and a necessity.

It will be replied, and very truly, that for all this, Socrates and Marcus Aurelius were grand specimens of humanity, rising to a noble height of moral greatness in an age of cruelty and licentiousness, and that we cannot expect them to have been all that we should expect from a Christian apostle or from a Christian king. Granted most heartily this. It only proves that Christianity has raised our standard of excellence and has raised the characters of those who embrace and follow it immeasurably above the highest standard and the noblest characters of the world, which had never heard of Christ.

I must bring my words, my most feeble and imperfect words in this high argument, to a close. I have tried to show that the life of Christ, and the teaching of Christ, as we have them recorded in the most unsuspicious records,—records which could not possibly have been the gradual concoctions and concretions of subsequent times, the careful afterthoughts of enthusiasts or impostors; that the life and teaching of Christ were original in the highest degree, not calculated to attract from any pandering to prejudice or to passion, that they exhibit the most marvellous ideal of simple grandeur or grand simplicity; that the power which they exercise is from no apparent effort—not even from reasoning and argumentation,—but from the strength of truth, and from their satisfaction to human want; that the power which they exercised, and yet exercise, is the greatest moral power ever tried upon man; that they have raised, and yet do raise, men and nations to a greater height of civilization, humanity, and purity, than anything has ever raised them before. And I ask, How can we account for the fact that all this has been done by the teaching of one unlettered Peasant in the most despised corner of a despised land? Is there any phenomenon in moral science, or in physical science, which demands a patient and honest investigation more seriously than this?

There are those who think the influence of Christianity is on the wane. I confess I can see no sign of this; though, without doubt, its enemies are many, and the wish is father to the thought. But I will just put my case in one other shape, which will more or less deal with this question of decay, and then I will end.

If an assembly of 500 or 1,000 persons could be gathered

together, in any city of Europe, or European America, it being provided that all of them should be intelligent, well-educated, high-principled, and well-living men and women; and if the question were put to each of them, "To what influences do you attribute your high character, your moral and social excellence?" I feel no doubt that nineteen out of twenty of them would, on reflection, reply, "To the influence of Christianity on my education, my conscience, and my heart." I will suppose a yet further question to be put to them, and it shall be this: "If you were to be assured that the object you hold dearest on earth would be taken from you to-morrow, and if at the same time you could be assured with undoubting certainty that Jesus Christ was a myth or an impostor, and His Gospel a fable and a falsehood, whether of the two assurances would strike upon your heart with the more chilling and more hope-destroying misery?" And I believe that nine-tenths of the company, being such as I have stipulated they should be, would answer, "Take from me my best earthly treasure, but leave me my hope in the Saviour of the world." This is the effect produced upon the most civilized nations of the world by the teaching of four years, and the agony of a few hours, of One who lived as a peasant, and died as a malefactor and a slave. "Whence had this man this wisdom and these mighty works?"

THE COMPLETENESS AND ADEQUACY

OF THE

EVIDENCES OF CHRISTIANITY.

BY THE

REV. F. C. COOK, M.A.,

CANON OF EXETER; PREACHER AT LINCOLN'S INN.

COMPLETENESS AND ADEQUACY

OF THE

EVIDENCES OF CHRISTIANITY.

THE evidences of Christianity form a department of sacred literature of vast extent, to which the most valuable contributions have been made in ages when the faith of the Church was most vehemently assailed, and her powers were developed by severe and protracted struggles.

It was the subject to which the ablest Christian writers of the first three centuries devoted their energies, carrying on in no alien spirit the work of the Apostles, meeting assailants at every point, demolishing with comparative ease the fabric of heathen superstition; winning a nobler and more fertile triumph over the intellect of Greece. Nor was the work thus well begun wholly intermitted during the ages which intervened between the overthrow of ancient, and the full development of modern, civilization; a civilization which owes whatever it has of life and power to its reception and assimilation of Christian principles.* But, as might be expected, the work had to be begun anew, new difficulties were to be met, new victories were to be achieved, when the spiritual and intellectual energies of Europe were set free by the vast upheaval of mind at the Reformation. The way was opened by representative men. Grotius, who combined in a most remarkable degree the accurate and profound learning and the clear dispassionate judgment characteristic of his countrymen, produced the first complete treatise, "*De Veritate Christianæ Religionis*," soon adopted as the standard work by Protestants, translated into every language of Europe, and by our own Pocock into Arabic, for the use of the East. England followed early in the field, and in the last century fairly won the place, which she still retains, among the foremost champions of the Cross. Nor did the persecution which arrested the progress of the Reformation in France, then, as ever, unhappy in her struggles for light and air, suppress the workings of spiritual thought. Of all advocates of the faith, none penetrated more deeply into its foundation, none ascended with a stronger flight or keener vision into its highest sphere, none combined more varied gifts of

* Midway stands Anselm, the father of modern metaphysics, with the scientific demonstration of the two fundamental truths of all religion, the existence of God and the Incarnation.

intellect and spirit than Pascal, a name bright with the gracious gleam of letters, dear to "science," dearest above all to Christian truth.* Germany, too, great in every field of intellectual power, has not been unmindful of the duty of maintaining and defending the deposit of truth—a duty specially incumbent upon her as first leader in the revolt against usurped authority—not wholly unmindful, though as yet she is far from having discharged her debt to Christendom, of late years perplexed and harassed by her reckless abuse of power. Still in the past, among other great names, Leibnitz, who represents, perhaps more fully than any one man, the peculiar characteristics of German intellect, laid the foundations of a system, in which the true relation between the Christian revelation and God's universe is examined. And at this present hour men sound in the faith, full of the love and light of Christ, are bringing the resources of profound learning and vigorous intellect to bear upon the chaotic turmoil of anti-Christian influences. Within this present year several works have appeared in which infidelity is confronted, both in the sphere of general cultivation, and in the abstrusest fastnesses of philosophy, by Luthardt, Steinmeyer, and Delitzsch.† One of the greatest

* Pascal, "Fragmens d'une Apologie du Christianisme," in the 2nd vol. of "Pensées du Blaise Pascal." Paris, 1814.

† Luthardt (Apologetische Vorträge, in two parts), presents in a form peculiarly adapted for general readers, a very complete survey both of

works at present incumbent upon the Church of Christ is to bring together into a compact and systematic body the results of previous investigations, which from their very extent are inaccessible to the generality of inquirers. It is a work for which this society has been formed; it will only be accomplished by the combined efforts of men varying in gifts and powers, but animated alike by one spirit of fealty and love to our Lord.

On this occasion I propose, with all possible brevity, to show that those evidences of Christianity which are accessible to every careful inquirer are complete and adequate; complete inasmuch as they meet the fair requirements of our moral and rational nature, and adequate with reference to their purpose, which is to bring us into contact with the central and fundamental truths of our religion, and with the Person of its Founder. It may be assumed that persons who meet to consider the evidences of revealed religion have previously satisfied themselves of the existence and the personality of God;

the internal and external evidences. Steinmeyer, Apologetische Vorträge, in three parts, discusses the historical evidence for the miracles, the death and the resurrection of our Lord, with special reference to the latest criticisms. Delitzsch's System der Christlichen Apologetik is of a more exclusively philosophical and dogmatic character. It has been reviewed in the Studien u. Kritiken, by Dr. Sack, of Bonn, whose own work, Christliche Apologetik, 1841, is one of the best on the whole subject of evidences.

or at least that they have not accepted the theory, once deemed too irrational to need refutation, that the universe is but an assemblage of forces, self-existent, and uncontrolled by a conscious will. That is a question antecedent to our present inquiry. It would be useless to discuss the proofs of a supernatural intervention with one who held that there is no supernatural power to intervene. Materialism under any form, and Christianity in any stage, are mutually exclusive. They are not even, properly speaking, antagonistic; since antagonism implies a common field of action, and the recognition of some principle to which disputants can appeal. We can only argue now with those who admit the possibility of a revelation, and are therefore willing to examine the evidences, and to accept the conclusions to which those evidences may lead.

Our first object will be to see what conclusions are fairly drawn from those broad facts which first present themselves in the history of Christianity, and which no one thinks of disputing. Put yourselves, if possible, in the position of an inquirer to whom the facts might be new, and who had simply to satisfy himself as to their bearings upon his own convictions and upon the state of man.

Here is one fact. At the central point of the world's history, central both in time and in historical import, equidistant from the end of what men are agreed to call the prehistoric period and our own time, the man Jesus arose, and claimed to be, in a sense altogther apart from other men, the teacher and the Saviour of the world. He claimed a direct mission from God,—nay, more, to be, in a sense hereafter to be ascertained, the Son of God. He assumed that the truth which He had to teach was new, inasmuch as it was one which man could not discover for himself, but at the same time one to which man's conscience would bear testimony, which could not therefore be rejected without sin. As credentials of His mission, He appealed to works which those who accepted Him and those who opposed Him admitted could not be wrought without supernatural aid.* To one work, as the crowning work of all, He directed His followers to appeal, as one capable of being attested, and incapable of being explained away, even His own resurrection from the dead.

And now observe, the fact of this assumption, quite independent of the evidence by which it was supported, stands absolutely alone in the world's history. Consider the existing religions of the world. Three are associated with the names of individuals as their founders. Of Mahomet we need not speak. His doctrine was avowedly derived from

* It is well known that both Jews and Gentiles admitted that the works were wrought, though they denied that the power came from God. Superstition, then as ever, opposed the faith of which it is the counterfeit.

Judaism, he claimed no special relationship to God, nor did he profess to work miracles; as coming after our Lord, we might have expected a far nearer resemblance in pretensions advanced by himself, and to some extent at a later period advanced by his followers. Two other men, however, stand before us with characteristics which attract our warmest interest, and enable us to understand the permanent influence they have exerted over the countless myriads of Asia. I know nothing in history more touching than the account of Siddartha * (called Sakya Monni, that is, monk of the royal race of the Sakyas), the founder of Bhuddism, whose tender and noble spirit was driven by the contemplation of human misery into desperate struggles to escape from this prison of the universe even at the cost

* The most interesting and accessible accounts of this man are given by M. Barthélemi S. Hilaire, "Le Bonddha et sa Religion;" and by M. Ampère, in "La Science et les Lettres en Orient." Siddartha lived about the end of the seventh century, B.C. The name "Sakya Monni" is an appellative, meaning the monk or hermit of the Sakyas, the royal race to which he belonged. The true end of all philosophy and religion in his system is to enter into Nirvana, *i. e.* (according to M. Eugène Burnouf, the highest authority on this subject), the complete annihilation, not only of the material elements of existence, but also, and more specially, of the thinking principle. In this view the majority of Oriental scholars agree; the few who differ, as Colebrook does, identify Nirvana with an endless and dreamless sleep. See M. S. Hilaire, l.c., p. 133. M. Ampère (p. 215) thus characterizes the system, "La fin suprême de l'homme à été de perdre le sentiment de son moi, de renoncer à sa liberté, de s'élever au dessus des affections les plus pures, d'arriver à un état, où il ne restât plus que le *vide.*"

of personal annihilation; but observe this, he did not even profess to support his strange gospel of despair by assertions or attestations which would necessarily imply the personality of God, and His sovereignty over the universe. If, again, you consult the four books in which Confucius * sets forth with singular simplicity and force the great principles of moral truth, you will find that he never presents them as revelations, as a message supernaturally imparted or attested, but as evolutions of man's inner conscience, as the product of a faculty inherent equally in all. Seekers after truth, honest, earnest, and noble seekers, to whom no Christian should refuse a tribute of admiration, the world has produced, but you will find no one man, save Jesus only, among the founders of existing religions, no one indeed within the historic period, who ever professed to be the *giver* of a truth at once absolutely new and attested by works such as God only could enable him to perform.

* The four books of Khung-fu-tseu were written in the second half of the sixth century, B.C. They contain the religions and philosophy of China in a dogmatic form. The second book, called "Tchung yung," represents most fully his moral code, of which the principle is obedience to natural reason, and the rule is observance of the *via media*, with due regard to times and circumstances. In one passage, ccxi., iv., Confucius says a man of strong virtue goes beyond this *via media* which prescribes indifference and exact conformity to natural law. For a just appreciation of the Confucian system, the reader may consult M. Ampère, "La Science et les Lettres en Orient," p. 98 ff.

And now consider this fact. The appearance of this man Jesus, unparalleled as it is shown to have been, was nevertheless *expected.* At present I have not to show that His person, His offices, His work, together with their permanent effect, had actually been foretold, or that the predictions referred to Him as accomplisher of a divine purpose; but this we know, as a fact beyond controversy, that when He began to teach and work, his countrymen were familiar with a long series of texts, beginning with the first, and continued to the end, of their sacred books, in which they recognized descriptions of such a teacher. You will remember that those descriptions included all particulars by which an individual could be identified. As for their accurate coincidence with what is recorded of our Lord, it is scarcely necessary to argue, since our ablest opponents hold that it is too close to be accounted for, save on the supposition that the records, whether consciously or unconsciously, were moulded so to produce the conformity. With that theory Mr. Row and others have dealt. I do not believe that it is likely to retain a hold on the minds of our countrymen, but it is a most striking attestation to an all-important fact which I request you most seriously to weigh, remembering that of this man Jesus alone in the world's history can it be asserted that such an expectation existed.

The next fact, again, is so obvious that men are in real danger of overlooking its significance. The faith in this Man took root. It took root at once, and so deeply that storms which might have sufficed to tear up any human institution, served only to fix it more firmly. This Man died, His followers were hounded to the death, man's passions, man's superstitions, man's intellect, during centuries of struggle, were opposed to this religion, and yet it prevailed. Will you say it did not prevail universally? Well, what is its actual extent? I answer, it is co-extensive with the civilization of the world. Is this assertion too strong? Look at the facts. Beyond the pale of Christendom, the great races of humanity, which in past ages have shown equal capacities for the highest culture, have at this present time no single representative nation, Turanian, Semitic, or Aryan, in which liberty, philosophy, nay, even physical science, with its serene indifference to moral or spiritual truth, have a settled home or practical development. The elements of civilization are there, capable undoubtedly of being evoked and energized, but as a plain matter of fact at this present time, after thousands of years for development, throughout the vast regions of Islamism, Buddhism, and Confucianism, not to speak of lower forms of paganism, they are stunted, distorted, and, to all human ken, in hopeless and chaotic ruin. It would not be diffcult to prove that the special evils which have choked the human mind, and blighted its energies, are in each case distinctly traceable to evils inherent in those religious systems; but we are dealing now with facts not depending upon argument, nor demanding lengthened inquiries. It suffices to state the bare fact that the religion of the crucified Jesus, with its doctrines that were a stumbling-block to the Jews, and foolishness to the Gentiles, is at this day conterminous with human progress, with all advance in liberty, science, and social culture, with all that is substantially precious in the civilization of the world.

To these facts others might be added of a similar character, such as the recognition of our Lord Jesus as the true Master and Teacher of the world, by men acknowledged in every age of Christendom to be conspicuous for moral worth and intellectual power; such, again, as the pre-eminence in Christendom, in every age, of nations which profess at least to acknowledge Him as their Lord, and as the rapid disintegration or ruin of communities which have corrupted or abjured His religion. But the broadest and simplest facts thus stated are sufficient for the one purpose we have now in view; sufficient to induce every one who cares to know the truth to go at once to that Man, to ask what He has to teach. The inquirer will do this, as I should think, before he enters into the lengthened and very difficult inquiry into the origin or interpretation of the predictions or the words of which we have spoken. He will do it because, after all, no evidence has anything approaching the weight which attaches to the personal influence of a teacher, in this case, of one who declares Himself to be ready to receive inquirers, and to satisfy their wants, who claims to be the living and ever-present Teacher of man. The inquirer will certainly do this if he feels the same moral wants, and experiences the same moral difficulties and perplexities which beset the most thoughtful heathen before the coming of this Man; feelings well expressed in the Phædo of Plato by Simmias, a good representative of sturdy, even sceptical, but thoroughly honest seekers after truth. These are his words: "It seems to me, Socrates, as probably to you also, that to know the certainty about such questions in this present life is a thing either impossible or exceedingly difficult; yet that, nevertheless, not to test thoroughly whatever is said about them, or to desist until we have done our utmost by inquiring in every direction, would be sheer cowardice. For some one at least of the following results we ought to attain about them, either to learn from others how the truth stands, or discover it for ourselves; or, if neither should be possible, then, at any rate, to take the best and most irrefragable of human theories, and use it as a raft, so to speak, to convey us, though in much danger, through the sea of life, unless, indeed, one were enabled to accomplish the passage, with no risk of error or mishap, upon the firmer conveyance of a word from God."*

The question now meets us, How can we be sure that we have His teaching? Where can we find His own words? Where can we learn what He really did? Have we a thoroughly trustworthy, not to say unquestioned, record of the words He uttered? of the works He is asserted to have wrought?

Now there can be no doubt, that of all assaults upon the faith, the most effective in this age are those which have been made upon the documents which compose the New Testament. The reason for this is obvious. An investigation into the authenticity of any ancient book demands an amount of knowledge and critical ability, a soundness and keenness of judgment, which are the very rarest of qualifications. Turn to secular literature, and you will find critics arguing for ages, without any approximation to a settlement, touching the genuineness of works attributed to men whose peculiarities of genius and of style would seem to defy imitation. Who would venture on his own judgment to determine how much of the Homeric poems belong to

* For a very remarkable echo of this passage, showing the depth and permanence of such feelings, see the words of Mr. Hutton, quoted further on.

> "That Lord of loftiest song,
> Who above others like an eagle soars ?"
>
> "Quel Signor dell' altissimo canto,
> Che sovra gli altri com' aquila vola." *

Look at the controversy between Grote, Jowett, and the latest German critics touching the authenticity of no small portion of the Platonic dialogues. Taken simply as a question of critical inquiry, no man of sense would venture to determine, on internal data, the authorship of any book in the New Testament, without years of laborious preparation. I will add, no prudent man at all conversant with the history of criticism would accept assertions, however confident, of critics whose known and avowed prepossessions would make it *à priori* certain that they would be averse to the acceptance of documents which, if genuine, supply substantial grounds for belief in supernatural works and a supernatural Person.

What then are we to do? Well, in the first place we may inquire whether any portion of the documents in that book is admitted to be wholly unaffected by the corrosive solvent of negative criticism. This will give us at once a most important set of documents, no less than those epistles of St. Paul † which contain the fullest exposition of Christ's

* Dante, Inferno, c. iv.

† Romans, Corinthians, and Galatians, accepted by all the Tübingen School. (See Mr. Leathes' lecture.)

doctrine, and the most explicit statements of the supernatural facts on which that doctrine is based; above all, the fact of the Resurrection. There you will find Christ speaking, according to His own promise, by His Spirit. But we are not to be cheated of our heritage by a criticism of which the main negative results are repudiated, not only by all who believe in any form or degree of objective revelation, but by a great majority of avowed rationalists. One by one we recover, with their concurrence, the other general epistles of St. Paul, the first of St. Peter and of St. John, the Gospel of St. Mark, the discourses in St. Matthew, the two treatises of St. Luke, and, though hotly contested, as might be expected, considering its vital importance, still triumphantly, and I do not fear to say irrevocably, secured, attested by external evidence ever more perfect, and by internal evidence * daily more convincing, as you can witness, the Gospel of St. John. I might go farther still, and point to the reception of nearly all contested portions by some or other of our opponents, and show the cogency of the reasons which overcame deep-seated

* In addition to the well-known work of Tischendorf, and German, French, and English commentaries, attention may be called to a valuable treatise by P. H. de Groot, of Groningen, "Basilides als erster Zeuge des Johannesevangeliums." Leipzig, 1868. The internal evidence has already been discussed by Dr. Lightfoot, who promises a complete treatise on the subject, with which no one can deal more effectively. Some good points are made by Mr. Hutton in Essays, vol. i.

prejudices; but it is sufficient for our immediate purpose to argue *ex concessis*. If we take at first those books only which the severest critics, with the exception of certain scholars of the Tübingen school hold to be indisputable, we have Christ before us, the characteristics of His Personality, the cardinal events of His life, the subject matter of His teaching. Even Keim and Rénan admit that His mark is unmistakably stamped upon those discourses to which every inquirer will naturally turn at once, when he seeks to know what Jesus taught.

And here let me speak out frankly my own opinion. The whole result of inquiry into the truth of Christianity will depend upon the effect produced upon you by the Personality of Jesus Christ. If a careful study of His words, of His works, does not constrain you to recognize in Him a divine Teacher, if it does not lead you to discern the Being in whom alone humanity attained to that ideal perfection of which philosophers had ever dreamed, but of which they deemed that the realization was impossible, nay, more, a Being in whom the moral and spiritual attributes of Deity, perfect holiness, and perfect love, were manifested, then indeed I admit, nay, I am in truth convinced, that no other evidences will have any real or permanent effect upon your spirit. The completeness of those evidences may fill your minds with anxious questionings, their adequacy may leave you without excuse for their rejection; but without a personal influence they will also leave you cold, and in a position, if not of outward antagonism, yet of inward alienation. If, on the other hand, you accept Jesus as your Teacher and Master, simply and wholly because He has won your heart and conquered your spirit, then all other evidences will fall into their proper place; they will not be set aside, contemned, or neglected—had they been needless, they would not have been given—but they will be used as subsidiary and supplementary; enabling you to give a reason for the faith which is in you, both for your own satisfaction, and for the defence and advancement of Christian truth. The one great evidence, the master evidence, the evidence with which all other evidences will stand or fall, is Christ Himself speaking by His own word.

Our first endeavour must therefore be to acquire a distinct and, so far as may be possible, a complete conception of the personal character of Jesus Christ. Here, however, we are met by the question, Are we to consider Him at first in His human nature separately, or must we, in order to appreciate Him truly, contemplate Him at once in the completeness of His Personality, combining the human with the divine? I answer, not without some hesitation, that the line seems pointed out by Holy Scripture. We are told there that His nature is twofold, that in Him we see God in man, that the whole work which He came to accomplish depended upon that nature; but, on the other hand, we find that the form in which He presented Himself to His contemporaries, and through the medium of historical records to the Church, in which and by which He drew mankind to Himself, was thoroughly human; and so it seems to me clear that our first duty must be to collect from the Gospel narrative all the characteristic traits of His humanity, and so learn to know Him as perfect man. We may or may not avail ourselves of external help in this part of the inquiry; but if we do, the utmost caution and discrimination will be needed. It is certain that all so-called lives of Jesus are written under some kind of prepossession, and convey impressions which, however fair and honest they may be, have a strong colouring of personal feelings. Doubtless by such lives as those by Neander, Baumgarten, Pressensé, not to speak of the "Ecce Homo," a student may have his attention drawn to traits which he might otherwise fail to appreciate: but I believe that, until the mind is saturated with the truth set forth with all plainness and in all completeness in Scripture, the loss will outweigh the gain. I do not say that, in an advanced stage of inquiry, those among us especially who have to consult the wants of other minds, may not profitably resort to these and similar writings for supplementary information or suggestions: but this observation is to some extent true of other works in which the false infinitely preponderates over the true; and if you once go outside of the Gospels for aid in the natural attempt to gain an independent position as an impartial inquirer, you may entangle yourself in the subtle webs of sophistry, such as are woven by Rénan, Keim, or Strauss. Speaking indeed of Pressensé's work on our Saviour's life, which, on the whole, approaches most nearly to a faithful and complete portraiture, a friend remarkable for sound strong sense remarked to me that a careful perusal served but to convince him of the needlessness of such remouldings of the sacred history. And for my own part, I do not hesitate to say that you will act most wisely if you keep to the gospel narrative exclusively until you have ascertained to your own satisfaction what are the true characteristics of our Lord. I do not entertain any doubt as to the result. No healthy moral nature ever came into contact with that Personality without recognizing its unapproached and unapproachable excellence. Nay, I will add, no human heart susceptible of tender or noble emotions ever fixed its gaze upon Jesus without acknowledging in Him the embodiment of love. Attestations to this effect might be adduced in abundance from writings of men who have passed their lives in ineffectual efforts to extricate themselves from the perplexity arising from their inability to reconcile that impression with their intellectual system: but we need no testimony from without. Go to Christ, hear Him speak, watch His actions, and you will have an evidence, at once complete and adequate, that in Him was a human nature which, in its entire freedom from all moral evil, and in its perfect development of all moral goodness, stands absolutely alone.

You may say this is mere assumption. I can only answer, You have to judge for yourselves. I do not profess to draw out the evidence, but simply to show what is its nature, and where it is to be found. I do not attempt to delineate that character; at the utmost, I could but give you but a very imperfect account of the impression which it has made on my own very imperfect nature. I simply assert that the evidence is there, and that upon you rests the responsibility of examining it. Its effect, as I doubt not, will depend upon your moral nature; not indeed upon your moral goodness—Christ speaks to sinners—but upon your moral susceptibility, your capacity to discern and appreciate moral goodness. If that character does not attract, subdue, and win you, I freely admit all other evidence will be useless so far as your innermost convictions are concerned. But numerous as are the cases o individuals who have remained in, or relapsed into, a state of scepticism from various causes, intellectual or moral, few indeed are the cases of men who have not borne with them into that dreary region an abiding sense of the personal and supreme goodness of Jesus.

But the more carefully you examine that character, the more forcibly you will be struck by the fact that this Man, of whom the most special and most distinctive characteristics are absolute truthfulness and absolute humility, speaks throughout with an authority which involves the assumption of a divine nature. This statement does not rest on particular texts open to misconstruction or evasion, but on the tenor of each and every discourse, on His acts not less than His words. He addresses man as man's Master; He speaks as the Son of God, as one with God. This fact is stated in strong, not to say irreverent, terms by the author of "Ecce Homo": "During His whole public life Jesus is distinguished from the other prominent characters of Jewish history by His unbounded personal pretensions." Two writers, differing widely in tone of mind, but alike in depth of thought and earnestness of purpose, prove, were proof needed, that those pretensions are justified by the truth of the Incarnation, and by that alone. (See the Rev. M. F. Sadler, "Immanuel," pp. 264—309; and Mr. Hutton's "Essay on the Incarnation.") You will, in fact, soon find that you have no alternative but either to give up all that has wrought itself into your moral nature, and intwined itself around the fibres of your affections, all your convictions of the moral excellence of Jesus, or to accept Him, even as He presents Himself, the God-man. His enemies felt this. They persecuted Him because He made Himself, as they said truly, equal with God. They crucified Him because He claimed the powers and attributes of the Son of God. Modern sceptics of loftier strain feel this keenly. They might be content to accept Him as a moral teacher; for, in that case, they could deal with Him as their equal by nature, receiving or rejecting His teaching as it might accord or not with their own judgment; if they reject Him, it is simply or mainly, as they will tell you, because He claims to be more than man, and, as they well know, to be no less than God. They ask (perhaps you will ask), how did He justify the claim? The answer, of course, involves the whole controversy; but I will once more state my own conviction. If you put yourselves under His teaching, He will not leave you in doubt. You will attain by degrees only to any real appreciation of His human goodness; but together with the growth of that appreciation will dawn upon you the consciousness, ever increasing in clearness and intensity, that in Him you are gazing upon the Incarnate God. You will have a twofold evidence: the evidence of a perfectly logical conviction, founded on sure inferences from sure premises, upon the inseparability of truth and goodness, self-knowledge and perfect wisdom, and the evidence of direct intuition; you will feel yourselves in the presence of God.

And now let me read a passage which is a very remarkable attestation to the effect produced upon a man of strong sense and thorough independence of character, by an honest and reverent study of our Lord's Person and teaching. You will find it in the treatise on the Incarnation, published within the last few months, in Mr. Hutton's Essays: "And now let me honestly ask myself, and answer the question as truly as I can, whether this great, this stupendous fact of the Incarnation is honestly *believable* by an ordinary man of modern times, who has not been educated into it, but educated to distrust it; who has no leaning to the orthodox creed, as such, but has generally preferred to associate with heretics; who is quite alive to the force of the scientific and literary criticisms of his day; who has no antiquarian tastes, no predilection for the venerable past; who does not regard this truth as part of a great system, dogmatic or ecclesiastical, but merely for itself; who is, in a word, simply anxious to take hold, if he so may, of any divine hand stretched out to help him through the excitement and the languor, the joy, the sorrow, the storm and sunshine, of this unintelligible life. From my heart I answer, Yes—believable, and more than believable, in any mood in which we can rise above ourselves to that supernatural spirit which orders the unruly wills and affections of sinful men ; *more* than believable, I say, because it so vivifies and supplements that fundamental faith in God as to realize what were else abstract, and, without dissolving the mystery, to clothe eternal love with breathing life."*

Let me call your attention to the remarkable resemblance, of which I believe the writer to have been unconscious, between these most striking words and those which I quoted from Plato. What the ancient inquirer longed for, but sought in vain, the modern has sought and found, and with it the one and the only imaginable solution of the mystery of life.

I speak to persons able to bring the stores of varied reading to bear upon these questions, and we live in a time when learning has fairly rivalled science in bringing regions of thought hitherto unknown, or known only to solitary students, within the cognizance of men of general cultivation. As a matter of a deep interest and importance, I would ask you, when you have attained to a complete conception of our Lord's Person, to compare His teaching with that of men whose influence has been most widely and abidingly felt in the world. I will not insult our Master by placing His name in juxtaposition with the founder of Islamism, nor indeed would it fairly enter into the inquiry; for if you separate the elements of truth

* Essays Theological and Literary, by R. H. Hutton; vol. i., p. 282.

derived from Judaism and from Christianity, through the medium of a corrupt tradition, the Koran will yield you but a mass of idle legends. It is indeed the fashion at present to speak of Mahomet as "a great and genuine prophet, with a Divine mission" (see Hutton's Essays, i. p. 277). Now I do not doubt his sincerity at the beginning of his career, or his steadfast adherence to the one great truth which he proclaimed; but it must never be forgotten that he invented a special revelation to justify indulgence in his master-sin (see the Koran, c. 66), and that he commanded the propagation of his religion by the sword. There are, however, three great names connected with those mighty revolutions of thought which have permanently affected the moral or religious convictions of mankind; I speak of them specially, because their character and teaching were wholly uninfluenced by revelation, and because they severally represent the highest development of pre-Christian character: Buddha, Confucius, and Socrates. Of two I have already spoken, and will now simply refer you to the clear and impartial accounts given by Ampère, Francke, and Barthélemi St. Hilaire, to justify my statement, that although, as might be expected, in some points of their moral teaching and in their spiritual aspirations they bear a true resemblance to Him in whom human nature was perfectly represented, yet each of them differed, as indeed all other men differ, from Him, in one special characteristic; each of them is the creature of his race and of his age; the influence of each is felt in the full development of the peculiar tendencies of his own section of the human family; in the one case, of physical languor and mental dreaminess; in the other, of a formal and conventional morality, and of political unity secured by the sacrifice of all independent action and thought. I turn to Socrates. There is a special reason why we should direct our attention to his character. It has at various times been brought into comparison with that of our Lord; even when that comparison is not distinctly brought out, it is often intentionally, or it may be unintentionally, suggested. That character has been delineated by Mr. Jowett, in the prefaces of his translation of the Platonic dialogues, with a sagacity beyond all praise, with an impartiality which trenches upon indifference, not merely in questions of merely speculative interest, but of moral concernment.* It is a noble work, representing the labour of long years devoted almost exclusively to the study of the master-mind of Greece. Socrates there stands before us. We enter into

* Notice the faint condemnation, if it be a condemnation at all, of the peculiar shame of Athens, as "greatly at variance with modern and Christian *notions*, but in accordance with Hellenic sentiment" (vol. i., p. 482, and compare p. 555).

his thoughts, we know him as a living man. His character may indeed have undergone some change of representation in passing through the mind of the most imaginative of human teachers, his greatest disciple, Plato; but it is a change which does but magnify and idealize his loftiest characteristics. Let us see, then, in what respects this wisest and best of men, this teacher whom the great Fathers of Christendom justly reverenced as a true though unconscious preparer of men's spirits for the coming Teacher, resembles, in what respects, not less than the other two, he especially differs, from our Lord.

This strikes us at a glance. Socrates is altogether and throughout a Greek. His intellect, his character, is Greek. The stamp of an exclusive nationality is upon him. He has the feelings, the prejudices, of a singularly exclusive section of an exclusive race. His code of morals tolerates, I will not say sanctions, habits and feelings "quite at variance," as Mr. Jowett says, "with modern and Christian *notions.*" Characters moulded to a great extent under his influence became living embodiments of some of the worst characteristics of heathenism, of force, pride (ὕβρις), and licentiousness, as, for instance, Critias, Charmides, and Alcibiades. Exquisite and perfect as was his sympathy with all that was noble, all that was graceful and beautiful in Hellenic culture, it went no further. Graces which to the Christian are the very foundation of spiritualist life, had no place, no name even, in his philosophy. I cannot recall, among all his sayings, one that expresses sympathy with man in his extremest degradation and misery, or indignation with his countrymen for their treatment of their slaves. I would not be unjust. I never turn to the pages in which his spirit breathes without recognizing its attractions for the lover of man and the seeker after God; but still the fact remains, and stands out more clearly the more fully that spirit is made known, that Socrates, in his best and in his worst characteristics, was out and out an Athenian by character, by temperament, by moral sympathy, and by religion also, not less than Confucius was a Chinese, and Siddartha a Hindoo.

I touch briefly on another important point. Socrates was a true, honest, earnest seeker after truth. I give this high praise unreservedly. As such, he represents the best tendencies of Gentile thought. As an honest seeker he had the fitting reward. So far as his search was not impeded by moral causes to which I have alluded, it was successful. He apprehended and taught truths of infinite value. But note this; he had not, did not profess to have, definite convictions upon the most important of all truths. Mr. Jowett says deliberately,* and as I think truly, "Socrates cannot

* See the preface to the Republic, in vol. ii. Compare also the words

be proved to have believed in the immortality of the soul." His speculations concerning a future state of retribution, recorded doubtless with a considerable admixture of Platonism in the Phædo, are deeply interesting; but they are speculations only, resting partly on grounds of which he recognises the insufficiency, or of which we cannot doubt the unsoundness. Socrates gave what he found. He sought for life and immortality; he drew very near to the region where they are to be found; he prepared the spirit of man for their announcement; but he did not bring them to light. That was the work of Him who at once declares the truth, and justifies its reception.

And now, keeping these characteristics in mind, let me ask you to consider them in reference to our Lord's teaching. One of our most popular and graceful writers —the Dean of Westminster—has done good service to the truth by pointing out repeatedly the very conspicuous and utterly peculiar characteristic of the Saviour, that He is wholly devoid of national exclusiveness. This is the more striking since His birth and all the circumstances of His early life would naturally have imbued Him with the pre-

of Socrates on his trial (p. 40 in the Greek, vol. i., p. 354, Jowett); they probably represent his views more truly than the brilliant speculations in the Phædo. One alternative which he seems disposed to accept, viz., that death may be "a sleep like the sleep of him who is undisturbed by dreams," resembles very nearly the Nirvana of Buddhism.

judices of the most exclusive of all nations : a nation which was intended to be exclusive, which could only fulfil its special mission by exclusiveness. Mr. Hutton puts this with his usual force, but somewhat harshly: "To trust in Him really, to believe that He can help us to reduce the vulgar chaos of our English life to any order resting on an eternal basis, is far easier if we believe that the very same mind is shining on our consciences which entered into the poorest of lots among nearly the most degraded generation of the most narrow-minded race that the world has ever known, and made it the birth-place of a new earth" (Essays, vol. i., p. 283). Christ speaks ever to man as man; His words find an echo in universal consciousness; in Him there is neither Jew nor Gentile, and, *note specially this point*, neither bond nor free.

At this point, however, we may be met with an objection which has been presented with considerable skill, and appears to have seriously affected the judgment of inquirers. It is asserted that, after all, our Lord was but a Jewish Rabbi, differing indeed in some remarkable characteristics from other teachers of the synagogue, but only to an extent which may be accounted for, partly by His position and education, and the influence of Essenian principles, partly by peculiarity of nature and gifts which our opponents admit to have been of the highest order, marking Him, as they would say, as a man of transcendent genius, one of the few in the world's history in whom men are compelled to recognise a master of the soul. Hebrew writers of great learning, by whom this notion is gladly accepted, in their efforts to establish it have done signal if unwitting service to our cause. They have enabled readers of general culture and unbiassed judgment to ascertain for themselves some important facts which were formerly known thoroughly to those only who had sufficient learning and leisure to enable them to penetrate into the depths of Rabbinical literature, the most intricate and repulsive which human labour ever produced. It is now comparatively easy to ascertain what was the true character of the Jewish Rabbi, and of Rabbinical teaching; what, too, was the special character of the Essenian teaching,* at and about the period when our Lord impressed His stamp upon the mind of man. Now I would challenge any controversialist to deny that our Lord's teaching differed from that of all the Rabbis, not merely in degree, but in kind. It differed in principle, in its processes, in its results, in its tone, its spirit, in every essential characteristic. This was felt at once by His hearers: the

Ritschl shows very conclusively that the Essenian principle was even more exclusive than the Rabbinical, and more antagonistic in principle to Christianity. See Altkatholische Kirche, pp. 179—203.

first and most abiding impression made upon the mass of His countrymen was that He taught *not* as the scribes. This was the secret of the attraction which drew and retained disciples. "*Where* shall we go? *Thou* hast the words of eternal life." This was the cause of the fierce antagonism on the part of the Rabbis. They felt that His system was incompatible with their own. The scribe, as such, was a mechanical instrument; his authority was that of the system under which he worked, he held the minds of his hearers bound down and crippled by fetters by which he was himself bound even more tightly. Properly speaking, he was not even an interpreter of the law, with the principles of which he was little concerned, but simply a referee on points of casuistry or of formal observance which had been settled in past ages. The one merit which he claimed was that of unswerving adherence to the old customs, the old interpretations, the old applications of the law. Of all disqualifications for the office of a scribe, the most fatal would be independence of spirit, originality of thought or feeling. Many sayings of the Rabbis express this principle with the utmost *naïveté*: *e.g.*, "A scribe will have no portion in the world to come, even should he be faithful to the law of God, and full of good works, if his teaching be not wholly in accordance with tradition." Our Lord's charge against them, that they made the word of God of none effect by their tradition, scarcely puts this point in a stronger light than their declaration "that it is highly perilous for any learned man to read the Bible, since he may be induced to trust to its guidance rather than to his teacher." For the more advanced disciple the rule was, "that for one hour given to the study of the Bible, two should be devoted to the Talmud." When we read of different schools of Rabbis, and learn that they represented different tendencies, we naturally suppose that there must have been some movements of spirit, some struggles of moral and intellectual spontaneity. And it is true that between the school of Shammai and that of Hillel and the Gamaliels there was a wide divergence, the one relaxing and the other enforcing rigorous observances, the one encouraging, the other condemning all genial culture; but when we compare the teaching of the two parties which is fully represented in the Talmud, we see that the liberality of the most advanced is bounded within very narrow limits. Hillel, the best of all, had the spirit of his caste. Eternal life, according to him, was the portion of those who had attained to a perfect knowledge of the unwritten and traditional system to which he devoted his own life.

It is quite possible to cull from the Talmud, especially from one section (the Pirke Aboth, *i.e.*, decisions of the Fathers) a set of maxims which breathe a high and grave morality, which enjoin temperance, chastity, gentleness, love of country, earnestness in the study of God's law, contempt for wealth, celebrity, and power; but the general spirit is cold, formal, casuistical, and the decisions are, on the whole, determined by considerations of interest and expediency. In short, errors of every kind,—errors of interpretation, errors in the foundations of moral truth, errors in the representation of God's attributes, errors originating in the grossest superstitions, and above all in narrow, bitter, exclusive prejudices,—bear an overwhelming proportion to the whole compilation, and belong unquestionably to that Talmudic atmosphere in which we are told that the pure and lofty spirit of our Master attained its natural development. It is true that the second portion of the Talmud, the Gemara, presents those characteristics in an exaggerated form; but the first part, the Mishna, is replete with a casuistry so trifling and repulsive as to make a continuous perusal almost impossible, save to one who has some special motive for the study. It contains not less than 4,008 mishnaioth, that is, decisions or precepts, of which the largest proportion is attributed to Hillel or his followers. Out of this vast collection it would be difficult to fix upon any consecutive series of maxims, say fifty, which would approve themselves to the moral sense.

Widely as our Lord's teaching differs from that of the Greek or the Asiatic, far more does it differ from that of

His Hebrew contemporaries: it belongs altogether to a different sphere, the sphere in which the human spirit was emancipated from all narrow, dark, exclusive prejudices, and all its powers developed by that Spirit which rested on Him without measure, which He received as man, and which He bestowed as God.

It may be said that if the evidence supplied by knowledge of the Person of our Lord be of itself complete and adequate for the highest purpose, further inquiries may be dismissed as superfluous. Nor is the remark unfair. It is, I believe, quite true that of the myriads who accept the Christian revelation an immense proportion, including spirits of every class, are moved chiefly, if not exclusively, by the personal influence of Jesus, by the intuition, so to speak, which they thus attain into the manifested truth. The sun shines with its own lustre, and needs no evidence to prove its existence. But our nature is full of inconsistencies. Our strongest convictions, after all, are held with a feeble grasp, and are liable to be wrenched from us by sudden assaults, most especially when they depend upon what in modern parlance are called subjective impressions. It is well, therefore, that even this strongest and deepest of all convictions should have outward and independent support, that it should appeal to palpable and ascertainable facts, never indeed surrendering its true position in the central stronghold of our spirits, but going forth when challenged, and examining at frequent intervals the state of its defences and outposts. Let us, then, very briefly consider some of those evidences which the Christian apologist recognizes as most important for the confirmation of faith.

Here, undoubtedly, we have first to look at the evidence of miracles, which has been discussed by Dr. Stoughton, and, among all miracles, first and foremost—with which all other proofs of miraculous intervention stand or fall—the miracle of the resurrection.* I take it in this place, not as it is often taken, as an antecedent evidence to be examined or rejected previous to examination of the character of our Saviour; but as an evidence of which the true force is inseparably bound up with the result of that

* Within the few last months, Steinmeyer has published a treatise on the history of the resurrection, with reference to the latest criticisms, which I would commend to readers of German. Serious attempts have been made in England to disjoin this cardinal truth from the doctrinal system of St. Paul, attempts which seem passing strange on the part of critics who accept him as a thoroughly truthful man, nay, as an inspired apostle, and who must know that he makes the resurrection the very centre or foundation of his teaching. Even Hegel, the very Corypheus of idealism, declares "Die Auferstehung gehört wesentlich dem Glauben an;" *i.e.*, the resurrection belongs essentially to the faith. See "Die Philosophie der Religion," p. 300. In a note on the same page, Hegel shows that he takes it as a real objective event: "wie alles Bisherige in der Weise der Wirklichkeit für das unmittelbare Bewusstsein zur Erscheinung gekommen, so auch diese Erhebung."

preliminary inquiry. The mind may indeed submit to logical inferences drawn from undisputed or demonstrated facts, but it will submit reluctantly, and will, sooner or later, shake off its shackles, unless those inferences accord with its sense of moral fitness, of harmony between the outward manifestation of power and the inward demands of conscience. All moral antecedent objection to the resurrection of Christ disappears when it is acknowledged that His character satisfies those conditions. The first apologist of Christianity—St. Peter at Pentecost—puts this in the very foreground of his argument: "God raised Him up, having loosed the pains of death, because it was not possible that He should be holden of it." It was impossible, considering the relation of the Son to the Father, and of the Father to the universe. The expectation, in fact, of the resurrection of one "approved by God" as perfect in holiness, such as Christians believe their Master to be, is actually admitted to be so natural that the most subtle opponents of revelation assume that it must have existed in the minds of the first disciples, bringing them into a state which prepared them to receive without questioning the rumours which were gradually moulded into a semblance of historical consistency. This theory at least proves this,—given the two facts of God's power and justice, and of Christ's nature, as acknowledged by the Christian, the resurrection, if proved on other grounds, will find no obstacle to its reception in our moral consciousness.

But the very fact that such a hope exists, one which, if fulfilled, transcends all human longings, carrying with it, as St. Paul shows, the pledge and the only pledge of our personal redintegration, will but make the inquirer careful to prove every link in the chain of evidence. And here we have to remark that, so far from having that assumed expectation, His disciples were utterly in despair after the crucifixion. With their Master's last breath their last hope departed. They treated the first accounts which reached them as idle, they did not believe till they had the evidence of their senses; "then were they glad, when they saw the Lord." It is a remarkable, not to say unique, combination of two conditions for the perfect establishment of an ascertainable fact, that on the one side it should be in perfect congruity with an eternal principle, and on the other that it should be witnessed by persons wholly unprepared for its occurrence, and attested under circumstances which make it impossible to doubt their sincerity. That the attestation was given, that it was confirmed by outward effects otherwise psychologically inexplicable, by an immediate and complete change in the character of the disciples, and by the rapid triumph of the religion so attested, these and kindred points you will find discussed in every treatise on Christian evidences: they are, in fact, not open to reasonable doubt. Weigh more especially the attestation of St. Paul, both as one who knew previously all that could be alleged against the belief, as one whose strong intellect and strong prejudices rendered him inaccessible to mere subjective impressions, and as a man of whose conversion no rational, no intelligible account has ever been given which does not involve the fact of a personal manifestation of Christ, and then you will have all that can be needed for steadfast conviction, evidence complete and adequate for its purpose, proving that Jesus was shown "to be the Son of God with power by the resurrection from the dead." (Rom. i.)

With an equal interest the student of evidence will now turn back to the inquiry into the teaching of prophecy. At the outset it sufficed to know the broad fact that the characteristics of the coming Christ were believed by His contemporaries to have been announced in predictions which, whether of divine origin or not, unquestionably moulded their anticipations. He is now able to test their accuracy, to satisfy himself as to their origin, and to study them with a far deeper and more intelligent interest than would be possible without the previous appreciation of our Lord's nature. At first his attention will naturally be caught by separate predictions, by their correspondence with outward occurrences in the Gospel narration; but as he advances in the study his whole spirit will be gradually absorbed in contemplation of their internal coherence, their unbroken continuity, their ever progressing development. Distinct, accurate, and in the strictest sense of the word evidential, those predictions are, taken separately and independently; as such they are recognised by one and all the sacred writers—by none more fully than by the two who stand pre-eminent among the disciples of Jesus—by St. Paul, who represents the highest development of the intellectual forces in Christianity, the acute disputant, the subtle reasoner, the spiritualist philosopher, or, as he has been lately called, the metaphysician of Christianity—and by St. John, whose spirit, insphered in the region of love, came into nearest contact with the divine, who represents the very highest of all faculties, that of spiritual intuition. Nay, those predictions are repeatedly and distinctly recognised as conclusive evidences by our Lord Himself. But their full significance is only discerned when we contemplate them as parts of a mighty whole, as a continuous and complete testimony of the Spirit of God. Two lines of light traverse the realm of spiritual manifestation, the one revealing the divine, the other the human characteristics of the future Saviour: the one ever expanding, but from the beginning broad, luminous, equable; the other advancing, so to speak, with varying progress, ever and anon bursting out in sudden flashes, each bringing into vivid light some event in the life, above all each event in the crowning work, of the Saviour. These two lines gradually converge until they meet in the Incarnation. From that point of meeting the Christian goes back; then he learns to combine and to comprehend their intimations. Under Christ's teaching, prophecy becomes to him a guiding light—an evidence so complete that if it stood alone he might dispense with other proofs, and feel it adequate for the support of his faith.

You will, however, remember that besides those predictions which apply directly to our Lord's person, an inexhaustible treasury of predictions refer to events in the providential history of the world, and they, too, are strictly evidential. Even writers to whom the very word revelation is distasteful, acknowledge in the Hebrew prophets true seers; that is, men whose spirit was in unison with the everlasting harmonies of the universe. But it is only when we know Christ as He reveals Himself, as the Lord of history, that the long series of prophetic intimations present themselves in their true light to our minds. The exact explanation of each specific prediction, such as are found in Isaiah and Daniel, taxes and rewards the industry of students, but the real interest consists not in the satisfaction of a rational curiosity, or the bearing upon controversy, but in the help which is thus supplied, enabling us to realize vividly the presence of Christ foreordering all events so as to make them work together for the accomplishment of His will.

If time allowed, I might here dwell on other topics. I might point out how deep thinkers, Pascal perhaps most powerfully, have shown that Christianity, and Christianity alone, fully recognises the two opposite and apparently irreconcilable aspects of our common humanity, its unspeakable misery and degradation out of God, and its capacity for restoration and reunion with the Divine, and, again, that it corresponds to an extent wholly incomprehensible, save on the admission of its divine origin, with those requirements of man's conscience and spirit which every system of philosophy recognises, but which one and all admit that they fail to satisfy. I might dwell upon the fact that between the acceptance of the entire truth thus made known to us, and utter negation of the supernatural and divine, the intermediate positions long defended as tenable have been, both here and on the continent, all but universally abandoned by the representatives of modern thought. I might point out that together with that abandonment, and as a direct result of that abandonment, a dark, drear hopelessness, not merely as to the immediate issue of the storms which convulse the atmosphere we breathe as spiritual, social, and intellectual beings, but as to the future and abiding consequences of those convulsions, appears to be settling down upon men's minds: a hopelessness for which there is no remedy save that which depends upon the triumph of righteousness and truth, a triumph to be achieved only under the banner of Christ. What I have attempted to do, none can feel as I do how imperfectly, has been to set before you in orderly sequence facts within the reach of all; facts of which the truth and power and far-reaching influences will be felt more and more in proportion to the earnestness and sincerity of your own inquiry; facts which once admitted are evidences complete in themselves, and adequate for their purpose in each stage of our spiritual development: evidences sufficient to constrain all who believe in God to believe also in the Son whom He has sent; to know Him as the way, the truth, and the life. In His school that rational conviction, retaining all its clearness, will undergo a process at once of development and transfigurement, and become a living faith.

EXPLANATORY PAPER

BY THE RIGHT REV. THE

LORD BISHOP OF GLOUCESTER AND BRISTOL.

EXPLANATORY PAPER.

Having been requested by the Committee of the Christian Evidence Society to draw up a short paper which might serve as a partial introduction to the Lectures, and especially might set forth their general plan and connexion, as originally designed by the Committee, I have much pleasure in submitting the following brief comments to the many readers of this valuable series. The Lectures were delivered in the course of the spring in the present year, to large audiences, in St. George's Hall, Langham Place, and were specially designed to meet some of the current forms of unbelief among the educated classes.

They were delivered at the request of the Christian Evidence Society, and represent a portion of the work undertaken by the Committee of that Society in the present year.

As they thus stand in such close connection with our Society, it may not be unsuitable for me to make a few explanatory remarks on the Society itself, and its general objects, as well as on the plan of the lectures which have been delivered at its request, and which are now presented to the reader in a collected and continuous form.

First, then, as to the Society, and its present working and design.

I. The Society was established in the spring of the past year. It had long been felt by earnest and thoughtful persons, both Churchmen and Nonconformists, that some combined attempt ought to be made to meet in fair argument the scepticism and unbelief which for the last few years have been distinctly traceable in all classes of society.

Into all the causes of this state of things it is not now our object to inquire. These are, probably, many and various, and may defy any formal classification. It is, indeed, seldom that those who live in the stream and current of a quickly moving generation can properly estimate the variously combined movements around them, or can always very successfully refer them even to their more proximate causes. We may, however, very profitably, as thus illustrating the general design of the lectures, pause to advert to two or three of what would seem to be leading causes of this present prevalence of doubt and scepticism.

We may, in the first place then, venture to express the

opinion that it does seem to stand in some degree of connection with the historical criticism, or, to speak more exactly, with the philosophical mode of treating ancient history, which, especially since the time of Niebuhr, has so honourably marked the present and the latter half of the preceding generation. It was obviously impossible that a system which appeared to yield results judged to be eminently satisfactory and trustworthy in regard of the general history of the past, should not be applied to sacred history, and to the various documents which together make up the Holy Bible. And it *has* been applied, sometimes cautiously and reverently, and with a due regard for the religious convictions of Christian readers, but sometimes also with an eagerness and persistence which may not unfairly be characterized as both inconsiderate and unjustifiable. This method of criticism, especially in its more unfavourable manifestations, may certainly be specified as one of the earlier causes of that suspended belief in the historical truth of several portions of the Old and New Testament, which many entertain at the present time, and make no scruple of avowing and justifying.

We may also as certainly specify as a second cause the tendency to over-hasty generalization that has of late marked the rapid development of some of the natural sciences. From true science true religion has nothing to fear. But it is otherwise when results newly obtained, and at present, from the very circumstances of the case, imperfectly tested and verified, are confidently put forward; and when inferences of perhaps doubtful validity are set, if not in actual opposition to the statements of Revelation, yet in such a studious juxtaposition, that comparison is challenged, and by consequence many an early conviction weakened and impaired. We say by consequence,—for no acute observer of the heart and its mysteries can have failed to mark how, even in minds of higher strain there is often a secret sympathy with the attacking party, not so much on the merits of the case, as from the simple fact that it *is* the attacking party; and that while on this side there is only the passivity of prescription, on the other there is all the vigour of assault and progress. This obvious fact, which,—like some other mental facts of a similar nature,—is, we fear, proved by almost daily experience, has not been sufficiently taken into consideration; but if estimated properly, it will account for much that is otherwise perplexing. It will even tend to reassure us, as it will enable us to assign to its true though hidden reason much of the present startling readiness with which scientific inferences, supposed generally to be unfavourable to received views, have received at least some measure of sympathy and approval. It may be, too, that this latent feeling of sympathy with the attack will be neutralized when it is found that the defence is not deficient in energy or vigour, and when English fair play seems to suggest that each side should be allowed to fight it out without having any advantages arising from prepensions or prejudice. However this may be, there is no doubt that the cause we have specified is a real and a prevailing one. Over-hasty scientific generalization is certainly one of the causes of the present state of modern religious belief.

One more cause we may also pause to specify, as it involves in it much that will minister comfort and reassurance. This cause is the eager and often impatient search for solid ground whereon religion and morality may be based. With all their faults, men are now certainly seeking for truth. There may be misapplications of historical criticism, there may be misuses and misapprehensions of the real testimony of science, but amid all there is clearly a searching for truth and firm ground. The processes of destructive criticism are in fact nearly over, and the difficult process of reconstruction is commencing. The due remembrance of this will help us in estimating a little more calmly, and perhaps also a little more fairly, some of the startling phenomena presented by the present state of religious belief. Let us, for example, take for a moment into consideration two remarkable characteristics of the present time,—first, the attempts to form a system of morality independent of revealed religion; and, secondly, the acceptance on the part of several earnest and truthful minds of such a system as Positivism. These really would seem to be at first sight two inexplicable phenomena. Both, however, are to be accounted for by that searching for something to rest on, which has just been mentioned. It has been assumed in the one case, far too hastily, that the uncertainties connected with the belief in the facts of revealed religion are so great, that no system of morality could be considered securely founded if it rested only on the Scriptures. It has been felt by many earnest thinkers that any such system, to be a true one, ought to rest solely on principles acknowledged to be of universal application, and on maxims that have received the assent of all the better part of civilized mankind. If the teaching of Scripture be in general harmony with such maxims and principles, its concurrence is not to be slighted; but it is not deemed as of more real moment than the concurrence of any other form of religious teaching that has exercised a real influence over any large portion of the human family. Religion generally is accepted as a buttress to the rising edifice of morality, but as nothing further. The tower is being builded really with the desire to reach heaven: if the sequel be what it was of old, it may still be conceded, with all fairness, that the attempt is not made in a bad spirit. To change slightly the allusion, the effort is not made in the spirit of the Titans who piled Pelion on Ossa, but with all the earnestness and anxiety of hoping, enquiring, and searching, though we are bound to add, mistaken men.

In the other case, though it may seem to many rash to say one word to mitigate the severity of the judgment that both is and ever will be passed on such a system as Positivism, yet, even here, let us be just and sympathising. There is, no doubt, in Positivism much that is plainly repulsive, and really calls for severity; still, even in this system, we may trace the prevailing desire to find something solid, something which appears to be proof to the changes of opinion or the fluctuation of creeds. So the attempt is made to secure a scientific basis, and to place thereon fact after fact, when each has become verified and established, and so to build onward—we cannot honestly say upward—until something like a system is so far constructed that succeeding generations may feel induced to continue it. So even in this sombre and cheerless system there is, we believe, really at work a desire to touch ground. To that desire, however, it must be sorrowfully added, every loftier aspiration, every nobler incentive, is necessarily sacrificed. Science and scientific truth is used in a way that warrants the apprehension that—if such is to be the use made of it—the progress of science may tend, first, to impair, and, next, to obliterate, the sense of *responsibility* on which the present and the future alike so solemnly rest. It is not without reason, then, that this is dwelt gravely upon by all sober thinkers; nor is it too much to say that this is now one of the gravest considerations connected with the advance of modern scientific investigations. The tendencies of such investigations certainly do *appear* to hinder the due recognition of these two momentous principles—first, the sense of responsibility; and, secondly, the sense of dependence on something higher than law, order, and evolution. This hindrance, we trust, is only in appearance; still that appearance is accepted by many as reality, and it is not without reason that we are again and again reminded that the acceptance of the truth of the Christian creed will with many depend on its power of assimilating the doctrine of universal causation, or, to speak more precisely, of demonstrating that that doctrine is itself only a form of a yet higher and holier truth.

We turn, however, back again to the design and working of the Society. It was established to meet this growing scepticism, and with a due recognition of the causes which have just been specified. It was not started, as has been sometimes said, with a little irony, for the purpose of restoring a belief in Christianity, but for the purpose of meeting argument with argument, and of supplying the many that are now fluctuating between belief and no belief with sober answers and valid arguments drawn forth anew from the great treasury of Christian evidences. This is the true design and object of the Society. Its mode of carrying out this design has hitherto been threefold—first, by means of lectures addressed to the educated; secondly, by the formation of classes under competent class-leaders, for the instruction of those in lower grades of society who are exposed to the thickening dangers arising from that organized diffusion of infidel principles which is one of the saddest and most monitory signs of the present time. Thirdly, the Society is endeavouring to stimulate private study by the circulation of useful tracts, and by the offer of prizes to such as may be willing that their private study should be tested by competitive examination. All these three modes of carrying out its work have been adopted during the present year; and, so far as can be inferred from the work that has been done, and from the various expressions of public opinion, with considerable success. Popular attention has naturally been directed more especially to the first of the modes specified—the lectures to the educated; but it is satisfactory to state, ere we pass at once to our explanatory comments on the plan of these lectures, that the formation of classes has answered even beyond expectation, and that, from the amount of the competition for the prizes that have been offered, examination in Christian evidences will form a large and most interesting portion of the future work of the Society.

II. We may now turn our attention to the lectures that are included in the present volume—our first year's work.

The number of the lectures was twelve. One of these, the lecture on the Internal Evidence of the Authenticity of St. John's Gospel, is unfortunately not included in the present volume, owing to the desire expressed by the learned writer that it should not be published. The absence is much to be regretted; first, on account of the value and importance of the lecture; and, secondly, on account of the partial break which has thus been caused in the sequence of the lectures.

The lectures were not delivered in the order in which they are here presented to the reader. The convenience of the active as well as distinguished men who consented to act as lecturers, had naturally to be consulted; adjustments had to be made, and interchanges of days of lecturing acceded to, so as to secure the continuous delivery of the lectures on the days specified. In this collective edition, however, the proper order is restored, and may now be briefly explained, as some criticisms have been passed on the subjects of the lectures, which would certainly have been modified if the whole series had been delivered in the order originally designed.

The first three lectures were designed to be preparatory and prelusive. They were directed against the three systems which are now more especially, in different ways, coming into collision with Christianity—Materialism and its theories, Pantheism, and Positivism. It was judged by those who sketched out the plan of the lectures, that until these subjects were shortly dealt with, and until the objections against Christianity, founded upon them or derived from them, were briefly noticed, the evidences for Christianity could hardly be expected to have a fair hearing. The internal arguments in favour of the leading truths of the Christian religion could scarcely be fairly estimated if there were to be antecedent objections of a grave and general character left wholly unnoticed and unanswered. Hence the three opening lectures: The first of these breaks ground by the consideration of some leading materialistic opinions, and especially by an exposition of the argument from design. It thus prepares the reader more fully to accept the deep truth so well and succinctly stated by Bishop Martensen,* that the "world

* Christian Dogmatics, § 63. (Clark.)

has not merely a cosmogonic but also a creational origin," and that the mysterious problem of creation and life can "never be solved in a merely natural way, but demands a supernatural solution, that is, a solution through a *creative teleology*."

The second lecture very suitably follows by a clear exposition of that great system which has of late been found to exercise such a fascination over thoughtful and cultivated minds that it becomes, to far more than we may suppose, the conclusion of all controversy. We allude to the system of Pantheism, into which of late many noble spirits have seemed willing to merge all their hopes and all their fears. Swayed to and fro, unable to accept Law for their God, and yet equally held back from the blessed truth that the God of the universe is a PERSON, thousands fall back upon the subtle and fascinating system which supplies a moving Principle, but withholds the blessed idea of a holy Will; which discloses to them a *natura naturans*, but denies the existence of a loving Creator and a personal God. It was thus very properly provided that the lecture on this subject should follow the lecture on Design in Nature, as exhibiting the true characteristics of that modified Atheism which only too often becomes the refuge of men whose minds have been shaken by the inferences of pure materialism, or who may have been drawn towards the disguised forms of it which lurk in many of our popular treatises on the origin and evolution of Man. After a careful study of these two lectures, the thoughtful reader will be enabled to recognize the true nature and force of the argument from design, and so will be led the better to appreciate the enduring validity of that great *natural* foundation for our belief in a personal God. Of the four great arguments by which man is permitted to rise to the knowledge of God, the argument from design, or, as it is technically called, the teleological argument, is the most important, as it, in fact, includes the moral argument, which, properly estimated, is only its subjective aspect. Apart from revelation we rise to the knowledge of God in two ways, by the consideration of ourselves, and by the contemplation of the world around us; what the moral argument is in the former method, that the teleological argument is in the latter. Hence the importance to the general reader of having an argument of such validity clearly set before him on different sides, and from different points of view.

The third lecture, on Positivism, completes the first group, and forms, as it were, a kind of useful appendix to the other two. Here we have the investigation of a special system,—a system that professes to be based on positive and observed phenomena, and claims to extricate the mental study of man from metaphysics and abstractions, and to place it in the realm of the realizable and the positive. Such a system, though neither now prevailing to any extent, nor ever likely to become prevalent or popular, is still worthy of attention, as it stands in close connection with current materialistic conceptions, and suggests some instructive contrasts to Pantheism. In the latter system we have, at any rate, some idea of pervading Deity; but in Positivism, if we understand the system aright, God, and all conceptions of God, are not so much denied as simply and entirely ignored. If Pantheism be deemed fascinating, Positivism will appear to most minds utterly repellent: still it is a system that claims some distinguished men among its professed exponents, and perhaps a larger number than we may suppose of conscious or unconscious adherents. It may therefore well claim from us investigation, and, in the position it occupies in the order of these lectures, may fairly be considered to be in its right place.

We have dwelt upon the first group of the lectures, as both the position and the importance of the subjects considered in it have seemed to require a fuller notice. On the remaining groups we may speak more briefly, as their connection and the special subjects on which they treat are much more self-explanatory.

The first three lectures having, as it were, cleared the ground, and having demonstrated, as we believe, successfully the untenable nature of the systems that have been placed in competition with Christianity, the two next lectures, which form the second group, deal with the chief difficulties arising from the supposed conflict between science and the Holy Scriptures. The first of these two lectures, that on Science and Revelation, enters into the subject generally, by showing how, on scientific considerations, a revelation was to be expected, and how, consequently, the evidences of Christianity have a strong claim upon the attention of every right-thinking man. The second of these two lectures is confined to a special but prerogative case, in which science and religion are supposed to be more particularly in opposition to each other,—viz., the case of miracles. Here it is necessary, not only to investigate generally the nature of the miraculous evidence to Christianity, but fairly to face the antecedent question, whether miracles, however defined, are not in themselves impossible. In facing that question, however, attention is rightly called to the nature of the weapons that are used in the conflict, and especially to the fact, so often overlooked, that all the assaults on the miraculous that can in any degree be deemed worthy of consideration, are carried on only with metaphysical weapons. The whole question really turns upon the belief in a personal God: if it be conceded that this belief is just and reasonable, then, as the writer of the lecture rightly observes, the presumed impossibility in reference to miracles at once melts away. The very idea of a free-creating God carries with it the possibility of new manifestations of the Divine will, whether in history or nature. The sustaining power of God, which we recognise in the form of law and orderly progress, changes whensoever it shall have seemed good to His holy will for it to pass into the creative; His immanent workings are then seen in the realm of the transcendental, and the result is that which Pantheism, Naturalism, and all similar systems must, if consistent, regard as impossible, a new movement from the Divine centre, an epiphany of a creative and overruling will, a wonder, a miracle. When Spinosa said that God and nature are one from eternity to eternity, he was quite consistent in adding that there is no transcendental beginning, and that miracles are impossible; but for any one who believes in a personal God, or who believes nature to be what it is,—not a system eternally fixed, but a system passing through a development characterised by design,—to deny the possibility of miraculous interpositions, reason and consistency must certainly, in this particular, be suspended or sacrificed.

The third group of lectures, which may be regarded as subdivided into two portions, naturally connects itself with, and follows, the subjects just specified. After the general consideration of difficulties connected with religion and Christianity, the attention ot the reader is now directed to the more special difficulties connected with the Holy Scriptures. In the first portion of the group the subject of the Gradual Development of Revelation, or, as the title was re-defined by the lecturer, the Gradual Nature of Divine Revelation, properly occupies the first place. It is followed by a lecture in which there will be found a careful consideration of some special instances of difficulty connected with the historical portions especially of the Old Testament. These two lectures were to have been followed by a consideration of the moral difficulties that have been felt in reference to some parts of the Old Testament; but for this subject, which, if properly treated, would have probably claimed a large share of attention, the Committee were not able to secure the services of a lecturer for the present year. This is to be regretted, as there is no subject connected with the Holy Scriptures which at the present time more requires a candid and sober consideration; no discussion which, if fairly conducted, would do more to remove many honestly felt difficulties, and to many minds to bring probably lasting reassurance. Without presuming to enter, however slightly, into such a subject in a discursive paper like the present, we will venture to make this general remark, which perhaps may be found helpful, viz., that in dealing with all such difficulties we must carefully distinguish between those connected with Divine workings, and those connected with human actions. The former are, in their real nature, utterly beyond the finite judgment of man. All that we may presume to consider is the way or manner in which they are brought before us by the writer, and all that we can either safely or wisely subject to criticism are the aspects or colouring under which they are presented. We really are not competent to sketch out theories of Divine government, even in the simplest matters, and with all the advantages of contemporaneous knowledge; nay, in the lives of ourselves and those around us, there are, as has been wisely observed, innumerable events of sorrow, and countless circumstances of suffering, of which the economic purpose cannot even be guessed at in our present state of knowledge, and of the exact purposes of which no sober or reverent thinker ever dreams of attempting to form any estimate whatever. It is thus utterly out of the question to attempt to consider the difficulties connected with the Divine workings, except as to the manner of their representation by the human narrator, whose human powers were the instruments by which God was pleased to communicate the outward facts of those workings to the children of men. In regard of the Divine workings themselves, especially when they come before us in the general forms of judgments on individuals or nations, all we may presume safely to do is to regard them as manifestations of Divine righteousness in judicial relations or contradistinctions to the sins or transgressions of men.

In reference, however, to the moral difficulties connected with recorded human actions, we may venture to go farther, and to take into consideration the fact already referred to of the gradual nature of God's revelation, and all the modifying thoughts which such a fact brings with it.

It is thus not only right, but necessary, to accept as our guide in all such investigations or discussions this sober spiritual principle,—that the Old Testament must be interpreted from the stand-point of the New Testament, and under the fuller light which is afforded by the later dispensation. If we cling to these two great truths—first, that the history of the past, as we find it in the Old Testament, ever involves a reference to final purposes; and, secondly, that every attempt to realize the deeper significance of that history must use Christianity as its basis—we shall probably find our way in this difficult domain of speculation as far and as safely as the finite powers of man can be deemed capable of advancing; we shall see as clearly as we can be permitted to see, when poor human reason is endeavouring to survey the adorable mysteries that surround the recorded workings of the manifold wisdom of God.

The second portion of this third group is more especially devoted to difficulties connected with the New Testament, the first place being naturally reserved for the questions relating to the life of our Lord and the Gospel narrative. The first lecture is thus directed to a consideration of the Mythical Theories of Christianity; the second to the Evidential Value of St. Paul's Epistles. As has already been mentioned, the lecture on St. John's Gospel, which would have occupied a position between the two just specified, owing to the request of the writer, has not been published, and the series in this part of it has in consequence suffered.

The two remaining lectures, viz., that on Christ's Teaching and Influence on the World, and that which follows it, on the Completeness and Adequacy of the Evidences of Christianity, form the last group, and worthily conclude the interesting series. A third lecture on the additional strength which is brought to the evidences of Christianity by the convergence of various lines of independent testimony, was intended to have been added to this group, but for this important and comprehensive subject, as in the case of another subject recently mentioned, the Committee were not able to procure a lecturer.

The series, as above described, is now commended to the thoughtful reader. It will be found to be marked throughout with learning, candour, and we believe also with gentleness and sympathy. On this last characteristic we ourselves lay great stress. If we would reclaim the wandering, or confirm the wavering, it is not by hard words and unkindly imputations, but by the expression of that love and gentleness which an apostle reminds us are numbered among the fruits of the Spirit. We must regard ourselves as far as possible in their places, endeavour to see as they see, and feel as they feel, and then it may be permitted to us to return from our charitable quest, bringing back the friendly wanderers with us, and ourselves sharing some portion of that holy joy which is felt in heaven and in earth when the doubter is led back to belief, and the lost is found. This rightful characteristic of all true Christian controversy is not, we believe, anywhere wanting in this volume, and we thus, with fullest confidence, commend it to the consideration of all who love the truth, and humbly seek it in history, science, and theology.

Lastly, we may call attention to the encouraging fact, that in this great work good men have agreed to forget minor differences. Among the distinguished men whose independent lectures are now, for convenience, gathered together in a common volume, are members of the Church of England and members of other religious communities. It is long that this co-operation has existed in the circulation of the Holy Scriptures; it is recently that it has again appeared in the effort to present those Scriptures in their most accurate form to the English reader; it is now again happily exemplified in the present attempt to defend and maintain the truth as it is in Jesus Christ our Lord.

These things are of good augury. Though there may be dissensions, sad and pitiful, within the Church, and assaults made upon it from without, often sadly characterized with the marks of political strife, yet we may thank God that in efforts such as the present, and in the calm and serenity of studies such as those which this volume commends, a true union has been felt and acted on. Yes, it is a cause for thankfulness and rejoicing that the love of Christ is more and more binding us together in companionships of high duty and gentle sympathy, and that reverence for His Holy Word, His Word of Life and Truth, is making us feel that our work is a common one, and that as we have in common freely received, so it is a blessed thing in common freely to give.

We may humbly pray then that God's gracious favour may rest on this Course of Lectures, and may be permitted to bear a blessing to those that read it. May they feel anew convinced in heart and spirit that we have not "followed cunningly devised fables," but that in the Holy Scriptures of the Old and New Testament there is light and truth, even because they bring us nearer to Him who is the Truth, as He is the Way and the Life, for evermore.

C. J. GLOUCESTER AND BRISTOL.

July 19, 1871.

NOTES TO
MODERN SCEPTICISM.

NOTES.

ON POSITIVISM.

1 "Does any one fancy that he sees a solid cube? It is easy to show that the solidity of the figure, the relative position of its faces and edges to each other, are inferences of the spectator—no more conveyed to his conviction by the eye alone than they would be if he were looking at a painted representation of a cube. The scene of nature is a picture without depth of substance, no less than the scene of art; and in the one case, as in the other, it is the mind which, by an act of its own, discovers that colour and shape denote distance and solidity. Most men are unconscious of this perpetual habit of reading the language of the external world, and translating as they read. The draughtsman, indeed, is compelled, for his purposes, to return back in thought from the solid bodies which he has inferred, to the shapes of surface which he really sees. He knows that there is a mask of theory over the whole face of nature, if it be *theory* to infer more than we *see*. But other men, unaware of this masquerade, hold it to be a fact that they see cubes and spheres, spacious apartments, and winding avenues. And these things are facts to them, because they are unconscious of the mental operation by which they have penetrated nature's disguise. . . .

"Our sensations require ideas to bind them together; namely, ideas of space, time, number, and the like. If not so bound together, sensations do not give us any apprehension of things or objects. All things, all objects, must exist in space and in time—must be one or many. Now space, time, number, are not sensations or things. They are something different from, and opposed to, sensations and things. We have termed them ideas. It may be said they are relations of things, or of sensations. But granting this form of expression, still a *relation* is not a thing or a sensation ; and therefore we must still have another and opposite element, along with our sensations. . . .

"We are often told that such a thing is *a fact*—a fact, and not a theory, —with all the emphasis which, in speaking or writing, tone or italics or capitals can give. We see from what has been said, that when this is urged, before we can estimate the truth, or the value of the assertion, we must ask to whom is it a fact? what habits of thought, what previous information, what ideas does it imply, to conceive the fact as a fact ? Does not the apprehension of the fact imply assumptions which may with equal justice be called theory, and which are perhaps false theory ? in which case the fact is no fact. Did not the ancients assert it as a fact, that the earth stood still, and the stars moved ? and can any fact have stronger apparent evidence to justify persons in asserting it emphatically than this had ?"—*Whewell's Philosophy of the Inductive Sciences*, 2nd ed., vol. i., p. 42, *seq.*

That the solidity of figures is in truth given by mental judgment, has been often proved experimentally ; see for examples, Huxley's Elementary Physiology, Lesson x., 13—16. The experiment with a coin, lens and pin, p. 259, is easy as well as conclusive, but Wheatstone's Pseudoscope more surprising to most observers. Compare on this curious subject Brewster's Natural Magic, Letter v.

[2] It is important to bear in mind that, from an admitted incompetency of our faculties to *know* the absolute, we cannot infer an impossibility of knowing its *existence.* To know that a thing *is*, and to know *what* it is, are two totally distinct degrees and sorts of knowledge. The moment this distinction is stated, every one sees its truth ; but many persons omit stating it to themselves when they reason upon these difficult subjects.

Ravaisson, after giving a brief account of Herbert Spencer's opinion, goes on to say : "Comment il y a, au fond de toute connaissance, un absolu, auquel correspond, comme son opposé, le relatif, c'est ce qu'établissait, il y a plus de vingt siècles, contre une doctrine déjà régnante alors de relativité et de mobilité universelles, la dialectique platonicienne, qui fraya le chemin à la metaphysique. Elle faisait plus : elle montrait que par cet absolu seul les relations sont intelligibles, parce qu'il est la mesure par laquelle seule nous les estimons. La métaphysique, entre les mains de son immortel fondateur, fit davantage encore : elle montra que cet absolu, par lequel l'intelligence mesure le relatif, est l'intelligence même. C'est ce que redisait Leibniz, lorsque, à cette assertion, renouvelée de la scolastique par Locke, qu'il n'était rien dans l'intelligence qui d'abord n'eût été dans le sens, il répondait : "sauf l'intelligence," et que, avec Aristote, il montrait dans l'intelligence la mesure supérieure du sens."—*Rapport*, p. 66.

Ravaisson then gives interesting extracts from Sophie St. Germain, and proceeds to show how Comte, without admitting any self-contemplating intelligence, and thus inferring the possibility of an Absolute, did in fact pursue the idea of Unity, and extended this idea to the universe, —a principle which, if fully grasped, must be fatal to Positive views. "D'accord maintenant avec Platon, Aristote, Leibniz, il déclarait que l'ensemble étant le resultat et l'expression d'une certaine unité, à laquelle tout concourt et se co-ordonne et qui est le but où tout marche, c'est dans cette unité, c'est dans le but, c'est dans la fin ou cause finale qu'est le secret de l'organisme."—*Rapport*, p. 76.

A special interest attaches to the work of Ravaisson as an authoritative French rating of the philosophic exchange between England and France. It is almost unnecessary to refer for a less abstract account of these relations to the widely known writings of M. Taine.

[3] It should have been stated in the text, as it was in the delivered lecture, that these questions were not forgotten by the eminent Professor. The passages referred to will be found in his eloquent address on the "Scientific use of the Imagination," p. 47, *seq.*, or in his volume of collected Essays, p. 163, *seq.* The reader may observe that, both in Professor Tyndall's pages and two sentences back in this lecture, Development is spoken of as a process or law in operation. The various kinds of philosophy which may be engrafted on such a law are severally determined by whatever reply is given to the questions above suggested. It would seem inappropriate here to state the possible relations between a law of development and such consequent (or inconsequent) philosophies.

Those who wish to consider them the writer may refer to his little volume entitled "Right and Wrong," for a brief discussion of this subject, and more particularly for the results to natural theology.

The following German sketch of an evolution-philosophy may not be without interest:—"Vermöge einer ewigen Kreisbewegung entstehen als Verdichtungen der Luft unzählige Welten, himmlische Gottheiten, in deren Mittelpunkt die cylinderförmige Erde ruht, unbewegt wegen des gleichen Abstandes von allen Punkten der Himmelskugel. Die Erde hat sich aus einem ursprünglich flüssigen Zustande gebildet. Aus dem Feuchten sind unter dem Einfluss der Wärme in stufenweise Entwickelung die lebenden Wesen hervorgegangen. Auch die Landthiere waren anfangs fischartig und haben erst mit der Abtrocknung der Erdoberfläche ihre jetzige Gestalt gewonnen. Die Seele soll Anaximander als luftartig bezeichnet haben."

Anaximander of Miletus was born about B.C. 610. Consequently he ranks early among European theorizers on development. The extract is from Ueberweg's Grundriss, t. 1, p. 40. Cf. Plutarch de Placit. v. 19, and Sympos viii. qu. 8, with Euseb. Præp. Evang. i. 8.

[4] The sight of a dualism apparently insoluble never fails to suggest some such questions as these: Was it always so? will it be so always? and were I at the centre of the universe, should I see it so now?

There are three possible ways of conceiving otherwise: 1, by reducing mind to matter; 2, by reducing matter to mind; 3, by comprehending both under a higher unity.

We need only write down these issues for common sense to perceive that Nos. 1 and 2 arise from, and end in, one-sided speculation. A man who lives shut up amongst machinery is apt to think of his own mind as a machine. Great chemists have ere now taken the human stomach for a laboratory, and were slow in awakening to those physiological facts which put the vital processes of assimilation in a nobler and truer light. Comte began by reducing all sciences to mathematical elements. Afterwards he discovered that to explain a higher order of things by a lower is the essence of materialism.

To a meditative spirit, the inner world is nearer than the outer; and therefore the evidence of its reality is stronger by wanting the weakness of a second link. But active life brings home to us the existence of both ; we suffer by defying or neglecting the laws of either ; and pain and sorrow are often the advanced guard of much stern unyielding truth. In a world where we all endure the friction of things external, it is hard not to believe in objective as well subjective realities.

The truth is, that the primary question belongs to the practical reason, and can be settled by no other criterion. There is a philosophical maxim that we can never speak of the Divine univocally, but only by analogy, figure, or similitude; the cause being that all attributes belonging to the Infinite require words which, if taken literally, must land us in self-contradiction. How vivid an idea do we gain of Omniscience or Omnipotence by saying that it is "a circle of which the centre is everywhere, the circumference nowhere." And what signifies the obvious inconsistency? Deny the Infinite, try to find a place for its centre or circumference, and the inconsistency remains, together with a host of absurd consequences. When of two hypotheses both cannot, but one must be true, and either position lands us in logical inconsistency, it is easy to see that our theoretical understanding will never clear up the inexplicable issue. A rule by which we live and act becomes the surest touchstone of truth or falsehood.

Let us see whether the two worlds in which we live can be practically treated as one. Suppose a bivouac into which a shell descends, certain in another moment, by physical law, to explode. Is the moral law—the effort of this man or that man to escape—equally certain? Arguing abstractedly, most people would hold it so, yet we know that the fact lies otherwise. There is a fatalism among soldiers—"every bullet has its billet"—as there is among nurses who believe that every epidemic must kill its destined prey. One may have trained himself to wish for death, another is indifferent, a third so undecided that he leaves the event to a doctrine of chances, a fourth is simply capricious. Each by a course of life and action has made or modified his present moment for choice, and any one may or may not draw back from the coming peril. Had the falling shell been a splash from a carriage wheel, every man would have shrunk from it. The latter risk is too simple for human ponderings or human self-direction, and in such cases people act by a proximate straightforward instinct.

But on what principles must he who shrinks from either risk really proceed? He is sure that his own movements are in his own power and contingent. He is equally sure that the movements of shell or mud are absolutely determined in calculable curves, and not at all contingent. Acting on these two conjoint data, he succeeds in avoiding death or dirt; and, whatever theorists may write, he would have perilled his success by acting otherwise. Nay, what is much to our purpose, all theoretical men would themselves act upon the like assumption in all cases of practical consequence and emergency.

Suppose dualism banished from the world in fact as well as in theory, the problems of education ought to be as demonstrable as those of geometry or chemical experiment. The paths of men and of comets being equally calculable, because equally subject to uniform law, how comes it that biography and history abound in the records of grossly falsified predictions? Let the courses of nations be tabulated, and statesmanship is made easy. We must owe it to some egregious oversight that criminal punishments are not invariably deterrent. Perhaps the law of the strongest motive has been neglected; if so, re-enact the code of Draco, and virtue will become universal. Till then the supposition must continue only an unverified hypothesis.

If we go back to our starting-point, and ask, can the practical dualism be reduced to a higher unity? our answer must confess a present condition of ignorance. We are so far from knowing what constitutes the thing we call matter, or what the entity we feel within us—our soul or mind—really is, that we cannot tell how they act and react on each other. We fail in tracing our own sensations from their outward antecedents to their impression on our consciousness; and, *vice versâ*, we cannot follow our energies from the springs of our volitions outward. While thus baffled, the longed-for unity floats before our inward eye like a dim vision of that intuitive faculty which pronounces subject and object to be ultimately identical, or as a revelation of that religious faith which accepts the incomprehensible, and reposes in the bosom of God.

[8] Since Comte's time it has been shown that mental development is no very difficult process, *provided* we assume that several principles which consciousness distinguishes and sometimes places in antagonism, may be

treated as equivalents, and be resolved into each other interchangeably. For example, we have been apt to reverence those who suffered the loss of all things rather than accept the Expedient as the Right, and who died resolute in disallowing the rule of policy to be pleaded *in foro conscientiæ*. We have also in common parlance asserted a distinction between these two principles, while holding that the one claims the other for its assured attendant. Honesty, we said, is the best policy; and we never meant thereby that thorough policy is the best policy. What we did mean was that a regard to expediency fails of the success which a straightforward observance of right deserves, and will at last obtain. But to make mental development easy, antitheses must appear fluent, the noble be convertible with the useful, the human with the merely animal. Thus, when Comte adored Clotilde, and Dante immortalized Beatrice, they rehearsed for a millionth time the loves of preadamite plants. Coleridge used to maintain that the test of a philosophy was its ultimate coincidence with common sense. In the theories under consideration, right is philosophically resolved into the greater happiness of the greater number, and this equivalent exactly coincides with the common sense of starving thinkers who are possessed by a fixed idea that the happiness of the impoverished many is promoted by an opportune pillage of the wealthy few.

It is less easy to verify mental development than to theorize upon it, yet verification may not be impossible! If disbelief in a future life, denial of responsibility, duty, and morality, as opposed to expediency, make sufficient way in the world, and if practice harmonize with speculation, progress may become more evidently regress, and Man be proved a brute animal at last. The promising events in France are patent to every one; a less known, but still more encouraging fact, which we learn on scientific authority, is that certain Basuto tribes have lately adopted the (to them) novel custom of cannibalism.

Pending the hoped-for verification, if an identity of human with animal nature be accepted as provisionally true, it may be as well to anticipate a few of its logical consequences. Eating the flesh of our instinctive congeners ought positively to be discountenanced; or, as men and women are simply animal, all carnivorous human beings should on compulsion become cannibals. Despotism being the form of government adopted by us with general applause, as regards the animal kingdom, it cannot be too soon transferred to our own mismanaged nationalities. In a word, our practices in reference to men, women, beasts, fishes, birds, and reptiles, ought to be made uniform. Above all, the new school-boards should be charged with the education of our poor relations, and the linguistic professors of Oxford and Cambridge be instructed to use every effort for the promotion of a universal language. Charity may be thought by some to begin at home, therefore a commencement may be made with the domesticated irrationals, finches, spaniels, cats, hackneys, sheep, mules, all asses, all pigs, and all monkey favourites. It is just possible that volatile creatures unaccustomed to habits of reflection (some tribes of light-minded birds, for example) may find abstract ideas and declarative sentences a little difficult. Yet, after all, it need not be such a long step in the case of contemplative owls; and we may then apply the old proverb, "Il n'y a que le premier pas qui coûte." At all events, the "Simious process," so successful in our world of fashion, will be likely to suffice with every well-disposed chimpanzee; the circle of knowledge will continually widen until the world of animals becomes identified with the world of man. Then, but not till then, the astonished psychologist may cease his useless labours, and record the inauguration of a new era by acknowledging

> "Omnia jam fient fieri quæ posse negabam;"

or, still more conclusively,

> "Thinking is but an idle waste of thought,
> And nought is everything, and everything is nought."

ON SCIENCE AND REVELATION.

[6] In an answer to this lecture by "Julian," it is replied that "Belief is the easiest thing possible for weak and ignorant minds." But Julian by belief means *acquiescence;* and every church-goer is aware that the worthlessness of mere acquiescence is constantly being urged upon them from the pulpit. It holds the same relation to faith that respectability—*i.e.*, acquiescence in the ordinary standard of morality—holds to holi-

ness. The subject is too difficult to be discussed adequately in a note; but in my first Bampton Lecture I have shown how belief, though gained by a struggle, is equally possible for the unlearned and the learned, but in every case it has to be won by an effort (Mal. xi. 12).

7 "Julian" asserts that there ought not to be any difficulty. "There ought not to be the least shadow of doubt whether a given book is from God or not" (p. 5): "If the handwriting of Jehovah in the Scriptures be doubtful, it cannot be divine." But, as Bishop Butler has shown in his "Analogy," there are no difficulties, as regards Revelation, different in kind from those which we daily encounter in common life. "Julian's" easy assertions involve a tremendous difficulty; for what he virtually affirms is that God ought to have acted, in matters of religion, in an entirely different way from that in which He has acted in the ordinary constitution of this world. The whole question turns upon something quite as much out of "Julian's" depth as it is out of mine; namely, what was God's purpose in creating man. By the study of "the constitution and course of nature," and of what is said in Holy Scripture, I arrive at the conclusion that God has, for some wise purpose, been pleased to place man here in a state of discipline. Such a state implies the existence of difficulties; the greatness and degree of these difficulties we can know solely by experience, being able only to guess at the reasons which have made a state of probation necessary for us. But the difficulties must not be insuperable; for if they were, then this present state would be a discipline no longer.

8 Mr. Darwin, in his "Descent of Man" (i. 201—206), enumerates the several stages through which man is supposed to have passed, of which the first stage is an imaginary "group of animals, resembling in many respects the larvæ of our present Ascidians, which diverged into two great branches—the one retrograding in development, and producing the present class of Ascidians, the other rising to the Vertebrata." He further describes these Ascidians as "hardly appearing like animals, and consisting of a simple, tough, leathery sack, with two small projecting orifices." I must own that in Mr. Darwin's book I can find no proof either of the degradation of the present race of Ascidians or of the de-

velopment of their cousins, whom Mr. Darwin has summoned into existence to serve his purpose, into apes. The work is full of interesting facts and ingenious speculations, but the speculations can scarcely be said to have consistency enough to merit the name even of a theory.

9 If this struggle existed, it seems unaccountable that we do not find creatures in every stage of evolution. We must suppose that these Ascidian larvæ existed by millions—at all events, many thousand species of animals exist, all according to this theory, evolved from them; and, as many have failed and become our present Ascidians, and others were content to remain as they were, the number of possible starters in this race must have been vast. Reasonably, then, we should expect to find creatures in every stage of progress, and at the head numbers pressing closely on man. Instead of this, we find an empty space between each several order, and that between man and the animal second in the race is enormous. "The difference between the mind of the lowest man and that of the highest animal is immense" (Darwin, i. 104).

10 A monkey must walk, and does so quite as frequently as man, but he walks very ill. "The gorilla runs with a sidelong shambling gait, but more commonly progresses by resting on its bent hands. The long-armed apes occasionally use their arms like crutches: . . . yet they move awkwardly, and much less securely than man" (Darwin, i. 143). Now the theory of revolution would require that, before men and monkeys separated from some common ancestor, their configuration was the same. How and when did the hands become feet, or, *vice versâ*, the feet hands?

11 I do not think that "Julian" can have observed this note. For he retorts upon me that dogs, monkeys, and jackdaws have a conscience, and that what I deduce from it as regards men, would justify a similar conclusion as regards cats and dogs. But I had already pointed out that whatever appearance of the higher moral qualities is to be observed in animals is apparently the result of contact with man. It is part of the present constitution of things that certain animals have been domesticated, and over these the "dominion" given to man (Gen. i. 28) is

very large. I cannot see how any animal could be domesticated if it were quite incapable of quasi-moral qualities. I see then no difficulty in a domestic animal having a sort of conscience: without it a dog could scarcely be faithful. And note, too, that this rudimentary conscience in a dog implies responsibility in it quite as much as man's more perfect conscience does in man. The dog's responsibility is to his master; to whom is his master responsible? Still, as regards these rudiments of conscience, I cannot see any real proof for more than a very curious influence of man's qualities upon those of animals brought into contact with him. With Mr. Darwin (i. 89) I hold that "man only can with certainty be ranked as a moral being;" and that as regards conscience "man differs profoundly from the lower animals" (*ib.*) I do not hold, however, as "Julian" imagines, that conscience is an unerring guide. The exact contrary is implied in Matt. vi. 23. Conscience needs more than itself to guide men aright.

[12] "Julian" considers that I must be "one of those who believe a stop occurs in the middle of the second verse of Gen. i., which severs the preadamite world from the world as it now is." I answer that I am one of those who know a little Hebrew, and I am therefore aware that the verb rendered *was* in verse 2 is not a copula, but means continued existence. As regards the geologic notions ascribed to me by "Julian," I can only express my regret that scientific men should persist in ascribing to theologians mere nonsense. Nothing is easier than to slay men of straw, but is it worth the trouble? I would recommend him to read a discussion upon the Mosaic record in the last chapter of [Mr. Capes'] "Reasons of Returning to the Church of England." He would then see that the opinions of theologians are not so puerile as he supposes.

ON MIRACLES.

[13] The publishers have asked me whether I have any remarks to make on "Julian's" Reply. A few lines will be sufficient for all I have to say.

"Julian" quotes (page 16) a sentence within inverted commas, as mine, which the reader will in vain search for in my Lecture.

He, on page 17, attributes to me, for the purpose of exciting ridicule, a statement which I never dreamed of making. Yet he adds: "The words are Dr. Stoughton's, and you may read them for sixpence."

He concedes the point maintained in the first twenty-six pages of my Lecture, by remarking: "We do not say that miracles are improbable or impossible."

Although I distinctly explain that my argument in the remainder of the Lecture is confined to the miracles ascribed to Christ, "Julian" simply indulges in an attack on the authenticity and genuineness of the Pentateuch. He concludes by saying: "The New Testament stands on no better foundation, although we need not enter on that question now." Most people will think this was the very question on which "Julian" ought to have entered, in answer to a Lecture on "The Miraculous Evidences of Christianity."

Exception has been taken to what I have said respecting remarkable coincidences between natural events and historical facts (p. 200). Some of my remarks, as the foot-note indicates, were suggested by one of the most thoughtful of modern Continental divines. I therefore subjoin the following passage:—

"There is a mysterious harmony between the natural and the moral, between facts of nature and facts of history, manifest in what we call the 'wonderful' (*mirabile*), as distinct from what is properly called the 'miraculous' (*miraculum*). While the miracle, properly speaking, implies a violation of the laws of nature, the wonderful, which is closely connected with it, is such a coincidence and working together of nature and history as reveals a supernatural result to the religious perceptions, while the natural explanation still holds good for the understanding. The march of Napoleon into Russia, pregnant with results, and the severe winter; the invincible Armada of Philip the Second, and the sudden storm (*afflavit deus et dissiparit eos*), serve as examples of the 'wonderful' in the sense referred to. There is in these things a surprising and unaccountable harmony of nature and history, and yet all is natural; no law is broken, but the coincidence is inexplicable. Wonders such as these continually present themselves to us, both in the world at large and in the lives of individuals. There is, generally speaking, an unaccountable power of nature which plays its part in the historical and moral complications of human life; and it cannot escape the notice of the careful observer that wonderful coincidences often occur, which to reason may appear only as an extraordinary, inexplicable *chance;* to the poet as a profound *play* of the spirit of the world, and an active presence of a divine phantasy in the world's progress;—combinations which lie beyond the range of rational computation, and which, like genii, scorn the narrow laws of human knowledge;—but in which the Christian discerns the *finger of God.* But he who truly recognizes the finger of God in these strange coincidences must be led on to a recognition of the actually miraculous. The wonderful is only the half-developed, unperfected miracle. The wonderful possesses that ambiguous character, half chance, half providence, half natural, half divine, just because the coincidence of the holy and the natural is external only; and faith must still demand a relation wherein nature and freedom—separate in the usual course of events—shall not only seek one another in wonderful configurations, shall not only approach one another, but be immediately and essentially united; faith must still long for an unequivocal sign, of which it can say, Here is God, and not nature. This sign is given in the sacred history of Christ; a sign which is spoken against, and which is set for the fall of many, and for the rising again of many."—*Martensen's "Christian Dogmatics,"* p. 222.

ON MYTHICAL THEORIES OF CHRISTIANITY.

14 The following quotation from Mr. Lecky, who is a witness of the most unexceptionable character, sets forth in a striking light the solitary grandeur of the character of Christ as it has been depicted in the Gospels. "It was reserved for Christianity to present to the world an ideal character which throughout all the changes of eighteen centuries has inspired the hearts of men with an impassioned love; has shown itself capable of acting on all ages, nations, temperaments, and con-

ditions; has not only been the highest pattern of virtue, but the strongest incentive to its practice; and has exercised so deep an influence that it may be truly said that the simple record of three short years of active life has done more to regenerate and to soften mankind than all the disquisitions of philosophers, and all the exhortations of moralists. This has, indeed, been the well-spring of whatever is best and purest in the Christian life. Amid all the sins and failings, amid all the priest-craft and persecution and fanaticism that has defaced the Church, it has preserved in the example and character of its Founder an enduring principle of regeneration."—Lecky's "History of Morals," vol. ii., p. 9.

Mr. Lecky distinctly admits that it is an historical fact that the Christ of the Gospels has exerted a power compared with which that of all characters, whether real or mythical, has been inconsiderable. A true philosophy must account for this unique power possessed by Jesus Christ. If the character is a fiction, why is it that it has exerted an influence compared with which all other fictions have been feebleness? If Jesus Christ was a great man only, why "has He done more to regenerate mankind than all the disquisitions of philosophers, and all the exhortations of moralists"? Why has He left immeasurably behind Him all other great men who have ever lived? The historical truth of the Divine character portrayed in the Gospels adequately accounts for this mighty influence. Nothing else does. A character which leaves every other human character indefinitely behind it, must belong to the supernatural, not to the natural, order of things. It is a moral and spiritual miracle. To suppose that such a character has been generated by the slow and gradual action of natural laws, contradicts alike the acts of history and the principles of philosophy. Nature recognizes no mighty leaps in her order of production.

Watson & Hazell, Printers, London and Aylesbury.